This border contains tall plants, such as *Filipendula rubra* 'Venusta', *Veronicastrum virginicum* 'Fascination', *Eupatorium purpureum* subsp. *maculatum* 'Atropurpurea' and some species of *Monarda* in a variety of colours.

Contents

Preface

'Piet can probably be described as the world's most famous and influential planting designer'

The Dutch have a reputation as one of the great gardening peoples of the world. Their country's soil, fertile and easy to work for the most part, must have helped, but so too must the nation's trading acumen. For it is trade that brings new plants across the seas and the continents, and it is new plants that quicken the hearts of so many gardeners. Trade has helped make the English a great gardening nation too, and it is interesting to note the similarities between the gardens that the two countries have made. Historically, both have a love of structure in the garden, the skeleton provided by clipped hedges and shrubs with clear geometrical shapes. This is tempered though by a shared love of flowers, of plants for their own sake, often grown exuberantly among the more formal elements. The creative tension that this contrast generates does seem enormously popular across the world, and the English garden is arguably one of the country's most successful cultural exports.

Dutch designer Piet Oudolf started off firmly in this tradition, although in the modernist vision of it (which the English missed out on). Over time however, the clipped structure has weakened and diminished, being displaced by another expression of structure, the natural, genetically-determined structure of perennials and grasses. Now, Piet can probably be described as the world's most famous and influential planting designer, largely through two projects in the United States: Chicago's Lurie Garden and New York's High Line, both of which are now stimulating many more urban public planting initiatives. Piet's achievement is to have developed an aesthetic which looks wild, but is actually a stylised version of nature, ideal for city planting.

Piet is very much a part of the naturalistic movement in garden design, and it is his love of wild plants, and the places in which they grow that was the basis of his 26-year friendship with draughtsman and garden designer Henk Gerritsen. It was this shared love of the natural beauty of

DREAM PLANTS
FOR THE NATURAL GARDEN

Over 1,200 beautiful and reliable plants for a natural garden

Piet Oudolf & Henk Gerritsen

Original title: Méér Droomplanten
© Terra Publishing Co., Warnsweld, Netherlands, 1999
Text: Henk Gerritsen and Piet Oudolf
All photographs by Piet Oudolf except:
Henk Gerritsen: 6–7, 21 above, 50 bottom, 78 below, 82, 83,
93, 98, 99, 114 above and below, 118 above, 129
Anton Schlepers: 62, 66, 109, 116, 119

Design: Erik de Bruin

Dream Plants for the Natural Garden first published in the
English language by Frances Lincoln Limited,
part of the Aurum Publishing Group,
74–77 White Lion Street, London N1 9PF
www.franceslincoln.com

Foreword by Noel Kingsbury copyright © Frances Lincoln Limited 2013
Index copyright © Frances Lincoln Limited 2000

A catalogue record for this book is available from the
British Library.

ISBN 978-0-7112-3462-8

Printed in China

9 8 7 6 5 4 3 2 1

Key to the symbols in the text

 Height

 Sun

Part shade

 Shade

 Time of flowering

ESp	early spring	EA	early autumn
MSp	mid-spring	MA	mid-autumn
LSp	late spring	LA	late autumn
ESu	early summer	EW	early winter
MSu	mid-summer	MW	mid-winter
LSu	late summer	LW	late winter

Usefulness zones

The usefulness zones given for each plant (except for
annuals) represent the range of zones in which the plant may
successfully be grown. The lower figure gives the coldest zone
in which the plant will be hardy without winter protection,
the higher shows the limit of tolerance of hot summer
weather. The zone ratings are those devised by the United
States Department of Agriculture. The chart below indicates
the average annual minimum temperature of each zone.

It must be remembered that zoning data can only give rough
guidelines. Plant hardiness depends on a great many factors,
and within any one zone particular regions may be endowed
with more or less favourable conditions, just as on a smaller
scale in any one garden plants can be positioned in individual
situations that will suit their needs to a greater or lesser
extent. In particular, it should be noted that the upper limit
hardly applies in western Europe, where summers are not
as hot as summers in North America. So most plants coded
as, for example, Z4–7 will grow happily in western European
zones 8 and 9.

CELSIUS	ZONES	°FARENHEIT
Below -45	1	below -50
-45 to -40	2	-50 to -40
-40 to -34	3	-40 to -30
-34 to -29	4	-30 to -20
-29 to -23	5	-20 to -10
-23 to -18	6	-10 to 0
-18 to -12	7	0 to 10
-12 to -7	8	10 to 20
-7 to -1	9	20 to 30
-1 to 4	10	30 to 40
above 4	11	above 40

plants that inspired this book, which in essence, describes the core of the 'New Perennial' flora – plants that fit into the contemporary, wildlife-friendly and nature-inspired garden style.

Henk sadly died in 2008, although his garden, Priona, survives and is managed by gardeners who aim to preserve and cherish its essential features. Different in style and atmosphere to Piet's work – wilder and more idiosyncratic – it has however always shared many of the same plants. Henk told me how when he started gardening, 'Piet just had the plants I wanted . . . they were different, they were unusual and people were sceptical but I just kept on coming back'. Henk had an interest in recreating wild plant communities at Priona, and his love of the wild places of The Netherlands comes through in his last book *Essay on Gardening,* where he outlines his philosophy of garden-making as rooted in an understanding of how nature works.

Any artist or craftsman who is good and successful is so to a large extent because they understand their materials. Which is where this book comes in. In it both men distil their knowledge not just of how plants look, and what conditions make them happy, but how they grow. The division of the book into three categories Tough, Playful and Troublesome (the latter with sub-categories for Invasive, Capricious and Demanding), tells us a lot about the technical focus of the book, as well as the sense of humour of the authors. Henk, in particular, has a wonderful way with words, and a dry, sometimes caustic wit. The gardening world is desperately short of the kind of spirited yet informed criticism of plants that comes across in these pages.

I remember asking Piet why roses hardly ever appeared in the gardens he designed and he said that they had 'weak form and lousy foliage'. In a similar spirit, he and Henk suggest in this book that astilbes have suffered at the hands of plant breeders who have produced plants that 'attempt to outstrip each other in sheer pomposity' and perhaps the 'entire genus can be thrown straight on to the compost heap'.

My experience with Piet is that he is quite ruthless in his plant selection. Over the years he has grown a vast range of plants from seed lists, collected seed in the wild, trialled innumerable plants bought in nurseries as well as those given him by friends and colleagues. Only a tiny fraction of these are judged good enough to be used in the gardens that he makes. Part of Piet's importance has been the way he has drawn our attention to plants that were never considered garden-worthy, such as umbellifers (the cow parsley family) and the sober-coloured but charming *Sanguisorba* genus. The fact that he and Henk can see beauty in plants that others have disregarded is in large part due to their ability to think of gardens as places which nature can, and indeed should, inspire.

Part of the dogma of traditional gardening that both Piet and Henk are keen to overturn is the idea of perfection: that as Henk puts it, a yellow leaf is a mistake. Piet once said to me, only half-jokingly that 'a plant is not worth growing unless it looks good when it is dead'. The ability to look and find beauty in dying flowers, frosted leaves and gaunt stems, is something that I learned from Piet. It is all part of the redefinition of gardening as a partnership with nature, which includes an acceptance of the death of nature as a subject in itself.

With projects like New York's High Line, which embrace a pragmatic blend of the horticultural and the locally native, the wilder garden look, to say nothing of the focus on perennials and grasses, the world has changed since this book first came out. The plants it covers have in many cases gone on to become new garden classics.

Noël Kingsbury, 2013

Introduction

Dream Plants for the Natural Garden describes 1,200 plant species selected from the practical perspective of natural gardens. This raises a number of questions: what does a practical perspective entail and what is a natural garden?

A practical perspective entails writing about plants on the basis of their dependable traits in a natural garden. In a natural garden, where your attempts at intervention are kept to the minimum, you cannot take on plants which are not to be relied upon: plants which have to be dug up regularly and pulled apart to stay alive or plants which suddenly just fall by the wayside.

We describe as reliable all plants which, over the years, can be maintained in an average garden without too much in the way of artificial props and bolstering. By artificial props and bolstering we mean pesticides, artificial fertilizers and armies of garden labourers. 'All plants' requires a little qualification, since we do not deal with trees and shrubs (which are all extremely dependable, as long as they are hardy), with the exception of a few shrubs which remain small enough to be combined with perennials. We have also omitted plants that need a special environment, such as water and bog plants, rock plants and plants which will only grow on floating islands, on beaches or in deserts.

'Specialist plants' have been shown no mercy either: plants which are probably dependable (or could be) but which are far and away too small or delicate to manage in a garden unless you keep an eye on them every day to make sure that their neighbours have not smothered them. We have not, however, been over-conscientious about this, since although we have considered some plants too small for this book, such as *Hacquetia epipactis* (which, of course, as true enthusiasts we tend lovingly in our own gardens), we do, even so, write about favourites like *Jeffersonia dubia* and *Cardamine waldsteinii*.

Nor have we given any space to ground-cover plants, which do not usually mix well with perennials and which are more suitable for swathing a whole border or forming a carpet beneath shrubs.

Finally, we have left out those plants which need special conditions, such as most of the plants from the Himalayas: species of *Meconopsis*, *Codonopsis*, *Morina* and *Primula*. Even if they have not already died of their own accord after the first two or three years, a whole army of slugs and snails lies in wait to devour them with relish.

What we do discuss in this book are those perennials, bulbs, grasses, ferns and small shrubs which – we promise – will be able to survive competition from one another or the vagaries of the weather (excepting catastrophes), and will do what is expected of them for many years to come: growing, flowering and setting seed. The backing for this comes for the most part from our own experience gained over the last twenty years in our own gardens and in the gardens we have designed for others. Moreover, we asked several colleagues for their advice – see the Acknowledgments – whenever our knowledge did not stretch far enough, when we felt unsure or when we just could not agree.

Furthermore, we make no claims to have written a scientific work. To do that we would have had to incorporate the experience of at least a thousand gardeners, and then some: so many gardeners, so much experience.

We also discuss tender perennials, annuals and biennials which self-seed in a way which enables them to compete with hardy perennials so that a few of their seedlings are always in evidence in the garden. This means especially the somewhat larger, more eye-catching species which grow quickly from seed and do not allow themselves to be pushed aside easily. There are only a few. There are hundreds, perhaps even thousands of glorious annuals and biennials which are too small or too weak to cope by their own efforts – therefore, we have not mentioned them.

In principle, we do not mention unreliable or troublesome plants either. However, there are so many extremely nice invasive plants that we have happily taken the extra time to write another chapter on them. We have also included some plants whose behaviour cannot be gauged exactly: one might grow on the same spot for twenty years without incident, the other keeps dying off. In such instances, we deal only with very well-known species.

Finally, we are of the opinion that a very familiar genus such as *Delphinium* cannot be omitted, which is why this notoriously troublesome genus has also been given attention.

As far as the natural garden is concerned, to be able to explain what we mean by the term we must first clarify what we understand by 'natural'. According to the old definition, much applied until recently, nature includes anything not brought about by mankind, and therefore is opposed to culture, or civilization: everything that has been created by mankind. This turns the phrase 'natural garden' into a contradiction in terms: a garden, created by man and his civilizing hand, can never be natural.

For the record, we do not agree with this. A natural garden can indeed be said to exist. However, you do need to be a little liberal with the contradiction between nature and civilization. And why not? In our opinion nobody is able to say any more what nature is in its strictest definition; everything which we recognize as 'nature', to the furthest corners of the earth, has been beneath the foot of man, used, abused, remoulded and altered. Moreover, it is undergoing an ever-accelerating process of change. For us, it is far simpler to consider man and his works, civilization, as being an inseparable part of nature. However, this outlook can also lead you into problem areas since you could then cite tarmac, concrete and plastic as being *ipso facto* 'natural', and that is taking things a little too far.

So, to provide a concrete definition of the word 'natural' would appear to be extremely problematic and since we are writing a gardening book and not a philosophical treatise, we shall not attempt to go any further into it.

A natural garden is difficult to describe. Gertrude Jekyll felt that her border designs lent themselves to nature but, nowadays, we would not agree at all. Mien Ruys also described her garden in Dedemsvaart as being wildly planted within a tidy design. This wild planting no longer seems nearly wild enough to us. The terms 'wild' or 'natural' are dependent on fashion and are subject to the ravages of time. What we now judge to be natural will be seen as hopelessly unnatural in fifty years' time. The best we can hope to do is define what we expect from a natural garden; not how it should look, since even the two of us cannot agree about that, never mind that we should dare pontificate about how someone else's garden should look.

In a natural garden, we expect a certain degree of balance. No pesticides, no artificial fertilizers and no army of gardeners to keep the plants alive. It is about a garden filled with animate life (insects and birds) which will happily share in the feast without becoming pests, since our plants can deal with them. These do not necessarily have to be indigenous or wild plants. We would rather have a vigorous monarda in our natural garden, produced through a lengthy selection process (in other words, cultivated), than a wild specimen which degenerates into a pathetic pile of mildew in our climate. Double peonies do not appear in our book, not because they are unreliable (in relatively decent soil they can live to a ripe old age), but because we do not consider them natural. As mentioned earlier, it is a question of taste or, if you prefer, fashion, which may be very different in another fifty years.

Summed up in a few words, plants in a natural garden may be permitted a sickly period, though not a continuous one (some plants fall prey to slugs and snails in extremely wet years but return cheerfully enough in a subsequent dry year; we define these as being dependable). In addition, we would emphasize in particular those plants which attract wildlife: insects, butterflies and birds. Furthermore, from our point of view, they must also have a natural appearance – not only have we sought to write as honest and reliable a book as possible, but we also have our own opinions.

We see no reason why plants in a natural garden should be indigenous. Many indigenous plants do not comply at all with the criteria set by this book. They may well be reliable and have a natural look about them but they are usually terribly troublesome because they seed themselves so copiously. A number of them are mentioned, none the less – mostly in the 'Playful' section – because we have felt they are worthy of a garden for their attractive flowers or leaf shapes. However, the majority of indigenous species are not like that. Just quickly consider stinging nettles, creeping thistles or ground elder. These are not garden plants, but rather a pain in the neck which you can spend a whole gardening lifetime fighting against.

Green public spaces

At this point, we should now like to make a plea for the return of perennials to green public spaces.

A renewed sense of the importance of nature and, in particular, the ground-breaking work of people such as Professor Zonderwijk at the Agricultural University of Wageningen in the Netherlands have led to many roadside verges experiencing a floral renaissance over the last twenty years. In the course of time, green public spaces in the new urban sprawl have undergone a facelift.

When economies have had to be made in recent years, the ability to produce an abundance of flowers on a blank patch

Drömparken in Enköping, Sweden

plants with large flowers in striking colours. Little thought was given to sensitivity to disease or the amount of maintenance they required, and absolutely nobody gave the slightest importance to how natural they looked, their winter aspect or their attractiveness to butterflies.

Delphiniums are a notorious example from the 'old' catalogue of plants. Every few years they need to be rejuvenated; during their flowering season they have to be supported extensively and given additional fertilizer and, to top it all, they are extremely vulnerable to attack by slugs and snails.

However, time does not stand still. Since 1980, a completely new range of perennials has been developed. What these plants have in common is not so much their striking flowers as their whole appearance: their habit, leaf shape, flowering, seed case and winter silhouette. As far as growth pattern is concerned, particular attention has been paid to whether the plant could support itself (and not collapse earthward after the first good shower of rain) and that it should not be susceptible to disease or attack from insects, or only marginally. In short, plants should require little maintenance.

Borders can be made using this new range which demand considerably less management and which are interesting to the eye throughout the whole year and not just in summer.

It is high time that some of this approach should be seen in our green public spaces. Choosing to create flower meadows on poor ground remains the most important option for larger green zones, but on a somewhat smaller scale it should also

of soil, deprived of nutrients, and with virtually no maintenance required, was just what we needed. These economies have led to remarkable improvements, especially when you compare them to the unimaginative stretches of shrubs and dog-fouled grass which distinguished residential districts in the 1960s and 1970s. However, on the grounds of public economy, what perennial borders you did now and then come across in public areas have been cleaned away, mostly on the grounds that they required too much maintenance and so were too expensive.

Admittedly, the former range of perennials, principally developed at the beginning of the twentieth century, was rather labour-intensive. In the past, people were interested in

Traffic island in Neuenburg, Germany

be possible for perennials to make a return appearance. The argument that it is too expensive is really outdated with the new range of plants on offer.

We feel that another counter-argument, 'it'll just be vandalized anyway', is too defeatist. Naturally, you do have to consider carefully the places where such efforts could be successful. We cite two extreme examples. Firstly, the low-maintenance, drought-proof planting which Ewald Hügin has created on traffic islands – where almost no one ever walks – in Neuenburg, southern Germany, could be created almost everywhere. In contrast, planting around a children's playground will almost never be without some damage somewhere – even if it has worked for Ulf Nordfjell in a park in a deprived area of Stockholm where drunks sleep off their hangovers on the benches every day. However, this is an exception. Intermediate approaches can certainly be imagined: places where a planting will never, or rarely, be destroyed and can still be enjoyed by a large public.

Vandalism apart, a perennial border such as this must also be able to withstand the effect of a heavy cloudburst or other extreme weather conditions (such as drought) over which man has no influence. When a border like this is designed carefully it can withstand a considerable amount of wear and tear, whether by people or the forces of nature.

Nature or culture

Once you take on board that such a garden (park, border) needs to be well designed, you once again come up against the dilemma of where nature ends and civilization begins: a dilemma to which we could find no clear answer earlier in this introduction.

Obvious designs are artificial, not natural, however wild or natural the perennials used might look. You can, however, suggest a natural environment by keeping the design loose and irregular.

A truly natural look arises with the incredibly large number of butterflies and other insects that are attracted by such plantings – a fact confirmed at any perennial nursery or perennial-filled garden whether urban or rural. A microcosm of nature which occurs all too rarely in 'real' nature.

Perhaps this is really the most important argument of all for introducing greater numbers of perennials: in the new century, in which we shall have to accommodate more and more people within an ever smaller space, public green spaces must be of the highest quality possible to generate the greatest possible value from the experience.

To return, just for a moment, to the argument that it is all 'too expensive'. We are currently having our own newly developed nature area maintained free of charge by a few Scottish Highland cattle we have driven in (only a few, otherwise they would eat everything in sight). While we do not suggest that all our parks could adopt the same policy,

Digitalis grandiflora

they can be maintained, not for free perhaps but certainly cheaply, by having one or two gardeners set loose on them. Not too many, as otherwise the park will become:

    a: too expensive

    b: too tidy

(cross out whichever is not relevant).

The private garden

Clearly the plants from Part 1 'Tough' should be earmarked for the low-maintenance requirements of public green spaces.

As far as private gardens are concerned, the situation is quite different. Any garden owner is free to employ just as much time and energy on his garden as he wants. That goes from the most labour-intensive rockeries and perfectly managed kitchen gardens to low-maintenance perennial borders and zero-maintenance fields of stinging nettles (the owner of the latter may find nightingales in his garden, so there is something to be said for it after all!)

The scope of this book is restricted to low- and relatively low-maintenance gardens. The 'relatively' particularly refers to those gardens where the other plants mentioned in this book are significantly employed: the self-seeding perennials, the invasive plants and the annuals and biennials you just cannot be rid of. These plants will take up more of your time and energy, of course, but on the other hand they offer an endless series of combinations with which you can let your creativity run riot.

Yet, even so, these plants are still low-maintenance. Truly labour-intensive plants have been omitted from this book: for example, plants whose seed you have first to collect and then sow in the greenhouse each spring before you can plant them in the garden, even though these plants include those which look very natural and which attract swarms of insects, such as *Gaura lindheimeri*. Although we do have to be careful about what we say on this since last summer we heard of a garden where the aforementioned gaura had seeded itself spontaneously and copiously. This is just one of the exceptions which proves the rule. In fact there is really only one basic rule in gardening: there is such a huge variety of plants within the plant kingdom and environmental conditions differ so enormously from one garden to the next that no rules really exist.

However, we have done our best to produce a basic book for anyone wanting to involve themselves in the 'natural garden' phenomenon. We hope this results in another rule which we would like to propose, which states that every gardener should enjoy his own garden above all others!

Acknowledgments

We owe thanks to our colleagues in the plant world who have provided us with helpful advice which we have used in this book.

Rita van der Zalm helped us in the compilation of the chapter on bulbs. We consulted Coen Jansen and Brian Kabbes on the reliability of a great number of the plants described in this book. We placed the genus *Senecio* under the magnifying glass together with Dirk-Jan Koning and Hein Koningen, with the latter also helping us on the behaviour of indigenous plants in the garden.

We also owe thanks to the many visitors to our gardens and nursery from whom we have gathered innumerable snippets of knowledge over the last twenty years and to those people who have given us the opportunity to design their gardens, enabling us to put our knowledge of plants to the test and adapt it under many very different conditions.

Finally, our thanks go to Anja Oudolf, who arranges and organizes everything for us in the background and without whom the nursery would be unable to function.

Henk Gerritsen
Piet Oudolf
Schuinesloot, Hummelo

Astrantia major 'Roma'

Tough **Perennials**

This section is devoted to all those perennials, ornamental grasses, ferns, bulbs and small shrubs that we dare promise are reliable plants which will grow and flower in all decent garden soils. They are absolutely hardy, will not invade their neighbours, will not seed themselves – or, at least, not to a troublesome extent – and will demand little attention. In short, the ideal plants for anyone who wants a pretty, natural garden but who has little time to manage it. (We are not writing for people who do not feel like working on their gardens; they are better off covering them in asphalt.) These are also the ideal plants for use in public parks, in office gardens and anywhere where space and desire may be present but money and time are not. They are perfect, too, for dyed-in-the-wool gardeners who spend all of their spare time in the garden. It can never do any harm to have a healthy base of plants you can depend on and with which you can achieve your wildest gardening fantasies.

It goes without saying that we can never say plants are 'always reliable anywhere', except, perhaps, for those indigenous or naturalized species that have been proven to be able to maintain themselves without human interference. And of course there are plants which prefer a little more moisture around their roots, or the opposite. This sort of information is provided for each species. We have doubtless missed out a whole group of species which under especially favourable conditions (warm and sheltered) are extremely dependable. However, we have not included them because they have not proved dependable under less favourable conditions. Of course, to be completely honest, we have to admit that we do not know about every last plant: it is simply not humanly possible. New species are still being introduced and trialled. It just never ends.

ACANTHUS *(ACANTHACEAE)* – bear's breeches

Extremely decorative plants with large, deeply cut leaves which served as the inspiration for the decoration on Corinthian columns. Since these plants can occupy 1m²/1yd² of space over the course of time, they are best suited either as single specimens or at the front of a border, in full sunshine or semi-shade in well-drained soil (especially in winter). Their sublime flower spikes reach approx. 1m/3½ft in height, with the flowers half concealed by decorative, spiky calyces. The most familiar species, *A. mollis*, has broad, soft leaves and is easily killed off by winter wet. The following species are generally more reliable:

A. hirsutus Z6–10 ↕ **50cm/ 20in**   **ESu–MSu**

Has prickly leaves and yellowish white flowers held in light green bracts. Hardy on well-drained soils in full sun.

A. hungaricus Z6–10 ↕ **1.2m/ 4ft**   **MSu–LSu**

Has small, deeply divided leaves without prickles and flowers particularly profusely, with whitish flowers within purple bracts; will tolerate quite deep shade but flowers best in full sun.

A. spinosus Z7–10 ↕ **1.2m/ 4ft** ⬡ **MSu–LSu** ☼ ▨

Looks very much like the previous species but has even prettier, finely spined leaves; produces flowers somewhat less abundantly. All species seed themselves (scantily) but that should not give rise to any problems. It can only be good news when you find a seedling from a plant as beautiful as this.

ACHILLEA *(ASTERACEAE)* – yarrow

Very familiar garden plants with flattened flower heads and fine, bushy, fern-like leaves. Countless cultivars are available in all manner of gorgeous colours. Sadly, they tend to be unreliable over time. If not easily killed off in winter, then when they seed themselves they revert to the wild type, which takes over the pretty cultivar in the twinkling of an eye. You will not be able to tell one of these seedlings apart from the others as they have the same leaves. There is only one species which you truly might call perennial:

A. filipendulina
'Parker's Variety' Z4–8 ↕ **1m/ 3½ft**   **MSu–LSu** ☼

Has deep yellow flowers.

ACONITUM *(RANUNCULACEAE)* – monkshood

Abundantly flowering plants with dark green, glossy leaves cut in a more or less palmate style. The remarkably shaped flowers do look like a monk's hood, with a little imagination, and are pollinated exclusively by bumblebees. Sturdy, erect plants with spikes or sometimes panicles of flowers which do not collapse or grow rampantly and which almost never seed themselves. Only following the very severest of winters will you occasionally discover thousands of little seedlings. In other words, virtually ideal. Moreover, they grow anywhere even if they could do with a little farmyard manure in poor soils. They are best in semi-shade or in cool soils in full sun. All parts of the plant are deadly poisonous but, according to Graham Stuart Thomas, have an 'evil beauty'. They should not be planted in too large a group in borders (with the exception of the late-blooming *A. carmichaelii*), because they quickly wither after flowering (even if the seed-heads are rather attractive), then fall over to leave a gap in the border.

Some confusion in their nomenclature has arisen. The majority of cultivars are originally hybrids of *A. napellus* (without branching flower stalks) and *A. paniculatum* (with branching flower stalks) and are classified under *A.* x *cammarum* or *A. napellus*. A definitive attribution for each of these cultivars would be a quite historic undertaking which, with our limited brainpower, we dare not attempt. Besides, some growers have not always been too precise over recording what has been crossed with what. We give the cultivar name only.

Acanthus hirsutus

There are only two undisputed species:

A. carmichaelii *Z3–8*   1–1.2m/ 3½–4ft   LSu–EA

Very sturdy, erect plant from Kamchatka which appears in very early spring but flowers only at the end of summer, with a compact raceme of blue-purple flowers. Shiny green leaves.

   A. carmichaelii var. *wilsonii* is much taller (sometimes even 2m/6½ft) and flowers even later, from mid-autumn until the beginning of winter. Indispensable in any border.

A. napellus *Z5–8*   80cm–1.2m/ 32in–4ft   ESu–LSu

The common European monkshood with a raceme of purple-blue flowers. Likes to grow in the wild in places where fertile debris accumulates, such as next to streams and rivers or where cattle gather. Simple but highly effective; however, it is hardly ever available in its pure form. Crosses with *A. napellus* are far more widespread.

Cultivars

'Bergfürst' *Z5–8*   1.2m/ 4ft   ESu–MSu

Has a broad, loose inflorescence of dark blue flowers.

'Bicolor' *Z4–8*   80cm–1.2m/ 32in–4ft   MSu–LSu

This is an old-fashioned cottage-garden monkshood with widely spaced panicles of blue and white flowers. Charming.

'Bressingham Spire' *Z5–8*   90cm/ 3ft   MSu–LSu

In relation to the plant's total height, this has an elongated inflorescence with only few side branches to its spike; purple-blue.

'Grandiflorum Album' *Z5–8*   1.2m/ 4ft   MSu–LSu

As the name suggests, it has large flowers, green when in bud, pure white when open. Few side branches. The best white monkshood.

'Ivorine' *Z5–8*   60–80cm/ 24–32in   LSp–MSu

This early-flowering, short cultivar has ivory white flowers with a high, narrow hood. The Scandinavian *A. lycoctonum* is probably one of its parents. Interesting for its early flowering but will not tolerate as much competition as the other monkshoods. Good soil and tender care would not go amiss.

'Newry Blue' *Z5–8*   1.4m/ 4½ft   ESu–MSu

A gorgeous cultivar; tall, virtually unbranched inflorescence with navy blue flowers in early summer. Vigorous.

'Spark's Variety' *Z5–8*   1.6m/ 5¼ft   LSu

Creates an airy, broadly branched plume with somewhat dusky, dark purple-blue flowers. Is a little weak and so needs support and a light backdrop to enhance its dark flowers.

'Stainless Steel' *Z5–8*   1.2m/ 4ft   MSu

Notable for the colour of its flowers: light blue washed with grey. Not quite stainless steel but the name is still rather charming.

ACTAEA (RANUNCULACEAE) – herb Christopher, baneberry

A genus of woodland plants with characteristic composite leaves like *Astilbe* and inconspicuous flowers in the spring. Their decorative value derives wholly from the large, shining berries borne by the plant in summer. Sadly, not all summer long since, while the berries may be extremely poisonous to us, they would not appear to be so to birds. These plants can live to a ripe old age so long as they have been well planted in a fertile, humus-rich, woodland soil. They will tolerate full sun where the soil has permanent moisture.

Above: *Aconitum* 'Grandiflorum Album'
Left: *Aconitum* 'Stainless Steel'

A. pachypoda Z4–9 90cm/3ft LSp–ESu
Syn. *A. alba*. A plant which would go unnoticed until its great, shining, porcelain white berries appear on short, reddening stems in mid-summer. 'There is nothing like it – a real treasure', says Graham Stuart Thomas, and he is right.

A. rubra Z4–8 40cm/16in LSp–ESu
A true shade-lover which only gets noticed when its gleaming, red berries appear on red stems at the end of the summer. *A. rubra* f. *neglecta* grows a little taller (80cm/32in) and has white berries. A selected form with translucent orange-red berries is available from nurseries under the name 'Neglecta'.

A. spicata Z3–8 50cm/20in LSp–ESu
Has black berries and thus is not so noticeable. It is a rare indigenous species occurring particularly in wooded ravines. It will seed itself a little. One for the real enthusiast.

AMSONIA *(APOCYNACEAE)*

A still relatively unfamiliar genus of virtually ideal garden plants; tidy in shape with regular leaves and pretty flowers, and extraordinarily hardy. It makes you wonder why they are not yet found in gardens everywhere. The time will come. As the name Apocynaceae implies, this is a member of the periwinkle family; so you now know just how the flowers will look.

A. hubrechtii Z5–9 70cm/28in ESu–MSu
Light blue racemes of tiny, star-shaped flowers at the top of stems densely surrounded by needle-shaped leaves. The flowers have less impact than the leaves, especially in autumn, when they turn spectacularly from yellow to orange to red.

A. orientalis Z5–8 50cm/20in LSp–LSu
Syn. *Rhazya orientalis*. Until recently, this plant was classified under another genus because this species is native to Thrace and is completely isolated from the rest of the genus (which grows in North America). It transpires that it can barely be distinguished from the American species and thus must belong to *Amsonia*. Relatively broad, grey-green leaves and grey-blue, star-shaped flowers emerging from dark blue buds: terribly pretty. It does require a good summer (for this species that means warm and dry), but it will then flower from the end of spring until mid-summer. The plant multiplies by sending out runners but never becomes a nuisance.

A. tabernaemontana var. salicifolia Z4–9   80cm/32in ESu–MSu
Grows slowly, but eventually forms solid clumps with elongated, willowy leaves. The flower stems are a beautiful purple-blue in spring. Produces abundant racemes of steel-blue, star-shaped flowers followed by attractive, oblong seeds; a pretty autumn leaf colour and will tolerate a fair amount of shade as well. In short, do plant it!

ANAPHALIS *(ASTERACEAE)*

Compact plants with woolly grey foliage and flowers borne in flat flower heads which, contrary to their appearance, will not tolerate dry conditions.

Anaphalis triplinervis Z4–9 60cm/2ft MSu–EA
Well-behaved with dense foliage and a profusion of flowers. In spite of this we find them rather severe and not particularly charming. Useful if you want something grey-leaved in a damp soil.

Above: *Actaea rubra* f. *neglecta*
Below: *Amsonia hubrechtii*

Right: *Anemone* x *lesseri*
Centre left: *Anemone multifida* 'Major'
Centre right: *Anemone hupehensis* 'Hadspen Abundance'
Bottom left: *Anemone rivularis*
Bottom right: *Anemone* x *hybrida* 'Honorine Jobert'

ANEMONE *(RANUNCULACEAE)* – **windflower**

A fascinating genus from the buttercup family. Species of anemone have been grown since the beginnings of history. To name just two: *A. coronaria*, the anemone found at the florist's, and the incomparable spring offering *A. nemorosa*, the wood anemone. All species have beautifully formed, often downy, leaves and 'true' flowers: five or six petals with a prominent stamen centre. This gorgeous genus should be split up, since the various species are far from being equally dependable, and also fall into different categories such as rhizomatous plants or invasive plants. For now, just the 'tough' species:

A. cylindrica Z2–8 ↕ **1.2m/ 4ft** MSu–LSu

Topping the long stems, the silvery down on its seed pods is what makes this species so decorative and not the greenish white flowers which precede them. Extremely subtle. You will need a large amount of these plants in your garden to achieve some effect. Particularly pretty in good garden soil, but will tolerate years of neglect in poor sandy soil as well. Vigorous.

A. x lesseri Z5–8 ↕ **30cm/ 1ft** LSp

For a while, we debated whether this anemone really belonged in this chapter; however, it responds really well in truly good garden soil, in a spot at the front of a border where you can keep an eye on it (it is intolerant of competition from larger plants). It is beautiful as well, of course, with its carmine-pink flowers and characteristic fluffy seed heads. The same applies to the similar *A. multifida* 'Major' and *A. multifida* (syn. *A. magellanica*) with pale yellow flowers. All three species often flower for a second time in the summer.

A. rivularis Z6–8 ↕ **80cm/ 32in** ESu–MSu

Side-stems branch out somewhat chaotically from rather large, downy leaves to produce pretty flowers, blue on the outside and white within, with blue stamens. *A. levellei* is a variant which flowers just as prettily a little earlier in the year and is somewhat shorter.

Japanese anemones

A collective name for a group of autumn-flowering anemones with deeply cut foliage and airy bunches of large anemone flowers on long stems. They need a good, well-drained soil where they can root deeply: only then will they become fully hardy. Cover them over with a mulch of dry straw or bracken during the first winter after planting.

A. hupehensis Z5–9 ↕ **60cm/ 2ft** LSu–EA

Does not grow so very tall, has a leaf composed of three leaflets and produces warm pink flowers. 'Hadspen Abundance' is more compact and produces deep pink-red flowers.

A. tomentosa Z5–9 ↕ **1.2m/ 4ft** MSu–EA

Has large, downy leaves divided into three leaflets. 'Albadura' produces white flowers, pink when in bud.

A. x hybrida Z5–8 ↕ **1–1.5m/ 3½–5ft** LSu–MA

A group of hybrids from both of the previous species and (probably) from a few others besides. Abundant in flower and vigorous. 'Honorine Jobert' has pure white flowers against dark green leaves. 'Robustissima' grows very tall, to 1.5m/5ft, has pale pink flowers and may become invasive once well established. 'September Charm' has semi-double pink flowers. 'Königin Charlotte' does not grow as tall and has semi-double, pale pink flowers with a dark pink underside. 'Pamina' is also low-growing and produces semi-double, wine-red flowers. Another shorter anemone is 'Whirlwind' with semi-double white flowers.

ANTHERICUM *(ANTHERICACEAE)* – **St Bernard's lily**

Clustering plants with grassy leaves and small, white, lily-like flowers for dry, open spaces. Though extremely vigorous, they will not tolerate any shade (or competition from larger plants).

A. liliago Z5–9 ↕ **40cm/ 16in** LSp–MSu

White, star-shaped, lily-like flowers on stems with few or no branches. Charming but needs to be planted in large groups. The same applies to *A. ramosum*, which grows taller (60cm/2ft), but which has even smaller flowers produced from strongly branching stems.

ARALIA *(ARALIACEAE)*

An extensive genus of plants from the ivy family which also includes trees such as the well-known Japanese angelica tree (*A. elata*). An attractive foliage plant for fertile, well-drained soil.

A. californica Z8–10 ↕ **3m/ 10ft** MSu–LSu

Gigantic plant with attractive, feathery foliage and greenish bunches of ivy-like flowers, which attract so many flies that they often appear black; later the blackness is of berries. You must have got the point: a plant for the true enthusiast. Extremely impressive, the plant grows as wide as it is tall. Very alike, but smaller by half, is *A. cordata* (Z4–9), which would be better in smaller gardens if its flowers did not appear so late in the year that the first night frosts destroy them.

A. racemosa Z5–9 ↕ **1m/ 3½ft** MSu–LSu

A beautiful plant when it takes. Sometimes it is totally devoured by slugs and snails year after year, and just when you think it really has disappeared for good, there it is suddenly, once again dangling bunches of black berries. So really, so far as we can tell, strong as iron.

ARTEMISIA *(ASTERACEAE)*

A large genus of mostly grey-leaved plants preferring drier soils, the majority of which are described elsewhere because they are shrubby, terribly invasive or not truly dependable in a changeable climate.

A. alba 'Canescens' Z5–9 ↕ **60cm/ 2ft**

Is relatively reliable in dry soil in full sun and has silver-white leaves cut like filigree. The flowers are unsightly.

A. ludoviciana var. latiloba Z4–8 ↕ **40cm/ 16in**

White sage. A relatively broad-leaved plant with so little tendency towards rampant growth that it is included in this chapter. The plant will start to flower in late spring, and at this point cut it back by about 20cm/8in to prevent the flower stems from collapsing into disarray.

The following species are of an altogether different type: they require a moisture-retentive soil, do not have grey foliage and do have pretty flowers:

A. lactiflora Z4–9 ↕ **1.5m/ 5ft**   MSu–EA

White mugwort. Tall border plants with prettily feathered, dark green leaves and attractive plumes of small, cream-coloured flowers. It is imperative to remember to plant them in a moisture-retentive soil. Just a few days of drought will cause the plants to wither away altogether.

Artemisia ludoviciana var. *latiloba*

Top: *Artemisia lactiflora* Guizhou Group
Centre: *Asarum europaeum*
Bottom: *Aster* 'Little Carlow'

A. lactiflora
Guizhou Group Z4–9 ↕ 2.2m/ 7ft MSu–EA

A hopeless name for a plant which nobody has yet been able to classify definitively. Nomenclature continues to be a stimulating subject. Changes arrive without warning and suddenly a whole genus has been renamed or has disappeared. You might well ask whether this really is a *lactiflora* type: in appearance it is most similar to a dark-leaved form of *A. chinensis* which in turn looks very like mugwort, *A. vulgaris*. This Guizhou plant was collected in China and has dark brown-red stems, purple-red younger leaves and almost white plumes of flowers standing very erect. There is also a cultivar, 'Rosa Schleier', which produces a pink inflorescence. Both require the same moisture-retentive soil as ordinary *A. lactiflora*.

ARUNCUS (ROSACEAE) – goat's beard

Indestructible plants which will grow almost anywhere provided they are given time to acclimatize. Their foliage is typical of the rose family, composite and divided, and they produce plumes of flowers.

A. dioicus Z3–8 ↕ 1.5m/ 5ft ESu–MSu

A wonderful plant if you are at your wits' end what to do: goat's beard grows everywhere, even in dry, shaded spots. It will not then grow as vigorously as in a damper location in sun but, none the less, it will grow. The cultivar 'Kneiffii' has very finely divided leaves and grows to half the height of the type.

A. 'Horatio' Z4–9 ↕ 1.2m/ 4ft ESu–MSu

A cross between *A. aethusifolius* and *A. dioicus*. Looks like an *Astilbe* but is more decorative and tolerates drier conditions.

ASARUM (ARISTOLOCHIACEAE)

Evergreen plants for planting in deep shade with pretty, dark green, slightly hairy leaves. Beautiful for ground cover but slow-growing, so you have to plant a great many in order to create a good effect.

A. europaeum Z6–9 ↕ 15cm/ 6in ESp–MSp

The most familiar species, with leaves that are shaped like human ears. Its notable dark brown flowers remain wholly hidden from view beneath the leaves.

ASPHODELINE (ASPHODELACEAE) – asphodel

A. lutea Z6–8 ↕ 90cm/ 3ft ESu–MSu

Clump-forming plants with grassy, blue-grey foliage from which long stems arise. The stems are covered for much of their length in spidery, light yellow lily-like flowers and later spherical seed capsules. Especially attractive, but requiring particularly fertile soil and a warm, sunny spot in order to thrive. They will not tolerate being shaded by other plants.

ASTER (ASTERACEAE)

A large and over-familiar genus of mainly autumn-flowering plants. A description is unnecessary. There are too many species to name them all. We feel that some of the small-flowered species which quickly naturalize are a little messy and so we have left them out. In the chapter entitled 'Capricious Plants', we describe a number of not entirely reliable species still worthy of garden use. Listed below are only the species which are both reliable and worthy of exhibiting. They will all grow in normal, moisture-retentive but well-drained garden soil.

A. cordifolius Z3–9 ↕ 1.2m/ 4ft EA–MA

Small-flowered species which you should allow to fall apart elegantly; do not support them. 'Ideal' produces light blue flowers. 'Little Carlow' is a violet-blue hybrid and 'Silverspray' is silvery white with a blue wash to it; the centres turn red.

A. ericoides Z3–8   ↕ 70cm/28in   EA–MA

Has flowers just as small but bushier than the previous species. Does not topple over. 'Blue Star' produces pale blue flowers, 'Esther' and the hybrid 'Pink Star' pink ones. The latter is a bit taller at 1.2m/4ft.

A. laevis Z4–8   ↕ 1.6m/5¼ft   EA–MA

Michaelmas daisy. A tall species with dark leaves and stems and elongated bunches of lilac-blue daisy flowers. Tends to topple over.

A. lateriflorus Z4–8   ↕ 60cm–1.4m/2–4½ft   EA–LA

Sturdy plants with small, darkly tinted leaves and small, white flowers. The most well-known cultivar, the low-growing 'Horizontalis', is sadly not terribly reliable. Much more dependable is the almost black-leaved and very tall (1.4m/4½ft) 'Lady in Black', which flowers very late (well into autumn). Also reliable is 'Coombe Fishacre', a hybrid flowering in early autumn with an abundance of pink flowers.

A. macrophyllus 'Twilight' Z4–8   ↕ 60cm/2ft   MSu–EA

A steadily spreading but non-invasive hybrid with fresh green, oval leaves which flowers early, producing fairly large, bright lavender flowers with a yellow centre. Will tolerate far more shade and less moisture than the other asters.

A. novae-angliae Z4–8   ↕ 1.4m/4½ft   LSu–MA

Michaelmas daisy. The best-known autumn aster, a dull mauve example of which annoyingly appears in every garden. There are far prettier cultivars which are indispensable in an autumn garden, partly because of the butterflies they attract. 'Andenken an Alma Pötschke' produces striking carmine-pink flowers, 'September Ruby' dark ruby red and 'Violetta' deep purple with contrasting yellow centres.

A. novi-belgii Z4–8   ↕ 30cm–1.2m/1–4ft   EA–MA

Michaelmas daisy. Sadly enough, indestructible. Endlessly bred, formal, in many colours which never quite live up to expectations. As far as we are concerned, these plants can become gardening history.

ASTILBE *(SAXIFRAGACEAE)*

Plants with beautiful pinnate leaves and plumed heads of flowers which look a little like *Spiraea*, which is why they are often so misnamed. However, the true *Spiraea* is a shrub which belongs to the rose family. Astilbes are thoroughly dependable unless grown in waterlogged locations. They cannot abide any kind of drought. They tend to be formal in habit, a characteristic which has been abused by growers on a wide scale with the result that hundreds of cultivars now exist which attempt to outstrip each other in sheer pomposity. Add to this the rather dominant (if not downright ugly) colours red and pink and, as far as we are concerned, you have an entire genus of plants which can be thrown straight on to the compost heap. However, as we have already remarked in the introduction, the term 'natural' is dependent on fashion, so who knows what people will think about these plants in fifty years time? For us, only a handful of cultivars come to the fore when employed in a natural garden.

A. chinensis var. taquetii 'Purpurlanze' Z4–8   ↕ 80cm/32in   MSu–LSu

A little formal, but that is a feature of *Astilbe*, with a compact, lightly branched, purple inflorescence. A nice plant to use architecturally, especially as it remains pretty in winter.

A. simplicifolia Z4–8   ↕ 30–50cm/12–20in   MSu–LSu

Just as formal as all other species of *Astilbe*, but because rather smaller and more dainty this is fairly good for incorporating into a natural garden. Importantly, its colours are restrained.
A. 'Dunkellachs' produces salmon-pink flowers against dark green, shiny leaves. 'Inshriach Pink' has subtle pink flowers against bronze-coloured leaves, just like 'Sprite' which is a little darker pink.

Top: *Aster novae-angliae* 'Violetta'
Bottom: *Astilbe chinensis* var. *taquetii* 'Purpurlanze' with *Eupatorium purpureum* subsp. *maculatum* 'Atropurpureum' and *Persicaria polymorpha*

A. thunbergii Z4–8   ↕ 80cm–1.2m/32in–4ft   LSu–EA

Taller and more ornamental than most of the other *Astilbe* species; like goat's beard but flowers later in the season. 'Betsy Cuperus' is a pale pink hybrid, 'Professor van der Wielen' is a tall white hybrid.

ASTILBOIDES *(SAXIFRAGACEAE)*

A. tabularis Z5–7   ↕ 1.5m/5ft   MSu–LSu

Syn. *Rodgersia tabularis*. A plant with giant, umbrella-like leaves which can measure up to 90cm/3ft across on thick hairy stalks and with cream-coloured plumes of flowers high above the leaves. Miraculous if successful: on fertile, moisture-retentive, woodland loam in a spot not too vulnerable to frosts. The plant can survive frost but will look much less impressive afterwards.

ASTRANTIA *(APIACEAE)* – *masterwort*

Astrantia species have become a real fashion in recent years, and rightly so with their miniature crocheted blanket of flowers: a subtly tinted envelope of bracts within which its tiny flowers are arranged. The trend has centred in particular around *A. major*, which seeds itself so copiously that growers are able to produce ever more new varieties of colours. Because of their prodigious self-seeding, they have been placed in the 'Playful' section, with the exception of a few sterile cultivars:

Above: *Baptisia australis*
Left: *Campanula* 'Burghaltii'

***A. major* 'Roma'** Z4–8   ↕ 60cm/ 2ft   LSp–EA
Produces flowers in a rather special muted rose colour over a long period. 'Washfield' is an attractive selection which, in colour, is somewhere between 'Roma' and the dark red cultivars.

A. maxima Z4–8   ↕ 60cm/ 2ft   ESu–MSu
Only grows well in heavy soils, so you need not bother trying this beauty elsewhere. Its shiny, three-lobed leaves and velvety, shell-pink bracts spread gradually but are not really invasive. We would not use the word 'troublesome' to describe such a gem. Happy in clay soils.

BAPTISIA (PAPILIONACEAE) – **false indigo**
Slow-growing plants which, if left in peace, become prettier every year. They prefer to grow in calcium-deficient soils where they root deeply (avoid spots where ground-water levels are high). They look a little like lupins but are far sturdier and have a more stately appearance.

B. australis Z3–9   ↕ 1.2m/ 4ft   LSp–MSu
Grows in robust clumps with blue-green leaves and an inflorescence resembling lupins in a soft indigo blue. After flowering is over, lovely round, grey pea-pods show up against the foliage which by autumn will have slowly turned coal-black. Is that distinguished or isn't it?

B. lactea Z5–9   ↕ 1.2m/ 4ft   ESu–MSu
Syn. *B. leucantha*. This cannot compete with the previous species even if its cream-coloured flowers are so very pretty. It becomes less attractive after flowering, so is better sited between shrubs than in a perennial border. Will tolerate above average moisture levels.

BERGENIA (SAXIFRAGACEAE)
A genus of plants having large, wavy-edged, evergreen leaves which hug the ground. They grow very slowly and, consequently, there is little to enjoy from them. However, they are incredibly tough and so belong in this list. The flowers, which appear early in spring, almost always die off again with a frost. The best species to incorporate are those with leaves that turn a lovely red in winter. At least you get something for your money then. There are several pleasant hybrids of *B. purpurascens*. A nice, smaller version of this is 'Baby Doll'.

BUPHTHALMUM (ASTERACEAE)
B. salicifolium Z4–9   ↕ 60cm/ 2ft   LSp–LSu
A literal translation of this name from its Latin and Greek components gives us willow-leaved ox-eye. Rather a mouthful and just for your information, particularly when you realize that it denotes quite an unpretentious plant with unexciting yellow daisy flowers, fairly crude leaves and weak stems. However, let it topple over; since the plant just goes on flowering it eventually creates a series of mounds. And devoid of pretension? Well, sometimes one needs something like that.

CALAMINTHA (LAMIACIAE) – **calamint**
C. nepeta* subsp. *nepeta Z5–9   ↕ 35cm/ 14in   MSu–MA
There are various species of calamint but this is the only one which rarely or never seeds itself and which stays where it is planted; at least it does when the location is sunny and well-drained in winter, otherwise it will just rot away. It creates little hillocks packed full of pale blue, lipped flowers. The whole plant smells so deliciously of real peppermint that you cannot resist touching it.

CAMPANULA (CAMPANULACEAE) – **bellflower**
Bellflowers have been familiar and much-loved garden plants for centuries. What few people realize is that the majority of them

flower only for a very short period and have little of interest to offer thereafter. Consequently, they cannot serve as the basis for an herbaceous border. Moreover, there are quite a few unreliable species which seed themselves like mad or which grow annoyingly rampant. You will come across a few bellflowers in nearly all of this book's chapters. Yet to give this somewhat sad tale a happy ending, they are, of course, absolutely beautiful and more than welcome in any garden. We have been tearing our hair out a little but we have found a few dependable bellflowers for you:

C. alliariifolia *Z4–8* ↕ *60cm/2ft*   *ESu–LSu*

Clump-forming plants with pretty, heart-shaped, light green leaves and rather sloppy, no, rather, informally bending stems carrying pendent milk-white bellflowers. According to Graham Stuart Thomas, well balanced and, according to the distinguished Dutch plant breeder Brian Kabbes, nicely informal. Something for everyone.

C. poscharskyana *Z3–9* ↕ *20cm/8in*   *ESu–MSu*

An indestructible species which will also grow on the very worst sites. It worms its way upwards through other plants with its long, stretching stems. A classic combination is with *Alchemilla mollis*. The species is blue. 'E.H. Frost' is white with a blue wash, 'Lisduggan Variety' is mauve.

Hybrids *Z5–8*

A number of hybrids derive from the Asian *C. punctata*, an invasive species, *C. takesimana*, a weak species with little decorative value, and also several European species which set seed abundantly. The surprising outcome is a number of spectacularly flowering and extremely respectable plants which neither run riot nor seed themselves. That is what we like to see. Carry on, plant breeders.

'Burghaltii' *Z4–8* ↕ *80cm/32in*   *ESu–MSu*

Produces lax stems which have to be either supported or allowed to grow up through other plants, with large aubergine-coloured buds from which lilac-grey flowers emerge that can be up to 7.5cm/3in long. Does well in drier soil.

'Kent Belle' *Z4–8* ↕ *1m/3½ft*   *ESu–MSu*

Found by Elizabeth Strangman. Produces large, shiny, purple-blue bellflowers on stems which happily intertwine through other plants. Often flowers a second time.

'Sarastro' *Z4–8* ↕ *80cm/32in*   *ESu–MSu*

Found by Christian Kress in Austria. The coarse *C. trachelium* is one of its parents. A sturdy plant, with coarse hairs and pendent, purple-blue bellflowers.

'Van Houttei' *Z4–8* ↕ *80cm/32in*   *ESu–MSu*

Similar to *C.* 'Burghaltii' but with darker flowers.

CARDAMINE *(BRASSICACEAE)* – meadow cress

The genus *Cardamine* (including *Dentaria*) accounts for a large number of marvellous spring-flowering plants, not least among them the ordinary lady's smock, or cuckoo flower, for cool, shady places. Most species are only grown in small numbers; it would seem that they are valued only by true enthusiasts. It is not easy either to sum up in a few words exactly what is so special about the regularity of their pink or white four-petalled flowers set against their characteristic pinnate leaves, the top leaf of which is always the biggest. On further consideration, we have come up with just one word to explain it: they look so healthy. Since they are so rarely grown, we mention just one:

C. waldsteinii *Z5–9* ↕ *20cm/8in*   *MSp–LSp*

A low-lying plant which forms large clumps. It has deliciously fresh leaves, each roughly dentate with three lobes with many large, white lady's smock flowers above during a short period in spring. The plant disappears below ground once it has flowered.

Above: *Campanula* 'Kent Belle' with *Nepeta sibirica*
Below: *Cardamine waldsteinii*

Above: *Leuzea centauroides*
Below: *Chaerophyllum hirsutum* 'Roseum'

CENTAUREA *(ASTERACEAE)* – knapweed

Composite flowers consist of a great number of individual flowers all bundled up and held together by a 'calyx'. In *Centaurea*, the calyx binds the flowers together from a rounded base made up of scaly bracts. This is slightly different in each species. There are hundreds of different ones, occurring mainly in southern Europe, including many very beautiful species which we all instantly want for our own gardens. Sadly, that does not always work out so well in practice. Many species produce only a few flower stems each season among a mass of rather coarse foliage. In the wild this is very pretty, but in the garden it is not enough. Of the other, more profusely flowering species which we have tried out, many have been rejected because they did not seem to be sufficiently reliable: the majority will not survive a winter which is either too wet or too cold. In the end, only a disappointingly small number remains – and one of these, which we used to know as *C. cynaroides*, has now been reclassed as *Leuzea centauroides*. This species has deeply cut leaves, green above, grey underneath, and lilac-pink artichoke-like flowers in early to mid-summer. It does well in good garden soil, in full sun, amid other shorter plants – where it looks like a miniature artichoke. The plant commonly known as *C.* 'Pulchra Major' is apparently the same species.

C. montana Z3–8   ↕ **45cm/ 18in**   ✸ **LSp–LSu**   ☼ ◩

This comes from central Europe and likes a normal, moisture-retentive garden soil, unlike most of the other species, and will tolerate a considerable amount of shade. It does self-seed a bit but not to the extent that it needs to be placed in the 'Playful' section of this book. The leaves are oblong, entire and a little greyish. The flowers, which appear in early summer, are like cornflowers (just as blue). It continues to flower on and off over the rest of the summer. A considerable number of cultivars are available in other colours which produce a slightly less abundant quantity of flowers. One extremely pretty one is *C.m. alba*, with enchanting white flowers; *C.m. carnea* is flesh pink.

CERATOSTIGMA *(PLUMBAGINACEAE)*

C. plumbaginoides Z5–8   ↕ **25cm/ 10in**   ✸ **LSu–MA**   ☼

Perennial with creeping stems and clusters of sky-blue flowers bursting from red buds. Flowers in autumn, while the leaves turn brown-red. Intolerant of shading by other plants.

CHAEROPHYLLUM *(APIACEAE)*

C. hirsutum 'Roseum' Z5–8   ↕ **80cm/ 32in**   ✸ **LSp–ESu**   ☼ ◩

Delicate umbellifer for moist, humus-rich soil. It expands in spring (literally: the flowering stems grow first in width, afterwards growing upwards) with light green, hairy, finely divided, pinnate leaves like chervil and pale pink flower heads. There is not much to it after flowering, so is best planted to the rear of a border, between plants which will later grow taller. The resultant shade will be very much appreciated by the plant during the hotter summer months.

CHELONE *(SCROPHULARIACEAE)* – turtle's head

Robust, not to say rigid, plants with striking snapdragon-like flowers that look a little like the back of a turtle's head, hence the common name. Indestructible in any moisture-retentive soil.

C. obliqua Z4–9   ↕ **1.2m/ 4ft**   ✸ **LSu–EA**

This is the most familiar species. The stiff, warm mauve-pink spikes of flowers are borne on densely leaved stems. The flowers remain intact even through the worst weather – not an unnecessary luxury for an autumn-flowering plant. Other species available once in a while are *C. glabra*, which is a little less bushy and has greenish white flowers, and *C. lyonii*, which has a more compact inflorescence.

CHRYSANTHEMUM *(ASTERACEAE)*

Autumn chrysanthemums are not necessarily the first flowers that you would think of for a natural garden, but among the vast number of large-flowered cultivars available in screaming colours there are a few which are more subtle, creating little groups which are not amiss anywhere. To flower well, they need to be planted in a warm spot where there is full sun even in autumn.

C. 'Anja's Bouquet' *Z5–9* ↑ 70cm/ ↓ 28in *EA–LA*
Produces pleasant mauve-pink flowers up until the first frost.

C. 'Herbstbrokat' *Z5–9* ↑ 80cm/ ↓ 32in *EA–LA*
Sturdy, compact plant with small, double, brown-red flowers.

C. 'Paul Boissier' *Z5–9* ↑ 1m/ ↓ 3½ft *MA–LA*
Brown-orange flowers which fit in perfectly with the season. It is not terribly robust but flowers so late in the year that this can be forgiven.

CIMICIFUGA *(RANUNCULACEAE)* – bugbane

According to the latest information, this should be included in *Actaea*. This is not yet official, fortunately for superficial plant enthusiasts like us, as they exhibit some considerable differences. In *Actaea*, it is only the berries which have any decorative value, whereas with *Cimicifuga* it is the whole habit (tall, slender, erect), the eye-catching, candle-like inflorescence late in the season and its winter silhouette. Therefore, *Cimicifuga* is a far better all-round garden plant. All species need a humus-rich, moisture-retentive soil and shade, and, in spite of their height, do not need to be supported.

C. dahurica *Z4–8* ↑ 1.8m/ ↓ 6ft *LSu–EA*
This has the most branched inflorescence of all the species with its fluffy, white flowers standing out a little further apart. Very elegant.

C. europaea *Z4–8* ↑ 1.5m/ ↓ 5ft *ESu–MSu*
The least of the bugbanes in all respects – the foliage is a little dull, the flowers unremarkably greenish – with the exception of its winter silhouette: the plumes of seeds are enchanting and persist throughout the whole winter.

C. foetida *Z5–8* ↑ 1.8m/ ↓ 6ft *ESu–MSu*
This is the only bugbane to produce yellow flowers in ornamental, drooping bunches. The dark green, prettily veined leaves are deeply cut and smell awful. A special plant for a shady garden.

C. japonica *Z4–8* ↑ 80cm/ ↓ 32in *LSu–EA*
The shortest species with white flowers and maple-like leaves which gleam a metallic grey-green in spring.

C. racemosa *Z3–8* ↑ 1.2m/ ↓ 4ft *MSu–LSu*
Black snake-root. A robust plant with many healthy leaves and particularly long flower spikes which develop all kinds of strange kinks and curves. Summer-flowering. Tolerates drier conditions than the other bugbanes but, in our experience, flowers poorly as a result.

C. rubifolia *Z4–8* ↑ 1.5m/ ↓ 5ft *LSu–EA*
Syn. *C. cordifolia*. Produces many large leaves like those of a Japanese anemone, against which the erect, branched spikes of creamy white flowers are a slight disappointment. For the best display of flowers, they should be planted in large groups. In smaller gardens where this is not possible it will still be a wonderful plant just for its leaves.

C. simplex *Z4–8* ↑ 2.5m/ ↓ 8ft *EA–MA*
Syn. *C. ramosa*. A number of cultivars have been produced from this very tall species, notable for their red-brown foliage. Atropurpurea Group, 'James Compton' and 'Mahogany' are among them. Unlike the other bugbanes, these cultivars need as sunny a position as possible to thrive. 'Brunette' wins the title of the brownest above the other cultivars but it does not grow as tall (1.2m/4ft). 'Prichard's Giant' is a green-leaved giant form.

Cimicifuga simplex Atropurpurea Group

C. simplex 1.5m/
var. matsumurae Z4–8 5ft MA–LA

This is the first bugbane to thrust its leaves above ground level in spring, remaining attractive all through the summer, and is the last to flower, with thick spikes of flowers. A celebration in the sombre autumn months. 'Elstead' has dark stems. 'Frau Herms' is a profusely flowering, compact form and 'White Pearl' is greenish white and has the prettiest leaves.

CIRSIUM (ASTERACEAE) – plumed thistle

A large genus of thistles which includes not only particularly troublesome weeds (such as creeping thistle) but also some sublime alpine plants. The majority, however, have such vicious spines as to make them not really suitable for gardens. One without spines is:

C. rivulare Z4–8 1.2m/
4ft LSp–MSu

This species grows throughout Europe, sometimes massed in meadows alongside rivers and streams, and can profusely self-seed in the garden. A more suitable garden plant is its cultivar *C.r.* 'Atropurpureum', which is sterile and thus never gets to be a menace. From a rosette of roughly dentate leaves rise long, unbranched stems crowned with a bundle of large, dark red-purple thistle flowers. Does not flower each year as vigorously as the last: sometimes not at all, sometimes all summer long. We do not know why it varies so, yet the plant is a perennial. Probably best in acid, moisture-retentive soil.

CLEMATIS (RANUNCULACEAE)

Most clematis are really climbing plants and therefore do not belong in this book. A small number, however, behave like perennials: they die back completely in winter only to emerge from the ground again in spring. A couple of species keep so compact that they deserve mention in this chapter. A number of the other species which grow rather bushier are discussed in the chapter 'Shrubs'.

C. integrifolia Z3–9 60cm/
2ft ESu–LSu

The leaf of this species is entire, which is unique in *Clematis*. The weak stems, which need supporting by willow wands or – better still – neighbouring plants, bear large, hairy, broad, bell-shaped flowers in purple-blue with a cream-coloured central mass of stamens and later, until far into the autumn, beautiful, fluffy seed pods. It is not fussy about soil type and eventually creates a dense cluster. A superb garden plant, though Graham Thomas describes it as 'dull'(!) Rare, but just as attractive, are the white variety, *C.i.* var. *albiflora* and the pink 'Pastel Pink'.

C. recta Z3–9 2m/
6½ft MSu–LSu

A tall plant which must have support and shows a tendency to creep along supports such as bamboo canes and tall neighbours. In fact, really a perennial with deeply cut leaves and garlands of little white flowers followed by fluffy white seed pods. Prettily flossy and pleasantly untamed. The cultivar 'Purpurea' has dark red-brown stems in spring.

COREOPSIS (ASTERACEAE) – tickseed

This genus of inoffensive, somewhat formal plants with bright yellow daisy flowers is a little old-fashioned. In a tidy, raked garden with a lot of peaty soil it is indeed the picture of ugliness but in a less kempt garden, combined with grasses, it is actually rather nice. (Do you have a specimen left on your compost heap? Go on, try it out!)

C. tripteris Z4–9 2.4m/
8ft LSu–EA

This is a robust plant to use as a backdrop in good, moisture-retentive garden soil. It produces a profusion of yellow daisies with brown centres. Not the prettiest of the tall yellow daisies, but slender, and fits in well within natural situations.

Top: *Cirsium rivulare* 'Atropurpureum'
Centre: *Clematis integrifolia*
Bottom: *Clematis recta* 'Purpurea'

C. verticillata Z4–9 ↕ 60cm/2ft   MSu–LSu

An unpretentious plant with unremarkable, needle-like leaves and many small, bright yellow daisies with brown centres. Does very well in drier, poorer soil. Attractive with grasses. Much more fashionable is the cultivar 'Moonbeam' which remains shorter and produces lemon-yellow flowers. It appears so late in spring that it is easily overgrown by other plants. You had better keep an eye on it.

CORYDALIS (PAPAVERACEAE)

A genus of delicate plants with ferny foliage and spurred, two-lipped flowers. There are many species with wide-ranging characteristics, so we have divided them over a great number of chapters. Only one species fits into this chapter:

C. elata Z6–8 ↕ 60cm/2ft   ESu–MSu

C. flexuosa cultivars have been all the rage in recent years. A fantastic bright blue but with the unfortunate property that they produce new leaves just before winter sets in, and because of this they are in danger of perishing unless they are given protection through the winter. Too much trouble to be included in this book. *C. elata* is the opposite of this. Extremely easy to grow, just as bright a blue but much taller, summer-flowering and – wisely – sheltering below ground in winter. It has a strong scent that is hard to describe. Dutch nurseryman Coen Jansen compares it to 'sweet camphor'.

CRAMBE (BRASSICACEAE) – **sea kale**

A deep-rooting plant which flourishes naturally under extreme conditions (heat, drought, salt and wind) and produces an abundance of flowers.

C. cordifolia Z6–9 ↕ 1.8m/6ft   ESu–MSu

This species forms a rosette of large, rough leaves, easily 1.5m/5ft across, from which a huge cloud of scented white flowers emerges in early summer. Requires a fertile, well-drained soil to enable it to root deeply and flower every year. In less fertile soil, the flowers will sometimes not appear for years at a time. In spite of its size, it is not really suitable for a border since it disappears for the most part once it has flowered, leaving a large gap.

C. maritima Z6–9 ↕ 50cm/20in   ESu–MSu

Common sea kale. This has large, wavy-edged, blue-grey leaves which are worth having in themselves. No less impressive is the inflorescence: rounded, full heads of white flowers. A shoreline plant but not on sand dunes. The plant does not appear to require salt as it also grows inland in gardens, although under otherwise similar conditions: dry, open to the elements, windy, on stony ground above fertile soil. If you have this to offer the plant then there is no more attractive foliage imaginable.

DARMERA (SAXIFRAGACEAE) – **umbrella plant**

D. peltata Z5–9 ↕ 70cm/28in   MSp–LSp

Syn. *Peltiphyllum peltatum*. A plant for boggy ground such as a river bank, with enormous, round, veined leaves, up to 50cm/20in in diameter, that die spectacularly in autumn in shades of yellow, orange and red. It spreads gradually by means of rhizomes but is not nearly as much trouble as butterbur (*Petasites hybridus*), and does not look nearly as unkempt, because *Darmera* does not get eaten away by snails in the summer. In early spring, before its leaves have unfolded, it produces hemispherical groups of pink flowers at the tips of long stems which are not hardy against frost. So they may not be successful every spring. However, the principal point about this plant is the foliage. There is a dwarf variety called 'Nana' for smaller gardens.

Top: *Coreopsis tripteris*
Centre: *Crambe maritima* on the beach at Dungeness
Bottom: *Darmera peltata*

DATISCA (DATISCACEAE)

D. cannabina Z8–9   ↕ **1.8m/ 6ft**   MSu–EA

Looks exactly like hemp but is totally unrelated. The plant does not have any intoxicating properties and can be planted anywhere without any legal restrictions. It grows anywhere equally well, even in poor, sandy soil. Although it originates from the Middle East, it is completely hardy. Deeply cut, palmate leaves and ornamental plumes of small, yellow-green flowers. Dioecious, so to ensure seedlings you must plant male and female specimens together.

DIANTHUS (CARYOPHYLLACEAE) – carnation, pink

The familiar double carnations are so hopelessly old-fashioned that you hardly even see them in florists' any more. This could be just the incentive you need to spur you on to do something creative with them. However, they are archetypal greenhouse plants which you cannot just plant in your garden without a second thought. Wild species of pink are standard features of rock gardens, which we are not going to discuss in this book. There are only two species which perform well in ordinary garden soil, one in the 'Playful' section and one in this chapter:

D. amurensis Z3–9   ↕ **25cm/ 10in**   MSu–EA

Plant right at the front of the border in full sun. Produces flowers in a lilac-mauve colour unusual in pinks.

DICENTRA (PAPAVERACEAE) – bleeding heart

Well known and much loved as bleeding heart is, it cannot be said to be very reliable. After much debate we have decided upon the following species:

D. eximia 'Snowdrift' Z4–8   ↕ **25cm/ 10in**    MSp–ESu

Syn. *D.e.* 'Alba'. An attractive woodland plant with light green foliage and pure white, cascading, heart-shaped flowers. It does not suddenly die or seed itself like *D. formosa* but rather tends to wander slowly but surely among other plants. You cannot really call it invasive. It is not fast enough for that.

DICTAMNUS (RUTACEAE) – burning bush

D. albus Z3–8   ↕ **90cm/ 3ft**   ESu–MSu

A very long-lived plant when given the right conditions: dry, chalky soil in full sun. It will take several years before it achieves its full glory but is worth waiting for: a stately plant with a robust spike of strangely shaped, white to mauve-pink flowers with darker veins. The flowers produce a volatile oil. If you hold a flame to them, the whole inflorescence will ignite, hence its common name. The plant becomes a target for slugs in wet years, but don't panic; it can withstand this and in a more favourable (drier) year it will grow back again as before. There is also a variety with pure white unveined flowers, *D.a.* f. *albiflora*. *D.a.* var. *caucasicus* can reach up to 1.5m/5ft in height. However, it takes at least ten years to get to that stage, so it is most appropriate for the 'eternal' border.

ECHINOPS (ASTERACEAE) – globe thistle

Stately plants with many prickly leaves and spherical flowers, each on its own stem. There is much confusion about nomenclature since there are many species which all look rather similar. We shall not attempt to clear it up. As they all look like one another we shall simply not describe them. Most species seed themselves profusely. We are reasonably sure of the names of the following cultivars and we know that they do not self-seed:

E. bannaticus 'Taplow Blue' Z3–9   ↕ **1.2m/ 4ft**   MSu–LSu

Produces grey-blue flowers and is taller than *E. ritro* 'Veitch's Blue', which has purple-blue flowers. Both are easy to grow almost anywhere.

Top left: *Datisca cannabina*
Top right: *Dictamnus albus*
Bottom: *Dianthus amurensis*

EPIMEDIUM *(BERBERIDACEAE)* – barrenwort, bishop's hat

Plants with leathery, thrice-divided, ternate leaves composed of typically lopsided, heart-shaped leaflets and fragile, pendent, four-petalled flowers in spring. Extremely effective as foliage and for ground cover: no weeds will push through it. The leaves of most species turn brown in winter, but that is attractive too. These pretty, brown leaves should be cut off in spring to let the flowers show. Fresh leaves appear from ground level in beautiful shades of bronze at the same time as the flowers. Indestructible when planted in (semi-)shade in a good, humus-rich soil.

E. grandiflorum Z5–8   25cm/10in MSp–LSp

Of all the species, this has the largest flowers, 2–3cm/1in across, which look like miniature columbines. Flowers are white; in 'Crimson Beauty' they are pinkish red; 'Lilafee' is purplish mauve, and 'Lilac Seedling' is even more decorative; 'Rose Queen' is pinkish mauve.

E. x perralchicum 'Frohnleiten' Z5–9   30cm/1ft MSp–LSp

In mild winters, this has evergreen leaves and bright yellow flowers. Spreads slowly.

E. pinnatum subsp. colchicum 'Black Sea' Z5–9   45cm/18in MSp–LSp

Produces pale yellow, unspurred flowers on long stems. The leaves shine in winter like the Black Sea. Well, a liver-coloured brown-red anyway. Isn't that lovely?

E. x versicolor 'Sulphureum' Z5–9   30cm/1ft MSp–LSp

A robust species which grows everywhere, even in poor soil. The flowers are sulphur yellow.

E. x warleyense Z5–9   30cm/1ft MSp–LSp

This has light green leaves and orange-yellow flowers. Does not grow into such a dense bush as the other species but is robust none the less. 'Orangekönigin' grows everywhere and poses no problems.

ERYNGIUM *(APIACEAE)* – sea holly

Eryngiums produce displays of teasel-like flowers surrounded by prickly bracts. There are many species, all of them very decorative but not all equally dependable. The dependable species are:

E. alpinum Z5–8   75cm/30in ESu–MSu

Has large, blue flower heads 5cm/2in long, surrounded by steel-blue bracts. A familiar sight at florists' and a problem-free plant for a garden where there is dry, chalky soil. It is easy to grow from seed but does not generally seed itself. 'When well grown is not surpassed in beauty by any other plant', according to William Robinson. 'Blue Star' is in all respects even bluer.

E. bourgatii Z5–9   60cm/2ft MSu–EA

A Pyrenean species with prickly, grey-green leaves veined in white and many branches bearing blue-green flowers approximately 1cm/½in in size.

E. x tripartitum Z5–8   60cm/2ft MSu–EA

Looks like the previous species but has green leaves and such an extremely branched inflorescence that it creates a veritable mound of purple-blue flowers.

EUPATORIUM *(ASTERACEAE)* – hemp agrimony

Impressive plants with robust leaves and large umbels of flowers in late summer which attract hoards of butterflies. Extremely resilient and attractive after flowering as well. They all do well in normal garden soil although they will repay a little extra water with improved growth.

Above: *Epimedium grandiflorum* 'Lilac Seedling'
Below: *Eryngium bourgatii*

Above: *Eupatorium purpureum* subsp. *maculatum* 'Album' with small tortoiseshell butterflies
Below: *Euphorbia palustris*

**E. cannabinum
'Flore Pleno' Z3–9** 1.5m/5ft MSu–EA

A sterile, double-flowered variety of wild hemp agrimony which neither seeds itself nor attracts butterflies. We mention it because the colour is very unusual: old rose. Likes a moisture-retentive soil.

E. chinense Z3–9 1.25m/4ft MSu–EA

This will not grow as tall as the other species but will spread wider. The flowering stems are much branched, ensuring that the plant remains in flower a long time; the flowers are slightly dull greyish white. In its favour is its flowering season at a time when most species of butterfly are at large (mid-summer); they crowd around it. Black and white map butterflies look particularly good against it.

**E. purpureum
subsp. maculatum Z3–9** 1.25–2.5m/4–8ft LSu–EA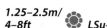

The species native to America, the Joe Pye weed, is not a very interesting garden plant. However, there are several spectacular cultivars which no garden should be without.

'Album' produces white flowers which fade to a dingy brown; the umbels are a little smaller than in other cultivars. It would appear to be the least desirable but it does grow to be the tallest (2.5m/8ft) and will definitely not topple over. 'Atropurpureum' has gigantic, purple-pink umbels on dark red stems, a great attraction for late-summer butterflies (red admirals and small tortoiseshells). It has a beautiful silhouette in winter. Reaches about 1.75m/6ft in height. 'Purple Bush' derives from the previous type. It is somewhat shorter and more compact with more flowers but borne in smaller umbels.

E. rugosum Z3–9 1.2m/4ft LSu–MA

A rather coarse but robust plant with stinging-nettle-like leaves and greyish white flowers similar to *Ageratum*. Interesting for flowering late in the season. Improvements made on this include 'Chocolate' with chocolate-coloured leaves and 'Snowball' with pure white flowers.

EUPHORBIA (EUPHORBIACEAE) – spurge

A large, extremely varied genus of plants with thousands of species ranging from little annuals to great trees, with many characteristics in common. The stems, which contain a poisonous, milky white sap (dangerous if in contact with the eyes), become more densely leaved towards the top of the plant. The flowers are inconspicuous but are surrounded by two eye-catching, usually green-yellow bracts. The most attractive species come either from southern Europe and, therefore, are not hardy, or from the Himalayas and do not survive wet winters. There are only two really dependable species:

E. palustris Z5–8 1.2m/4ft MSp–LSp

Marsh spurge grows naturally in marshland wherever it encounters a slight accumulation of vegetable debris. It will also grow in regular garden soil provided you add plenty of coarse, well-rotted compost. It creates an impressive bush even in early spring.

E. polychroma Z4–9 50cm/20in MSp–ESu

Grows in neat clumps and flowers profusely in spring. A much brighter yellow than the other *Euphorbia* species. Perhaps not very subtle and a little formal but at least it is reliable and very suitable for a slightly wilder shade garden.

FILIPENDULA (ROSACEAE) – meadowsweet

Plants with the large, irregularly cut and deeply veined leaves characteristic of the rose family and similarly characteristic flowers: plumes which are flat on top but which taper to a point beneath to form rough triangles.

F. camtschatica Z3–9 2m/6½ft MSu–LSu

Originally from the Siberian peninsula of Kamchatka where the plant attains unearthly proportions when growing next to warm geysers. In cool temperate gardens with a good, moisture-retentive soil, it will grow to a hefty size but not out of this world. The large, cream-coloured plumes are set off attractively by a woodland backdrop.

F. purpurea Z4–9 ↕ 80cm–1.4m/ 32in–4¹/₂ft MSu–LSu

Looks just like the typical wild species but has pink flowers; cerise, to be precise. Grows in all soil types, if moist, and gradually spreads to create hefty clumps which will tolerate a lot of competition. 'Nephele' flowers profusely and grows 1.2m/4ft tall, 'Pink Dreamland' is shorter (80cm/32in) and has red flower stems, 'Rhapsody' looks like *F. rubra* 'Venusta' but is shorter (1.4m/4¹/₂ft) and is not invasive.

F. vulgaris Z4–9 ↕ 60cm/ 2ft ESu–MSu

Dropwort. Unlike its relatives, this *Filipendula* does not like damp conditions, preferring a dry, chalky soil. Its feathery leaves which look like yarrow (and not like carrot leaves as Graham Stuart Thomas attests) give a compact plumed effect above which appear the branching umbels of flowers. A little bit scrawny. *F. vulgaris* 'Multiplex' is more effective.

GENTIANA (GENTIANACEAE) – gentian

Plants with bell-shaped flowers in eponymous gentian blue which anyone would happily have in their garden. Unfortunately, most species require a very specific environment (alpine, chalk grassland, peat bog) which a normal garden cannot usually provide. Two species are reliable as garden plants:

G. asclepiadea Z6–9 ↕ 70cm/ 28in LSu–EA

Willow gentian. Reliable when planted in moisture-retentive, woodland loam, preferably chalky. The older it gets, the prettier it becomes. Delicate stems with willow-like leaves bend beneath the weight of true gentian-blue flowers. *G.a.* var. *alba* has white flowers.

G. lutea Z5–8 ↕ 1.2m/ 4ft  ESu–MSu

The yellow gentian is an unusual species with its large, veined, ovate leaves (like *Veratrum*) and yellow flowers wreathed around the stem. A regal appearance which can only be seen after it has been allowed to grow for years in the same spot. When it flowers for the first time, it rests the following year only to flower even more abundantly the next year. Eventually, gigantic clumps of these plants are formed. It has no particular requirements as regards soil type except that it should be well drained: the plant needs to root deeply. Never move it once established.

GERANIUM (GERANIACEAE) – cranesbill

Geraniums are ideal garden plants. They will grow well under virtually all conditions anywhere. They have neat round leaves which are lobed or deeply cut and palmate. The flowers have five petals and have seed cases that look like cranes' bills. They range from 3cm/1¹/₄in to 1.25m/4ft high and you can find them in any colour except yellow and orange. There's one to suit any spot in the garden you care to mention: from the deepest, driest shade to a marsh, from a moisture-laden meadow to a rockery. There are so many reliable species that it would be impossible to name them all. A selection, therefore (see also under the 'Playful' section and the 'Invasive plants' chapter):

G. 'Brookside' Z4–8 ↕ 60cm/ 2ft LSp–EA

Grows as wide as it does tall and produces bowl-shaped, purple-blue flowers. The main flowering season is late spring but the plant will continue to flower (modestly) afterwards.

G. 'Dilys' Z4–8 ↕ 30cm/ 1ft MSu–LA

Produces red-purple flowers late in the season on long, lateral stems which spread out over a large area (but which do not take root). Ideal in combination with spring-flowering perennials which die back after flowering such as *Papaver orientale*.

Above: *Filipendula purpurea*
Below: *Gentiana asclepiadea* var. *alba*

G. erianthum Z3–9 | 45cm/18in MSp–LSp

A fairly undemanding species with purple-blue flowers 4cm/1½in in size early in the year and deeply cut leaves which turn red in autumn. Modestly repeat-flowering.

G. ibericum Z5–8 | 45cm/18in  LSp–MSu

A pretty species with deeply cut, hairy leaves and blue, purple-veined flowers 5cm/2in across.

G. 'Johnson's Blue' Z4–8 | 45cm/18in LSp–MSu

An old cultivar but still one of the most attractive and abundantly flowering with blue flowers 5cm/2in across.

G. x magnificum Z4–8 | 60cm/2ft LSp–ESu

An old-fashioned hybrid with large purple-blue flowers in healthy bunches. Flowers for a short time then collapses. Very robust.

G. 'Nimbus' Z4–8 | 60cm/2ft LSp–MSu

A new, pretty cultivar with delicately cut leaves which appear green-yellow in spring and blue-purple, delicately veined flowers with a white centre. The petals are quite narrow.

G. x oxonianum Z5–8 | 30–70cm/12–28in  LSp–EA

A collective name for a group of cultivars, *G. endressii* x *G. versicolor*, all of them vigorous, flowering all summer long and tolerant of a great deal of shade. 'Claridge Druce' is the most natural-looking, threading its way between other, taller plants, with mauve-pink flowers. It copes in seemingly impossible locations. 'Summer Surprise' is comparable but a little less wayward and produces warm pink flowers. 'Phoebe Noble' has dark red-pink flowers while those of 'Rebecca Moss' are pale, shining pink. *G. x o.* f. *thurstonianum* is a top grower with strange flowers: very narrow petals in flesh pink, just like little worms. Narrower still are the petals of 'Sherwood'. 'Wargrave Pink' is an old standard which produces robust sheets of salmon-pink flowers even in deep shade. 'Wageningen' is similar but is more compact.

G. 'Patricia' Z4–8 | 75cm/30in LSp–MA

Spreading, repeat-flowering plant with magenta flowers with black centres. Step-child to *G. psilostemon*.

G. 'Philippe Vapelle' Z6–8 | 40cm/16in ESu–MSu

A hybrid of *G. renardii* with beautiful, grey-green, puckered leaves and dark blue flowers. Elegant.

G. psilostemon Z4–8 | 1.2m/4ft ESu–LSu

A magnificent, tall species which flowers abundantly over a long period producing magenta flowers with black centres. Flamboyantly pretty, it peps up any border. The plant has a tendency to self-seed, but with a plant as attractive as this that should not pose a problem.

G. sanguineum Z4–8 | 25–40cm/10–16in LSp–MA

Bloody cranesbill. This is native to many sunny limestone areas in Europe. It does not necessarily need a dry location as the plant also grows vigorously in the Burren, a limestone plateau in the west of Ireland with ridiculously high levels of rainfall. A sunny spot at the front of the border and well-drained soil are all it requires. The blood-red flowers appear throughout the whole summer.

G. 'Sirak' Z5–8 | 50cm/20in LSp–MSu

Hairy leaves and relatively large lilac-pink flowers. One of the better new introductions.

G. soboliferum Z6–8 | 30cm/1ft MSu–EA

An unassuming, summer-flowering species with lilac-pink flowers and beautiful autumn leaf colour.

Top: *Geranium ibericum*
Centre: *Geranium* 'Philippe Vapelle'

Bottom left: *Geranium* 'Sirak'
Bottom right: *Geranium* 'Spinners'

G. 'Spinners' Z4–8 ↕ 80cm/ 32in ESu–EA

Slow-growing but eventually a hefty plant, repeat-flowering with nice purple-blue flowers.

G. wallichianum 'Buxton's Variety' Z4–8 ↕ 30cm/ 1ft MSu–LA

A gorgeous species with long, creeping stems which need to work their way through other plants, veined leaves and blue flowers with white centres. Flowers until the first night frost. Has the reputation of not being completely hardy but in our experience it is, given a well-drained soil.

GILLENIA (ROSACEAE)

G. trifoliata Z4–8 ↕ 1m/ 3½ft ESu–MSu

A plant of steel which does well in any well-drained soil, even in dry shaded spots. It has a shrubby appearance with a profusion of white, butterfly-like flowers on red stems. The plant does not always flower beautifully every year, probably because of occasional very late frosts.

HELENIUM (ASTERACEAE) – sneezewort

H. autumnale Z4–8 ↕ 1.8m/ 6ft MSu–EA

This prairie plant has an abundance of yellow daisies with brown centres. The species as found in the wild is grown hardly anywhere, which is only right: it grows too tall, blows over and could only be used in a very wild garden indeed. For years, people have been growing cultivars which do not grow nearly as tall and which are sturdy through and through. That would seem ideal, were it not for question marks hanging over the brown-flowered varieties in particular regarding their longevity. Too much rain in the spring (snails!) would appear to be the principal culprit.

Cultivars Z5–8

In our opinion, the most reliable cultivars are 'Moerheim Beauty', 1.2m/4ft tall, early-flowering with radiant, red-brown flowers; unfortunately, the plant is quick to fall over and thus needs supporting. 'Flammendes Kätchen' grows very tall, 1.8m/6ft, 'Kupferzwerg', 1.2m/4ft, orange-red with dark centres, 'Rubinzwerg', 1.2m/4ft, shorter, browner with great abundance of flowers, and 'Zimbelstern', 1.4m/5ft with yellow-brown, speckled flowers.

HELIANTHUS (ASTERACEAE) – sunflower

As well as the familiar annual sunflower, this genus also contains a large number of perennials, most of which are coarse, ugly and invasive. Graham Stuart Thomas grumbles 'I cannot write about these with any enthusiasm', and proceeds to summarize a whole array of these rampant plants. We shall not bother doing that. We shall only list the species which enthuse us:

H. 'Lemon Queen' Z5–8 ↕ 2.4m/ 8ft MSu–MA

A sturdy, non-invasive cultivar which from mid-summer until far into autumn is covered in lovely, little lemon-yellow sunflowers. Humming with bees and packed with butterflies.

H. salicifolius Z6–9 ↕ 2.5m/ 8ft MA–LA

A unique plant with tall stems filled with long, drooping leaves which provide a gorgeous, woolly effect at the back of a border. A little like an ornamental grass, but different! It flowers too, producing floppy versions of dandelion flowers in late autumn, but they are irrelevant. An architectural plant which should be used a great deal more.

HELIOPSIS (ASTERACEAE)

Extremely robust and reliable plants with large, bright yellow 'daisies'. Terribly dependable and thus a genus worthy of mention.

Top: *Gillenia trifoliata*
Centre: *Helenium* 'Rubinzwerg'

Bottom left: *Helianthus salicifolius*
Bottom right: *Helianthus* 'Lemon Queen' with *Sanguisorba canadensis*

Sadly, their appearance lacks a certain something. This genus alone is responsible for the present-day lament: 'I don't like yellow!' We still see far too much of it in ugly gardens, usually alongside a nasty pink phlox. Enough – we have mentioned it and having done so will move swiftly on.

HELLEBORUS *(RANUNCULACEAE)* – **hellebore**

A real craze for this genus has developed in recent years and everyone now knows about these fabulous winter-flowering plants, sometimes known as Christmas roses. However, the true Christmas rose (*H. niger*), widely available in winter from garden centres and market stalls, is often a difficult garden plant. While it performs well in heavy, fertile soils, the flowers will not tolerate sharp frost and this, of course, is a first principle for winter-flowering plants; the flowers simply collapse at a few degrees below zero. In addition to *H. niger*, there are many other species which are just as delightful or more, but which appear to be extremely sensitive to leaf-spot in a damp climate: these plants turn black and collapse. Sadly, there are only a few species which will, under normal conditions, flower well. Normal conditions for *Helleborus* species mean a nutrient-rich soil with plenty of humus, which is moisture-retentive without being waterlogged. In the wild, all these species grow in deciduous woodland, which means that they receive full sunlight when in flower in the winter and spring and lie in the shade in summer.

For years, botanists have been arguing about the correct names for these plants. We have decided, therefore, to distance ourselves from the debate and all names are conditional as a result.

H. argutifolius Z7–9 60cm/ 2ft LW–LSp

Syn. *H. lividus* subsp. *corsicus*. A generally hardy species with beautiful, three-lobed, serrated, jade green leaves and large, long-lasting, apple green flowers. The flower buds can be damaged by hard frost, but the plant itself usually survives.

H. multifidus Z5–9 40cm/ 16in LW–MSp

This is a plant with especially delicate leaves, deeply incised and almost feather-like, and pale, green-veined flowers. Slow-growing. The leaves of *H.m.* subsp. *hercegovinus* are even prettier, like those of a palm tree, but whether this subspecies will ever become a good garden plant is still open to debate.

H. odorus Z5–9 40cm/ 16in LW–MSp

An enthusiast's plant. The young leaves are covered in silky down. Its apple green flowers also produce an apple scent.

H. orientalis Z4–9  50cm/ 20in MW–MSp

Lenten rose. Definitely the hardiest species. The true species flowers profusely, producing long-stemmed flowers ranging from pink to green. These lie prostrate on the ground during frosty periods, but perk up again when it thaws. Each plant exhibits a differently speckled pattern on its flowers. The species suffers either little or not at all from leaf spot but is sadly hardly ever available in its true wild form. It has been submerged by a sea of hybrids, each more beautiful then the last: pure white, speckled, green, metallic grey, purple, near black or with double flowers. You name it, somebody is bound to have grown it. If you are buying young plants that have yet to flower, it is important to know whether they have been propagated from seed or by division. The flower colour of seed-raised plants will always be a surprise. Moreover, some hybrids are rather susceptible to leaf spot. Hellebores tend to be expensive, so do be careful. We can't say too much, though, because we make blunders ourselves sometimes.

H. purpurascens Z5–8 25cm/ 10in LW–MSp

Deciduous. The flowers, purple on the exterior and greenish within, emerge from ground level in spring before the leaves appear. One of the hardier species.

H. torquatus Z5–8 30cm/ 1ft LW–MSp

Flower hue is variable and so difficult to describe: greyish on the exterior with a purplish edge, greenish within with purple veins. Neat and elegant. *H. atrorubens* from Croatia is similar, but generally has purple flowers and less deeply indented leaves.

Top: Helleborus atrorubens
Bottom: Helleborus multifidus

Helleborus orientalis hybrids

Above: *Hemerocallis* 'Princess Blue Eyes' in front of *H.* 'Green Flutter'
Below: *Heuchera micrantha* 'Purple Ace'

H. viridis ↕ 30cm/ 1ft LW–MSp

Green hellebore. An unpretentious and hardy species with yellow-green flowers. The plant was used in the past in veterinary science and is extremely poisonous – as are all the other species of *Helleborus*.

HEMEROCALLIS *(HEMEROCALLIDACEAE)* – daylily

A genus of plants as strong as iron which performs well in any reasonable garden soil. Large clusters of grassy leaves and large lily-like flowers which are produced in great numbers in the summer months. Each individual flower lasts only one day, hence the common name.

H. altissima Z6–9 ↕ 1.6m/ 5¼ft MSu–LSu

A rare species with relatively small, bright yellow flowers on exceptionally long stems.

H. citrina Z3–9 ↕ 1m/ 3½ft ESu–MSu

A large plant with abundant lemon-yellow flowers with narrow petals. The flowers open in the evening, remaining closed during the day, and are sweetly scented.

Hybrids Z4–9 ↕ 50–80cm/ 20–32in ESu–LSu

Daylilies have been popular garden plants for centuries and in the course of time thousands of cultivars have been grown in all the colours of the rainbow, mostly under the slogan 'the bigger the better'. That is not our motto, but we have still managed to find a number of cultivars with attractively coloured flowers which can be placed in a natural setting. 'Corky' produces small yellow flowers speckled red-brown on the exterior early in the season. 'Gentle Shepherd' has primarily white flowers with yellow-green centres, 'Green Flutter' is rather formal but produces especially beautiful, fresh yellow flowers with green centres, 'Pardon Me' requires no apology at all for its dark red flowers with green-yellow centres, 'Princess Blue Eyes' is a somewhat muted purple-red, green within, and 'Red Toy' is a jolly miniature producing red flowers with green centres.

HEUCHERA *(SAXIFRAGACEAE)* – coral flower

Plants with small flowers and beautiful, maple-like leaves which need a humus-rich, moist soil to grow well. Not too moist, as they then tend to become woody and lift themselves above ground level, rendering them vulnerable to decimation by frost. Not too dry or else they will do nothing at all. We find just one species particularly interesting because of its leaves:

H. micrantha Z4–8 ↕ 40cm/ 16in LSp–MSu

With nondescript little creamy white flowers but beautifully cut, brown leaves, this does very well to fill in spaces at the front of a border. A growing number of cultivars is being produced with a variety of different leaf forms: wavy-edged or wrinkled, red-brown, chocolate-coloured, pewter-coloured or metallic green with brown veins. American growers especially stand out as having thought up the most extraordinary names for these cultivars. We shall not trouble ourselves to describe them; you have to see them for yourself in order to make a choice. Just enjoy the names: 'Chocolate Ruffles', 'Eco Magnififolia' (large-leaved), 'Emerald Veil', 'Palace Purple' (one of the oldest), 'Pewter Moon', 'Purple Ace', and 'Stormy Seas' (in silver, lavender, pewter and charcoal-grey). Go on, try them out!

HOSTA *(HOSTACEAE)* – hosta, plantain lily

The *Hosta* genus is too well known to need description. We feel it would be more useful, therefore, to speak seriously about ecology for a moment. Hostas are famous for their susceptibility to attack by slugs and snails and should perhaps not be mentioned in this chapter because of that. That would be true except that they are not at all vulnerable to snails when planted correctly! Why is that? In nature, hostas will grow in rocky places, mostly facing away from direct sunshine. In your garden, this means that they need a well-drained spot that is (semi-)shaded, which never gets too wet and whose soil is not too nutrient-rich. A sandy soil with a moderate amount of nutrients is ideal for growing compact, robust hostas which are unpalatable to slugs and snails. All other soil types, especially heavy clay and peat soils, quickly become waterlogged and are too fertile. This will cause them to grow too fast so that the leaves become large (splendid visually) but too thin, providing a delicacy for snail palates. We are aware that this advice will not endear us to many except to the (usually unfortunate) owners of gardens with poor, sandy soil. We disagree with all other gardening books, which all advise that hostas need a nutrient-rich soil with a lot of fertilizer to produce large leaves. What all those books forget to add is that in so doing you are serving up a snail banquet. We do not write this because we are keen to broadcast a different opinion; it is a fact borne out by our experience which we feel should be shared. It is a pity, but it has to be said: natural gardening (without pesticides) in heavy clay or peat soils does not go hand in hand with growing hostas. For those now not-so-unfortunate owners of gardens with poor, sandy soil there now follows a selection from the enormous and complex range available:

H. clausa Z3–9 40cm/16in MSu–LSu
A ground-cover species, not to say rather rampant, with lilac flowers which do not open. The flowers do open in *H.c.* var. *normalis*.

H. 'Halcyon' Z3–9   45cm/18in MSu–LSu
This is a small cultivar with attractive, flawless, oblong, blue-grey leaves.

H. montana Z3–9 1m/3½ft ESu–MSu
Slow-growing but eventually an enormous plant with large, oval, gleaming green leaves.

H. plantaginea var. grandiflora Z3–9 50cm/20in LSu–MA
An exception to the rule. What a relief to gardeners with fertile soil! This species with light green leaves and large, white flowers in late summer needs a warm, sunny spot in fertile, moisture-retentive soil, without which it struggles.

H. sieboldiana var. elegans Z3–9   75cm/30in MSu–LSu
A familiar species with large, rounded, blue-grey, deeply quilted leaves. The pale lilac flowers scarcely rise above the foliage. 'Frances Williams' is comparable but has a wide green-yellow leaf margin; gorgeous, but the pale lilac flowers clash and are best cut off.

Above: *Hosta plantaginea* var. *grandiflora*
Below: *Hosta* 'Blue Angel'

Hybrids *Z3–9*

'Big Daddy' and 'Blue Angel' are both giants, at least 1m/3½ft tall and wide, with large, blue-green leaves. The first also has puckered leaves. 'Blue Impression' does not grow as large but produces exceptionally abundant lilac flowers against its blue leaves. 'Krossa Regal' has long, upright, blue-grey leaves and especially long (1.25m/4ft tall) stems with white flowers. 'Midas Touch' is a medium-sized hybrid with deeply puckered leaves which turn gold in the course of the summer. The lilac flowers clash. 'Moody Blues' is a particularly well-balanced plant whose lilac flowers go well with its blue-grey leaves. Finally, 'Sum and Substance' is a giant with enormous, thick, yellow-green leaves and lilac flowers.

INULA (ASTERACEAE) – fleabane

A large genus with large as well as small species. Only the large ones meet our requirements. They have huge, hairy leaves which hang from the plants like doormats when they die off in autumn. It may sound strange but we think this looks rather attractive! Yellow daisy-like flowers. In spite of their large leaves, they prefer drier locations.

I. helenium Z5–9 1.8m/ 6ft   ESu–MSu

Elecampane. According to gardening manuals this one belongs in the herb garden. Just why is anyone's guess. An attractive wild plant with large, tapering leaves and fairly small flowers borne at the top of the stem. Self-seeding but not obnoxiously so.

I. magnifica Z4–8 2.2m/ 7ft MSu–LSu

The scientific name leaves nothing for us to add: magnificent! Large flowers with long, wispy, ray-florets. 'Sonnenstrahl' is a superior version.

IRIS (IRIDACEAE) – iris

Irises are yet another of the familiar plant genera whose total unsuitability for the natural garden we have with some sadness to report. The well-known purple flag (*I. germanica*), of which there are numerous wonderful hybrids, is a notorious steppe plant which requires heat and will not tolerate competition from other plants. That is all very well in a traditional garden where plants are given plenty of space to themselves, enabling the sun to warm the rhizomes unimpeded. Most irises cannot cope when combined with either plants of the same height or ground-cover plants as the rhizomes become overshadowed. They start to languish, with snails quickly bringing their dismal existence to a sorry end.

There is, in fact, only one species which we find grows well in normal, moisture-retentive garden soil and which can be combined close to other plants:

I. sibirica Z4–9 1m/ 3½ft LSp–ESu

Its elegant, blue flowers are fleeting but the familiar sword-shaped leaves are effective for the whole summer. There are quantities of cultivars which principally vary in terms of flower colour: white, all shades of blue, purple. A close relation is *I. chrysographes*, with black-purple flowers, which thrives only in fertile (heavy) soil.

JEFFERSONIA (BERBERIDACEAE)

J. dubia Z5–9 25cm/ 10in MSp

A delicate woodland plant with a cluster of saucer-shaped, blue-green leaves on brittle, red stems and lilac-blue flowers about 4cm/ 1½in across. Can live for ages in a nice shaded spot. Only flowers for a short time and afterwards disappears below ground. A plant for enthusiasts.

KALIMERIS (ASTERACEAE)

K. incisa Z4–9 75cm/ 30in ESu–EA

Syn. *Aster mongolicus*. An unpretentious plant which builds into a pleasant cluster of endlessly remontant, lilac-blue daisy flowers. Strong and reliable, it combines well everywhere. 'Alba', with white flowers, is most frequently available.

KIRENGESHOMA (SAXIFRAGACEAE)

K. palmata Z5–8 1m/ 3½ft LSu–EA

Beautiful woodland plant with sycamore-like leaves and soft yellow, bell-shaped flowers (like shuttlecocks) in early autumn and pretty seed capsules after that. Flourishes in humus-rich, moisture-retentive soil in shade. One of the few plants to flower abundantly even in places never reached by the sun's rays.

Top: *Inula magnifica* 'Sonnenstrahl'   Centre right: *Jeffersonia dubia*
Centre left: *Iris sibirica*   Bottom: *Kirengeshoma palmata*

KITAIBELA (MALVACEAE)

K. vitifolia Z6–8 ↕ 1.8m/ 6ft ESu–LSu

A stately plant with a calm demeanour, not spectacular. Elegant, vine-like leaves and small mallow flowers. Reliable as a perennial in moderately fertile, well-drained soil and then does not grow as tall.

LAMIUM (LAMIACEAE) – dead-nettle

Dead-nettles do not, of course, fit in with this chapter. They either run rampant or seed themselves or (disaster!) do both. The following, albeit rather fussy, cultivars are reasonably manageable:

L. maculatum 'White Nancy' Z4–9 ↕ 25cm/ 10in LSp–EA

This has silver leaves and white flowers. 'James Boyd Parselle' flowers in pink.

LATHYRUS (PAPILIONACEAE)

A large and varied genus of annuals and perennials. Among the perennials are many species which are particularly charming in the wild in southern Europe but which prove disappointing in the garden. However, one which does work is:

L. vernus Z5–9 ↕ 40cm/ 16in   MSp–LSp

Spring vetchling. This produces clusters of delicately divided, almost fern-like leaves and racemes of red-purple sweet-pea flowers. With a little luck, you will get to see its elegant, chestnut-brown pods as well. An easy plant for a shaded garden. There are varieties in different colours too, such as 'Alboroseus' in white with pink, although these are not of such good quality.

LAVATERA (MALVACEAE) – mallow

These are favourites of gardeners and look very similar to *Malva* (so much so that even the *Flora Europaea* cannot explain what the difference is between the two genera). However, the shrubby lavateras, deriving from the southern European *L. maritima* and *L. olbia*, are not hardy. One which is hardy is:

L. thuringiaca Z7–9 ↕ 1m/ 3½ft MSu–EA

Vigorous and flowers over a long period. 'Ice Cool' is the prettiest, with a greenish tint to the white flowers.

LEUCANTHEMELLA (ASTERACEAE) – daisy

L. serotina Z4–9 ↕ 1.6m/ 5¼ft MA–LA

A tall, sturdy species which late in the season produces white daisies with green centres that turn to follow the path of the low-lying sun.

LIATRIS (ASTERACEAE) – blazing star, gayfeather

Generally loathed plants with narrow, grassy leaves and a rigid, thistle-like, purple inflorescence. The flowers characteristically open from the top of the spike downwards. Since the rediscovery of the North American tall grass prairie, we now understand what to do with them: they are best presented combined *en masse* with grasses and *Echinacea*. However, the most familiar species, *L. spicata*, which is commonly used in cut-flower arrangements, remains rather formal. More attractive examples are:

L. ligulistylis Z7–10 ↕ 60cm/ 2ft MSu–LSu

This species' flowers are not borne in a cluster but rather are staggered; the flowers open on the spike from the top to the bottom, from eye-catching, flame-red buds.

L. pycnostachya Z4–9 ↕ 1m/ 3½ft MSu–LSu

This looks like *L. spicata* but grows taller and has a sleeker appearance.

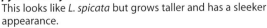
Top: *Lathyrus vernus*
Above: *Leucanthemella serotina* with *Aster* 'Herfstweelde'
Right: *Liatris ligulistylis* in bud

LIGULARIA (ASTERACEAE)

A genus closely related to groundsel (*Senecio*), with attractive, large leaves and bright yellow spikes of flowers which in appearance come somewhere between daisies and dandelions. They only like growing on boggy ground, preferably marshland or heavy soil, in full sun. The leaves are usually eaten by snails and droop in hot weather. However, this is not such a problem as these plants look very rugged anyway. They look at their best when planted in a more informal setting.

L. dentata Z4–8 ↕ 1.2m/ ↓ 4ft MSu–LSu ☼ ☀

This has large, heart-shaped, dark green leaves and robust stems bearing racemes of large, orange-yellow daisies. 'Desdemona' and 'Othello' are well-known cultivars in which the underside of the leaf is dark red.

L. 'Gregynog Gold' Z4–8 ↕ 1.8m/ ↓ 6ft MSu–LSu

A cross between *L. dentata* and *L. veitchiana* with large, heart-shaped leaves; its large, orange-yellow daisies are borne not in racemes but on huge, tapering spikes. Spectacular!

L. japonica Z4–8 ↕ 1.5m/ ↓ 5ft ESu–MSu ☼ ☀

This has eye-catching, deeply cut leaves and large yellow flowers on long stems, followed by attractive fluffy seed heads.

L. macrophylla Z4–8 ↕ 1.5m/ ↓ 5ft MSu–LSu ☼

Syn. *Senecio macrophyllus* and *S. doria* subsp. *macrophyllus*; general confusion all round. The plant is certainly quite unique. Its inflorescence is a panicle of many small florets and does indeed more closely resemble a *Senecio* than a *Ligularia*. Large, oblong, grey-powdered leaves which feel like suede. Is far more tolerant of dry conditions than other species of *Ligularia*.

L. x palmatiloba Z4–8 ↕ 1.5m/ ↓ 5ft MSu–LSu ☼ ☀

A cross between *L. dentata* and *L. japonica* with the large, orange-yellow flowers of the former species and the cut leaves of the latter.

L. przewalskii Z4–8 ↕ 1.8m/ ↓ 6ft MSu–LSu ☼ ☀

This has deeply cut leaves like fingers and oblong, bright yellow flowers borne on black spikes. It has a slightly invasive tendency.

L. stenocephala Z4–8 ↕ 1.2m/ ↓ 4ft MSu–LSu ☼ ☀

This has triangular, deeply toothed leaves and an oblong inflorescence. 'The Rocket' is a better hybrid with purple flower spikes.

L. veitchiana Z4–8 ↕ 1.2m/ ↓ 4ft MSu–LSu ☼ ☀

Broad, heart-shaped leaves, branching flower spikes and eye-catching seed heads. *L. wilsoniana* looks just like it.

LIMONIUM (PLUMBAGINACEAE) – sea lavender

Fields of sea lavender in bloom in salt marshes along the coast are an unforgettable sight to anyone who has seen them. There are dozens of species which occur from the coasts of Europe all the way to the Siberian salt steppes. A number of these do not seem to have salt as a requirement for their well-being and will grow quite happily in gardens given a sunny spot and well-drained soil. All species have large, shiny, leathery leaves and elegantly branching inflorescences suitable for dried flower arrangements.

L. gmelinii Z4–9 ↕ 50cm/ ↓ 20in MSu–LSu ☼

Produces erect plumes of lavender-blue flowers.

L. platyphyllum Z4–9 ↕ 40cm/ ↓ 16in MSu–LSu ☼

Syn. *L. latifolium*. Just as lavender-blue as *L. gmelinii*, but the flowers fan out more broadly.

Top: *Ligularia veitchiana*
Centre: *Limonium gmelinii*
Bottom: *Lindelofia anchusoides*

LINDELOFIA *(BORAGINACEAE)*

L. anchusoides Z6–9 ↕ **80cm/ 32in** **ESu–MSu**

Syn. *Adelocaryum anchusoides*. The inflorescence of these boraginaceous plants (the 'scorpioid cyme') unfurls as if it were a fern. In the process, this species displays kingfisher-blue flowers against blue-grey leaves. This is an extremely reliable plant in any well-drained garden soil. May self-seed a little.

LYTHRUM *(LYTHRACEAE)* – **loosestrife**

Loosestrifes are bog plants which tend to dominate entire stretches of ditches, canals and marshes in summer with their jolly red-purple spikes of flowers. They seem able to grow well in normal garden soil that is reasonably moisture-retentive.

L. salicaria Z4–9 ↕ **1.2m/ 4ft** **MSu–EA**

Purple loosestrife. The species self-seeds aggressively and is not included in this chapter. However, there are several cultivars which are less problematic: 'Blush' produces light pink flowers that are slightly crumpled making them look double. Very attractive. 'Morden Pink' flowers in a mauve-pink and 'Zigeunerblut' in a luminous red-purple.

L. virgatum Z4–9 ↕ **1m/ 3½ft** 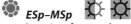 **MSu–LSu**

This tends towards pinker flowers than the ordinary purple loosestrife. It is also more branching and generally sleeker and more refined.

MARRUBIUM *(LAMIACEAE)* – **horehound**

A characteristic feature of *Marrubium* is the way it produces flowers in wreaths around the grey-haired leaves along the stem. A southern European genus from which the following species have proved to be relatively hardy, given dry, well-drained soil and full sun:

M. incanum Z3–9 ↕ **40cm/ 16in** **MSu–LSu**

The whole plant has a felt-like down and the flowers are white. When the plant sets seed and the stems die back, a fresh rosette of leaves appears at the base.

M. peregrinum Z7–9 ↕ **60cm/ 2ft** **MSu–LSu**

This species' flowers are unsightly but it is a vigorously branching plant which creates a large silver-white cluster. Attractive when used to create a break in a border.

M. velutinum Z7–9 ↕ **50cm/ 20in** **MSu–LSu**

Both flowers and foliage on this plant are a yellowish green.

MERTENSIA *(BORAGINACEAE)*

A genus closely related to *Pulmonaria*, with blue-grey leaves and azure, bell-shaped flowers.

M. pulmonarioides Z4–9 ↕ **50cm/ 20in** **ESp–MSp**

Syn. *M. virginica*. Virginian cowslip. In very early spring, fat, purple buds emerge from ground level and open out to reveal grey-blue leaves and showers of bright blue flowers which gradually turn paler. The plant disappears below ground after flowering. Should be given a nice spot in the shade.

M. sibirica Z3–8 ↕ **40cm/ 16in** **LSp–ESu**

A nice plant for a shaded spot in fertile, woodland loam.

MOLOPOSPERMUM *(APIACEAE)*

M. peloponnesiacum Z4–8 ↕ **1.5m/ 5ft** **LSp–ESu**

From southern Europe, but not from the Peloponnese. Grows into a large plant with deeply cut, gleaming dark green leaves and rounded umbels of yellow-white flowers. Flowers only after the first few years and only in well-fertilized soil.

Top left: *Lythrum salicaria* 'Blush'
Top right: *Lythrum salicaria* 'Zigeunerblut'
Centre: *Mertensia pulmonarioides*
Bottom: *Molopospermum peloponnesiacum*

MONARDA (LAMIACEAE) – bergamot, horsemint

One of the most important of plant genera in gardening: everything about the plants is attractive. The stems are robust and do not collapse. The leaves are deliciously scented. The flowers are plentiful and persist for a long time. The bracts beneath the inflorescence form an important part of these plants' wonderful beauty. Hordes of butterflies descend on them during the flowering period, adding a fabulous finishing touch. Their winter silhouette is not to be sneezed at either. After all this euphoria, just a few caveats because these plants are not altogether problem-free. In fact, we even considered moving the entire genus to the chapter entitled 'Capricious plants' but felt that the species can be sufficiently depended upon under certain conditions, especially in sandy, well-drained soil. These plants will sometimes unexpectedly die off in more moisture-retentive soil following a wet winter. And then there is mildew to contend with. Sometimes too damp an environment appears to be responsible. Sometimes the opposite is true. It is likely that other, unknown factors also play a role in this since, fortunately, the plant does not suffer uniformly from it every year. As these plants are so pretty and flower well for so many years, we have awarded them a place in this chapter regardless. You should not have too many problems with the following:

Hybrids Z4–8   ↕ **80cm–1.8m/ 32in–6ft**   MSu–EA

'Aquarius', 1.3m/4¼ft, light purple-violet; alternate flowers. 'Balance', 1.2m/4ft, vivid pink, 'Beauty of Cobham', 1.2m/4ft, light pink flowers with dark red bracts, 'Blaustrumpf', 80cm/32in, purple, 'Cherokee', 1.6m/5¼ft, pink with green centres and brown bracts, 'Comanche', 1.8m/6ft, deep pink, red bracts, 'Elsie's Lavender', 1.4m/4½ft, light lavender with green bracts, 'Fishes', 1m/3½ft, shell pink with a lime-green centre, 'Mohawk', 1.6m/5¼ft, lilac-pink, dark bracts, 'Ou' Charm', 80cm/32in, pale pink with dark red bracts, 'Pawnee', 1.7m/5½ft, lilac-pink with green centres, 'Purple Ann', 1.2m/4ft, purple-red, 'Scorpion', 1.4m/4½ft, bright violet with dark bracts, 'Sioux', 1.6m/5¼ft, white with a hint of lilac, 'Snow Queen', 1.4m/4½ft, white with a hint of lilac, 'Squaw', 1.2m/4ft, red and 'Talud', 1.2m/4ft, pinkish red.

NEPETA (LAMIACEAE) – catmint

Plants with an abundance of tubular flowers and slightly unpleasant-smelling leaves (musty lemon) which induce erotic feelings in felines: cats rub themselves up against them. The following plants are robust and manage to survive this:

N. govaniana Z5–9   ↕ **1m/ 3½ft**   MSu–EA

An erect, well-branched plant with large, light yellow tubular flowers on long stems. Needs a cool, moisture-retentive soil.

N. racemosa Z4–8   ↕ **30cm–1.4m/ 1–4½ft**   LSp–EA   ☼

This is the familiar catmint with soft blue flowers and ribbed, grey-green leaves. A little floppy, but ideal for weaving in among other plants. It grows anywhere sunny. 'Superba' is low-lying at 30cm/1ft high and produces an endless succession of larger, purplish blue flowers. 'Walkers Low' is not low-lying at all at 80cm/32in and is an improvement on the hybrid 'Six Hills Giant' with more powerful purple-blue flowers.

N. subsessilis Z3–9   ↕ **1m/ 3½ft**   ESu–EA

Only grows in well-fertilized, moisture-retentive soil, where it becomes a formidable plant with fresh green leaves and bright blue flowers on compact spikes. If you crush the leaves it smells like a gasworks. In other words, don't. This plant is for visual appeal only.

OPHIOPOGON (CONVALLARIACEAE) – lilyturf

O. planiscapus   ↕ **30cm/ 1ft**
'Nigrescens' Z6–9

Interesting as a gap filler with black, grassy leaves. The late-summer flowers are not significant. Indestructible as long as you do not allow it to become overgrown by larger neighbours.

Top: *Monarda* 'Ou' Charm'
Bottom left: *Monarda* 'Talud'
Bottom right: *Nepeta subsessilis*
with *Astrantia* 'Roma'

PAEONIA (PAEONIACEAE) – peony

Fully mature peonies are the pride of every gardener even if they flower for only a few days. They seem to radiate an elemental power which is probably due to their antiquity: peonies, together with magnolias, are among the most primitive (in other words, the very oldest) flowering plants in the world. Their stalwart simplicity makes them, as Graham Stuart Thomas states, 'just the very type of plant we are all looking for'. The beautiful flowers are followed by gorgeous seed pods. Peonies require a very good fertile soil, lime-rich and well-drained as well as a position in full sun. It is best not to move them once established. If they are not flowering well any more, nutrient-deficiency is to blame: add bonemeal. If they are suffering from fungal diseases, the conditions are too damp.

In this section, we shall discuss only the single-flowered types. The doubles have too many disadvantages to integrate well into a natural setting: they collapse and the flowers turn brown immediately after a shower of rain.

P. emodi Z5–8 — 60cm/2ft — LSp
This has deliciously scented, pure white flowers with golden centre of stamens.

P. mascula Z7–9 — 80cm/32in — LSp
P.m. subsp. *arietina* 'Northern Glory' produces translucent pinkish red flowers. The more lime-enriched the soil is the better.

P. mlokosewitschii Z5–8 — 50cm/20in — LSp
When it flowers you must phone all your friends straight away to come and look as the display often lasts only a few days. The large, pale yellow flowers are indescribably beautiful.

P. mollis Z5–8 — 40cm/16in — LSp–ESu
A profusion of pink, saucer-shaped flowers with yellow stamens at the centre set against grey-green leaves with a hint of purple.

P. officinalis Z3–9 — 70cm/28in — LSp–ESu
The cottage-garden peony. A vigorous species, readily producing wine-red flowers with yellow centres.

P. peregrina Z5–8 — 60cm/2ft — LSp
Nice, fresh green, shining leaves and intense scarlet flowers.

P. tenuifolia Z4–8 — 45cm/18in — LSp–ESu
Its poppy-red flowers with large centres of yellow stamens are half-buried among a mass of finely divided, pinnate leaves.

P. veitchii Z5–8 — 35cm/14in — LSp–ESu
An elegant shorter species with half-cut leaves and pale magenta flowers with pink stamens. The flowers of *P.v.* var. *woodwardii* are light pink.

P. wittmanniana Z5–8 — 90cm/3ft — LSp–ESu
This has coarse, lobed leaves and white flowers with a green-yellow tint to them plus red stamens. The flowers last for an even shorter time than *P. mlokosewitschii*, so a phone call to your friends will not suffice: you have to give them all alarm clocks as well.

Hybrids Z4–8

A large number of elegant, single-flowered cultivars exists which can be incorporated into a natural garden very effectively. We can mention only a few of the most beautiful: P. 'Bowl of Beauty', fuschia pink with a large heart of stamens tending to white, P. 'Jan van Leeuwen', extremely robust, white flowers with a yellow centre of stamens, P. 'Mai Fleuri' and P. 'Clair de Lune', a hybrid with *mlokosewitschii* blood having pale yellow flowers and orange-yellow stamens at its centre.

Top: *Paeonia mlokosewitschii*
Centre: *Paeonia veitchii* var. *woodwardii*
Bottom: *Paeonia* 'Mai Fleuri'

Russian vine (*Fallopia baldschuanica*) overgrowing a macleaya

Battling with ground elder

To avoid the charge of writing a gardening book while wearing a pair of rose-tinted spectacles, we must donate some space to ground elder (*Aegopodium podagraria*). Weeds grow in every garden. In a traditional garden with a lot of bare earth around the plants, you are constantly busy getting rid of unwanted annuals (field weeds) and tap-rooted weeds, such as dandelions. This is less of a problem in a natural garden where you aim to achieve all-over cover, even if you may occasionally have to remove a sow thistle or some willow herb. However, sooner or later you will come up against 'running' weeds: perennials that can spread like lightning through the garden by means of root runners or rhizomes, such as couch grass (*Elytrigia repens*), bindweed (*Calystegia sepium*), the field horsetail (*Equisetum arvense*) and ground elder, or a decorative plant that you introduced yourself such as the creeping bellflower (*Campanula rapunculoides*) which becomes ineradicable once you have it. Yet of all these plants, ground elder is the worst: it is totally and utterly indestructible.

If you have decided to start afresh and replant your existing garden, you can try to fork it out completely. The garden then needs to be cleaned up completely, and so

do your neighbours' gardens. If you leave just one specimen standing you can be sure of what lurks beneath. (Did somebody mention weedkillers? You have to do what you have to do, of course, but you did not hear it from us!) However, even if you start anew with a totally clean garden, you will still be bothered by rooting weeds whenever your attention slackens. Then there is only one thing to do: weeding, weeding and yet more weeding. That is, if you are not inclined to start all over again.

As awful as the prospect might seem, it need not be all that bad; it is useful to know that rooting weeds prefer to grow (and grow fastest) in fertile soil with a disturbed profile: in other words, gardens. The more you dig, turn over and rake the soil, the faster they will grow. Experience teaches that running weeds gradually enjoy it less and less in well-thought-out, stable gardens where all species are in harmony with one another and where therefore you rarely need to take any remedial action. One annual maintenance session in spring is usually sufficient: pulling up surface weeds without being too rigorous and disturbing the soil profile too much. Some reappearances will occur later in the summer but these will not show up very much in between perennials which in the meantime have grown much taller. Experience also teaches that it is very hard, in practice, to achieve a stable garden. Therefore, combating running weeds usually turns into a battle: in the case of ground elder, a battle that has to be pursued not just in spring, but in summer too, year in year out. We sometimes tell over-enthusiastic admirers who comment on how terribly happy we must feel that 'gardening is just like doing the dishes; as soon as you've finished, you can start all over again.'

And think hard before leaving everything a year, perhaps because you do not have the time or you have just lost heart. If you do, then the next year there will only be ground elder and you will definitely have to start all over again: everything out and new plants back in. As you know, we want absolutely nothing to do with weedkillers! 'Is there no hope at all then?' you will be asking, doubtfully. The answer to that is definitely 'No!'

Let us throw a few words of comfort in your direction: 'One must suffer for art.' There is nothing else to be said. And just imagine if everything were straightforward and you had nothing to do at all any more. Why, it doesn't bear thinking about.

PAPAVER (PAPAVERACEAE) – poppy

Poppies need no introduction. The majority can be found in the 'Playful' section and in the chapter entitled 'Annuals'. The only real perennial is:

P. orientale Z4–9 ↕ 60–80cm/ 24–32in   LSp–MSu

Oriental poppy. This species is almost indestructible in any sunny spot with well-drained soil. It will even tolerate years of neglect. The best-known type has bright orange-red flowers which lie flat on the ground after the first passing shower. So rather than name that one, we shall mention: 'Flamingo', white with an orange-red margin and black stamens at the centre; 'Karine', with slightly smaller, saucer-shaped flowers in pastel pink, does not topple over; 'Kleine Tänzerin', with an abundance of fairly small, raspberry-pink, darkly mottled flowers; 'Lilac Girl' produces flowers with patches of lilac-pink.

PATRINIA (VALERIANACEAE)

P. scabiosifolia Z6–9 ↕ 1.2m/ 4ft   LSu–EA

Looks just like valerian with the same composite leaves and the same panicles of flowers but in bright yellow and at the end of summer. For well-drained soil.

PENSTEMON (SCROPHULARIACEAE)

A large genus of plants with foxglove-like flowers in all colours of the rainbow. Sadly, most of the species are extremely unreliable, but almost every grower has a species by which he will swear: 'This one really is hardy!' When other growers give it a go, it turns out not to be the case. So it is with some hesitation that we propose the following two species as being dependable:

P. digitalis Z3–9 ↕ 80cm/ 32in   ESu–LSu

'Husker Red', in particular, with dark leaves and white, slightly purple-flushed flowers seems to be reasonably reliable provided it is grown in a well-drained soil.

P. hirsutus Z4–9 ↕ 50cm/ 20in   LSp–MSu

A plant producing an abundance of dark, hairy stems and blue flowers with a white lower lip.

PERSICARIA (POLYGONACEAE) – knotweed

An attempt to classify more logically the extremely variable *Polygonum* genus went a little out of control and may be blamed for all those species now having to be called *Persicaria*. Is this really a logical reclassification? The problem is, it makes for an unfortunate association with redshank (formerly *Polygonum persicaria*), a troublesome weed whose seeds remain viable for hundreds of years. So much so that wherever you stick your spade in the ground, redshank will be the first weed to greet you. The reclassification is doubtless correct in terms of nomenclature, but nobody is very happy about it. The species we shall be mentioning would not look like redshank from any distance and are not in the least bit troublesome.

P. amplexicaulis Z5–9 ↕ 1.2m/ 4ft   MSu–MA

This ranks among the very best garden plants. (Wasps think so too, so beware!) Strong as an ox, it will grow almost anywhere. It grows into a fair-sized clump of pretty, bronze-green, oval-oblong leaves and produces long, slim, dark red spikes of flowers which bloom ever more abundantly until the first frost puts an end to them. The straight species is available almost nowhere, but there are many cultivars, the most important of which are: 'Alba', pure white, though it flowers less profusely than the other types, 'Firedance', which can be combined with other garden plants despite its fiery colour, and 'Rosea', light pink, not so eye-catching but all the better for that when used to 'knit' everything together.

Top: *Papaver orientale* 'Flamingo'
Centre: *Penstemon digitalis* 'Husker Red' with *Achillea* 'Martina'
Bottom: *Persicaria amplexicaulis* 'Alba'

Top: *Persicaria amplexicaulis* 'Rosea'
Centre: *Persicaria bistorta* 'Hohe Tatra'
Bottom: *Persicaria polymorpha*

P. bistorta **50cm/**
'Hohe Tatra' Z4–8 **20in** LSp–ESu
A non-invasive type of snakeweed (see under 'Invasive plants'). Often flowers again later in the year. Moisture-retentive soil.

P. bistorta **60cm/**
subsp. *carnea* **Z4–8** **2ft** ESu
A close relative of *P. bistorta* from the Himalayas which is content with less moisture and is absolutely not invasive. Produces lovely pink flowers and often repeats in early autumn too.

P. milletii Z5–9 **30cm/**
1ft LSp–MSu
Slim, pointed and tapering leaves and short carmine-red flower spikes. Grows in fertile, moisture-retentive garden soil. A gem.

P. polymorpha Z4–9 **2m/**
6½ft LSp–EA
A gigantic plant – as wide as it is tall – which neither invades others nor topples over. It produces large, cream-coloured panicles which slowly turn pink and then brown-red. It is begging for some superlatives and since other authors have not provided them, we shall do so ourselves: staggeringly beautiful, it successfully manages to remain the border's focal point for the whole season. Viewed superficially, it looks a little like goat's beard, but an endlessly remontant one. Owing to its slowly changing colours, it always fits in with the other colours in the border. It is notably tolerant of significantly drier conditions and in waterlogged soil grows less tall.

P. weyrichii Z5–9 **1.2m/**
4ft LSu–EA
In appearance, it somewhat resembles *P. polymorpha* but is shorter and spreads wider. Russian vine type of inflorescence. Best in moisture-retentive soil.

PHLOMIS (LAMIACEAE)
A large genus from southern Europe with large, prettily formed lipped flowers clustered around the stem. Eminently desirable, but there are only a few hardy species.

P. pungens Z6–10 **1m/**
3½ft MSu–LSu
Syn. *P. taurica.* A sturdy plant with mauve flowers.

P. russeliana Z4–9 **80cm/**
32in ESu–MSu
Spreads gradually with substantial, grey-green leaves. The woolly flowering stems with their wreaths of pale yellow, lipped flowers only appear in a warm, sunny spot with good garden soil. Also remains decorative until long into the winter when the flowers have gone.

P. tuberosa Z4–9 **1.5m/**
5ft ESu–MSu
The harder the winter, the better the flowers on this plant from the Ukraine. The flowers are often disappointing after a mild, wet winter. It produces large, ribbed, heart-shaped leaves and long, robust stems covered in wreaths of mauve, lipped flowers. The straight species is a little sloppy; 'Amazone' is a noticeable improvement which never topples over.

PHLOX (POLEMONIACEAE)
Here we go again. Karl Foerster has been quoted time and again, but he was right and so we shall do it one more time: 'Life without phlox is a mistake.' Only not in heavy, chalky clay, as phlox will not grow there. Otherwise, phlox grows well in any humus-rich, moisture-retentive garden soil. They are at their best on warm, damp summer evenings when they diffuse their intoxicating scent. In older gardens with older cultivars, problems such as eelworms and mildew can sometimes arise. In gardens like these it can sometimes take years before phlox can be planted again. Up until now we have had no problems (touch wood) and so shall not moan about diseases.

P. divaricata Z4–9 **40cm/**
16in LSp–ESu
A low-growing species which must be given a cool spot in the shade

to ensure reliability. It will flower abundantly if such a space is available and fill the garden with its scent. 'Blue Dreams' produces lilac-blue flowers, 'Clouds of Perfume' is pale blue and 'May Breeze' is white and pale blue when in bud.

P. maculata Z4–8 80cm/32in MSu–EA
A healthy species which is not too tall, with ornamental, narrow leaves and slender stems. A little too well-behaved. 'Alpha' is pink, 'Delta' is white with lilac centres.

P. paniculata Z4–8 1.5m/5ft MSu–EA
Phlox in the wild is almost disease-free and flowers abundantly with large panicles of small flowers in lilac-pink or, in the evenings and during overcast weather, in a luminous blue. It does tend to topple over, unfortunately, and is a little invasive, but in wilder natural gardens that is not really going to be a problem. *P.p.* var. *alba* has white flowers with a hint of pink.

P. paniculata cultivars Z4–8
We shall describe a number of cultivars which suffer few or no problems from disease. A few old ones which have proved themselves over the years, and a few new ones. We highlight the brand new cultivars by Coen Jansen (CJ), which are exceptionally beautiful, healthy and very different from the old phloxes.

'Blue Evening' 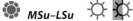 1.3m/4¼ft 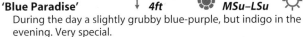 MSu–LSu
Lilac-pink, in the evening pure blue; looks a lot like the parent species but does not collapse.

'Blue Paradise' 1.2m/4ft 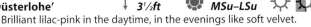 MSu–LSu
During the day a slightly grubby blue-purple, but indigo in the evening. Very special.

'Casablanca' 1m/3½ft MSu–EA
(CJ) Small white florets, flowers in mid-summer, then stops and flowers again in late summer.

'Düsterlohe' 1.1m/3½ft MSu–LSu
Brilliant lilac-pink in the daytime, in the evenings like soft velvet.

'Grace' 1.1m/3½ft MSu–LSu
(CJ) Produces small lilac-white flowers with reddish centres.

'Hesperis' 1.4m/4½ft MSu–EA
(CJ) Flowers just like dame's violet, red-purple with small flowers in pyramidal panicles. Lovely.

'Lavendelwolke' 1.6m/5¼ft MSu–LSu
A healthy old hybrid with large, white flowers and lavender-coloured centres.

'Lichtspel' 1.2m/4ft MSu–EA
We refer irreverently to this as 'bike-stand phlox'; it is so sturdy that you could park your bicycle up against it! Unpretentious, light lilac-pink. So unpretentious, in fact, that you will usually want lots of it. Does well in shaded areas too.

'Luc's Lilac' 1.2m/4ft MSu–LSu
(CJ) Robust, deep lilac and in the evenings a magnificent blue.

'Matineus' 1m/3½ft ESu–MSu
(CJ) Extremely early to flower in white with a touch of lilac and red centres. Repeat flowering until late summer.

Top: *Phlomis russeliana* with *Centranthus ruber*
Centre: *Phlomis tuberosa* 'Amazone'

Bottom left: *Phlox paniculata*
Bottom right: *Phlox* 'Düsterlohe'

Top: *Phlox* 'Rosa Pastell'
Centre: *Platycodon grandiflorus*
Bottom: *Podophyllum hexandrum* 'Majus'

'Rosa Pastell' — 1m/3½ft — MSu–EA
Large flowers in very gentle pink with dark red centres.

'Rosa Spier' — 80cm/32in — MSu–LSu
An old favourite of Mien Ruys. A rather robust pink which fades to light pink.

'Schneerausch' — 1m/3½ft — MSu–LSu
Large, overlapping, velvety flowers opening from lilac-coloured buds.

'Utopia' — 1.8m/6ft — MSu–LSu
Grows very tall but does not topple over. Large, light pink flowers.

PLATYCODON *(CAMPANULACEAE)* – balloon flower

In good, moisture-retentive soil these are perfect plants which can live to a ripe old age. They do need some attention because they appear so late in spring that they are easily swamped by other plants and will not be able to cope.

P. grandiflorus Z4–9 — 40cm/16in — MSu–LSu
Atop robust stems covered by grey-green leaves appear hefty, balloon-shaped buds which spring open to reveal large, purple-blue, bell-shaped flowers. *P.g. albus* is white, 'Hakone Blue' has a second, smaller flower within the first purple-blue one and 'Perlmutterschale' is a pearly pink.

PODOPHYLLUM *(BERBERIDACEAE)*

Plants for a cool, fertile spot in the shade with improbably large, beautifully cut leaves on fleshy stems; they unfurl like umbrellas. The plants are poisonous except for their fruits.

P. hexandrum Z5–8 — 40cm/16in — LSp–ESu
Produces pink flowers before the brown-red leaves emerge from the ground in twos. Ovate, coral-red fruits are hidden beneath the leaves. 'Majus' is a large selection with delicately marbled leaves.

P. peltatum Z4–9 — 30cm/1ft — LSp–ESu
The May apple from North American broad-leaved forests, with deeply cut green leaves. The proportionally large, pure white flowers and subsequent yellow, plum-like fruits remain beneath the leaves.

POLEMONIUM *(POLEMONIACEAE)* – Jacob's ladder

Jacob's ladders are generally short-lived plants which self-seed copiously. There are a few exceptions, one of which is:

P. 'Lambrook Mauve' Z4–8 — 45cm/18in — MSp–ESu
A sterile hybrid which produces abundant mauve-purple flowers over several weeks in spring.

POLYGONATUM *(CONVALLARIACEAE)* – Solomon's seal

Solomon's seal is a true shade plant which will grow in almost any soil type as long as it is not too warm. It slowly extends its territory by means of running roots. From each of these, one stem emerges on which upward-pointing, ovate leaves appear which are veined lengthways, with clusters of white, bell-shaped flowers hanging beneath them. The leaves turn bright yellow in autumn. The plants are sometimes completely eaten by large sawfly grubs which have the same colour as the seed pods (blue-grey). This is not a disaster as the grubs are extremely attractive and it does not happen every year (sawflies have to survive too). There are a great many reliable species which differ from one another only in detail. That may be fun for specialist collectors but not for us. We shall list the most important:

P. x hybridum Z4–9 — 60cm–1m/2–3½ft — LSp–ESu
A cross between the following two species with rather more 'garden impact' than its parents. On first emerging, 'Betberg' has blue-grey,

almost black, stems; 'Pruhonice' has grey-blue leaves and bears an
abundance of berries; 'Weihenstephan' grows to more than 1m/3¹/₂ft
tall and is larger in all respects – very attractive; 'Striatum' syn.
'Variegatum' has white variegated leaves.

P. multiflorum Z3–9   ↕ **60cm/ 2ft**   **LSp–ESu**

The general description given for the genus perfectly fits this species
which will even grow reasonably in poor, sandy soil.

P. odoratum Z4–9   ↕ **50cm/ 20in**   **LSp–ESu**

A more compact species with more foliage than the previous one
and bearing slightly larger, cream-coloured flowers in ones or twos.
Will spread far in light, chalky soil.

P. verticillatum Z4–9   ↕ **1.2m/ 4ft**   **LSp–ESu**

This differs strongly from the rest because the lance-shaped leaves
form wreaths around the stem. Each wreath has a ring of small,
green-white flowers. Found in the wild only in ancient woodlands so
requires a lot of humus. The flowers are red in *P.v. rubrum*.

POTENTILLA *(ROSACEAE)* – cinquefoil

A large genus of strawberry-like plants, most of which either behave
like weeds in the garden or else are too small to earn a place in this
book. A small number of Asian species and their hybrids are solidly
reliable garden plants given a sunny spot in any reasonably good
soil.

P. atrosanguinea Z5–8   ↕ **45cm/ 18in**   **ESu–EA**

Grows into a luxuriant clump of strawberry leaves with clusters of dark
red flowers.

P. x hopwoodiana Z5–8   ↕ **50cm/ 20in**   **ESu–LA**

Pale pink flowers with a dark red centre. A little bit limp and needs
to be draped through other plants.

P. nepalensis Z5–8   ↕ **40cm/ 16in**   **ESu–EA**

Abundant velvety flowers ranging in colour from dark crimson to
pink or orange.

Hybrids Z5–8   ↕ **45cm/ 18in**   **ESu–EA**

'Etna' has velvet red flowers and silvery leaves. 'Flamingo' has fire-
red flowers. 'Volcan' is dark red and double and 'William Rollison' is
double, orange and, notwithstanding, still appealing.

PRIMULA *(PRIMULACEAE)*

There are huge numbers of incredibly lovely primulas from China
and the Himalayas which make one feel very greedy. Sadly, though,
they are without exception extremely difficult to grow. The well-
known candelabra primulas from China and Japan will cope in wet,
peaty soil by self-seeding, but we are not very taken with their
screaming colours and thus choose to omit them. After some
hesitation, we have decided on two native species which can be
depended upon in a well-drained soil that is not too nutrient-rich,
where they will even self-seed a little. They are extremely small but
are very charming none the less:

P. veris Z5–9   ↕ **25cm/ 10in**   **MSp–LSp**

Cowslip. Produces rosettes of the characteristic crenulated leaves
and, at the tip of the stem, clusters of trumpet-shaped flowers in
egg-yolk yellow.

P. vulgaris Z6–9   ↕ **10cm/ 4in**   **LW–MSp**

Primrose. Eventually forms large clumps and blooms early with
virtually stemless, subtly pale yellow flowers, about 2cm/1in across,
held just above the light green rosette of leaves. Many cultivars from
this species exist with larger and often brilliantly coloured flowers
but these are all less attractive than the straight species.

Above: *Polygonatum* x *hybridum* 'Betberg'
Below: *Potentilla* 'Volcan'

PULMONARIA *(BORAGINACEAE)* – **lungwort**

There are many garden-worthy species of lungwort but most are self-seeding and so have been placed in the 'Playful' section. The following species is not self-seeding:

P. angustifolia Z3–8 ↕ 25cm/ 10in   LW–MSp

One of the first plants to flower in spring. Eventually forms large clumps of unmarked leaves and clusters of gentian-blue flowers. The plant disappears below ground after flowering. 'Blaues Meer' has slightly larger flowers which are a little darker blue, just like 'Blue Crown'; but the latter has speckled leaves and thus has clearly been crossed with another species of *Pulmonaria*.

RANUNCULUS *(RANUNCULACEAE)* – **buttercup**

Ordinary buttercups are so commonplace that there is little need to put them in the garden. Moreover, most of them will behave like annoying weeds. Two clearly different ones which cause no trouble are:

R. aconitifolius Z5–9 ↕ 90cm/ 3ft   MSp–LSp

Fair maids of France. Once you have seen the fields of white buttercups which in the alpine regions of Europe generally flourish around hillside springs, you will forever be mad about this plant: a regular buttercup, in fact, but with slightly darker leaves and large panicles of pure white flowers. The plant disappears below ground after flowering. Plant in humus-rich, moisture-retentive to waterlogged soil. Although we generally don't like double flowers, 'Flore Pleno', a very old cultivar, is a real gem.

R. gramineus Z7–10 ↕ 25cm/ 10in ❁ LSp–ESu ☼

A plant with blue, ribbed, grassy leaves and fresh, yellow buttercup flowers. The leaves appear as early as autumn and disappear immediately after flowering. Does self-seed a bit.

RHEUM *(POLYGONACEAE)* – **rhubarb**

Giant plants with enormous, rough leaves and huge panicles of flowers. Indestructible once established, which happens only in very rich, moist soil that has been well composted and manured.

R. australe Z5–9 ↕ 1.5m/ 5ft ❁ LSp–MSu ☼

Has broad, entire leaves and enormous white panicles of flowers which turn pink.

R. palmatum Z5–9 ↕ 2.5m/ 8ft ❁ ESu–MSu ☼

Grows as broad as it is tall with cut leaves which can reach up to 1m/3½ft across and gigantic flower heads which turn cherry red. *R.p.* var. *tanguticum* has somewhat more formal, less spectacularly coloured flower heads (whitish) but the leaves are deep purple on both sides.

RODGERSIA *(SAXIFRAGACEAE)*

Rodgersia are exceptionally elegant foliage plants with large, bronze-green, divided, palm-shaped leaves and lovely panicles of flowers, followed by elegant seed heads. The various species bear many similarities to one another; they differ in leaf composition. They grow best in moisture-retentive, humus-rich soil in semi-shaded positions. They are even more attractive when planted in full sun in a waterlogged soil. They perform well even in fairly dry soil but will not then tolerate the slightest ray of sunshine, nor will they flower so abundantly. There are many cultivars which differ little from one another. We have not made a selection in this instance since all of the plants are equally dependable and attractive.

R. aesculifolia Z5–8 ↕ 1m/ 3½ft   ESu–MSu

Has horse-chestnut-like leaves on hairy stems and a svelte, cream-coloured inflorescence. In 'Irish Bronze', the leaves are an even stronger bronze colour.

R. pinnata Z5–8 ↕ 1.25m/ 4ft   ESu–MSu

This species has the most abundant flowers. It has pinnate leaves and soft pink flowers. A well-known cultivar is 'Superba' with bronze-green leaves. 'Maurice Mason' is an improved version. The renowned plant breeder Ernst Pagels has produced 'Die Anmutige', 'Die Schöne' and 'Die Stolze', all equally lovely with small differences in the shape and colour of the inflorescence (from cream to dark pink).

R. podophylla Z5–8 ↕ 80cm/ 32in   ESu–MSu

Has palm-shaped leaves, the component parts of which are serrated like a duck's foot. The flower heads are whitish, not as spectacular as the leaves, which in spring emerge a bronze colour that changes to green in summer and die in autumn an elegant copper. The leaves are red-brown initially in 'Braunlaub' and mahogany-red in 'Rotlaub'. 'Smaragd' has luminous green leaves in summer, 'Pagode' an attractively regular composition to the flowers. 'Saarbrücken' emerges a liver colour.

R. purdomii Z5–8 ↕ 80cm/ 32in   ESu–MSu

The young leaves are liver-coloured, the flower panicles are cream.

R. sambucifolia Z5–8 ↕ 1m/ 3½ft   ESu–MSu ☼☼

Has the composite leaves of an elder and produces airy, elongated clusters of cream-white flowers. 'Kupferschein' has a coppery hue to it. 'Rothaut' has dark green leaves on tall, brown-red stems.

RUDBECKIA *(ASTERACEAE)* – **coneflower**

Familiar garden plants whose yellow daisy-like flowers have distinctive, usually cone-shaped centres. Not often very inspiring but they can be employed in some situations and there are exceptions (*R. maxima*). They are all easy to grow in any reasonable garden soil.

R. fulgida var. speciosa Z4–9 ↕ 1m/ 3½ft   MSu–EA ☼

This grows into hefty clumps of erect stems displaying bright yellow daisies with black centres. Very prim and doubtless very useful, even if we don't quite know how. Still more worthy, and with larger flowers, is *R.f.* var. *sullivantii* 'Goldsturm'.

R. 'Herbstsonne' Z5–9 ↕ 2m/ 6½ft   MSu–EA ☼

Looks like *R. laciniata* but the leaves are less deeply cut and the flowers are larger. Rather coarse, if not downright ugly, except that the long green seed cones after flowering make it worthwhile.

R. laciniata Z3–9 ↕ 1.8m/ 6ft ❁ MSu–EA ☼

Long, loosely branching stems with deeply cut leaves and daisies with yellow ray-florets and green, cone-shaped centres. A little messy but perfectly serviceable combined with grasses in wilder gardens.

R. maxima Z6–9 ↕ 1.8m/ 6ft ❁ LSu–EA ☼

This species deviates from the norm by having extremely attractive, large, bluish, waxily ribbed leaves like a hosta and a few long-stemmed, drooping daisies with deep yellow ray-florets and eye-catching, long black central cones. Demands a well-fertilized, moisture-retentive soil.

R. occidentalis Z6–9 ↕ 1.2m/ 4ft   MSu–EA ☼

A somewhat indeterminate plant with special flowers: instead of ray-florets, it has only the black, central cone left. Curious and only effective when planted in large numbers.

SALVIA *(LAMIACEAE)* – **sage**

The sage genus is characterized by its tubular, two-lipped, hooded flowers which constitute an ingenious mechanism for pollination. As there are an awful lot of attractive species which all behave differently, we have spread the individual species throughout this book. Only the following group of cultivars is truly dependable:

Above: *Rodgersia pinnata* 'Die Anmutige'
Below: *Rodgersia podophylla* 'Saarbrücken'

Above: *Rudbeckia fulgida* var. *sullivantii* 'Goldsturm'
Below: *Rudbeckia maxima*

Top left: *Sanguisorba canadensis*
Top right: *Sanguisorba tenuifolia* 'Alba'
Centre: *Sanguisorba menziesii*
Bottom: *Sanguisorba tenuifolia* 'Purpurea'
with *Persicaria polymorpha*

S. nemorosa cultivars Z5–9   40–90cm/ 16in–3ft   LSp–EA

Direct descendants of *S. nemorosa* belong to this group; they are recognizable from the fact that they set seed (and sometimes seed themselves as a result). Also included are the (often sterile) crosses of *S. nemorosa* and *S. pratensis* (*S. x sylvestris*). They are all plants with relatively small flowers and prettily coloured bracts borne on long, compact spikes which flower repeatedly over a long season. If you cut them back half way through the flowering season, you will assure yourself of a full repeat performance. Once again, many cultivars have been produced by Ernst Pagels. 'Amethyst' grows tall and flowers in mauve-pink. 'Blauhügel' is low-lying and compact with true blue flowers. 'Brightness' is medium-sized with pink flowers in purple-pink bracts. 'Dear Anja' is an erect cultivar having blue flowers with a white lower lip. 'Forncett Dawn' has very small flowers in pale pink. 'Lubecca' is a dark purple-blue and low-lying (45cm/18in). 'Lye End' is large and rough with lavender-blue flowers. 'Mainacht' starts producing slightly larger, deep purple flowers as early as late spring and is low-lying. 'Ostfriesland' is the best-known, dark purple-blue, medium-sized cultivar at 60cm/2ft tall. 'Porcelaine' has blue-tinted, white flowers. 'Puszta Flamme' is a monstrosity without flowers but with bracts propped open on top of each other in purple. It looks like an amaranth but is fun none the less. 'Rubin' is a lanky plant but has an attractive colour (ruby). 'Rügen' is purple-blue, early-flowering and compact. 'Schneehügel' is like 'Blauhügel' but white. 'Superba' is dark purple-blue and tall (90cm/3ft). 'Tänzerin' is an improvement on this, a little shorter but more ornamental. 'Viola Klose' is a plumper version of 'Mainacht'. 'Wesuwe' is also like 'Mainacht' but sleeker, a less muted purple-blue and even earlier in bloom.

SANGUISORBA (*ROSACEAE*) – burnet

Plants with ornamental pinnate leaves and small flowers held in cylindrical spikes (as in bottlebrush plants) which lend a 'wilderness' look to any border. They grow well in any garden soil that does not dry out excessively. The leaves turn a charming autumn colour.

S. canadensis Z3–8   1.8m/ 6ft   LSu–EA

Robust plant with erect white flower spikes in late summer.

S. menziesii Z3–8   80cm/ 32in   LSp–ESu

An early-flowering species with finger-length, blood-red spikes.

S. 'Tanna' Z5–8   70cm/ 28in   ESu–LSu

Originated in Japan. Supposedly a cultivar of *S. officinalis*, but we do not believe a word of it. A ground-cover plant which spreads slowly with blue-grey leaves and red flower heads. Tolerant of dry conditions.

S. stipulata Z3–8   80cm/ 32in   ESu–MSu

Syn. *S. sitchensis*. Looks like *S. canadensis* but flowers earlier and is shorter.

S. tenuifolia 'Alba' Z4–8   1.8m/ 6ft   MSu–LSu

An especially ornamental plant with narrow leaves and long, white, pendent flowers. *S.t.* 'Purpurea' is a rather variable form with dark red flower spikes, sometimes long and drooping and sometimes shorter and more erect. In the latter instance, it looks very like *S. officinalis*. This species is closely related.

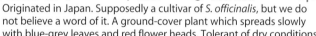

SAPONARIA (*CARYOPHYLLACEAE*) – soapwort

Most species of *Saponaria* are rock-garden plants. Ordinary soapwort runs far too rampant to be included as a garden plant. However, one very suitable candidate for a nice spot at the front of the border is:

S. x lempergii 'Max Frei' Z4–8   40cm/ 16in   LSu–EA

A cross between *S. cypria* and *S. haussknechtii*. A robust plant with a fragile appearance. It resembles common soapwort but is not at all invasive.

SAXIFRAGA *(SAXIFRAGACEAE)* – **saxifrage**

Most species of saxifrage are strictly rock-garden plants. Several species will also grow in ordinary garden soil, given the necessary attention, but, oh, they are so small... you turn your back on them for a moment and they have been swamped by a neighbour. The following two species perform very respectably in a humus-rich, moisture-retentive spot in the shade.

S. cortusifolia Z6–8 ↕ **30cm/1ft**   MA–LA

A woodland plant from Japan with dark green, round, lobed leaves and small, airy clusters of white flowers late in the year. In 'Rubrifolia' the underside of the leaves, leaf stalks and flowers are dark red.

S. pensylvanica Z5–8 ↕ **90cm/3ft**   LSp–ESu

Produces large, fleshy, hairy leaves and thick red flower stems and is exciting when in bud. It is a little disappointing when the green flowers open up, but remains, though gauche, still subtle.

SCOPOLIA *(SOLANACEAE)*

S. carniolica Z5–8 ↕ **50cm/20in**   LW–MSp

A plant with coarse foliage which very early in the year emerges from the ground in an exciting purple and starts to flower immediately. In the straight species, the flowers are a dark brown which you can hardly see, but the unpronounceable *S.c.* var. *hladnikiana* produces light yellow flowers. Also good in dry, shaded locations.

SCUTELLARIA *(LAMIACEAE)* – **skull cap**

A large genus containing around 200 species easily recognized by the masked flowers and even more so by the remarkable seed pods which look like baseball caps. There are quite a lot of species which could be promoted to the status of garden plants, but until now there is only one which has achieved this:

S. incana Z4–9 ↕ **60cm/2ft**   LSu–EA

A robust plant with grey-blue leaves and soft blue flowers held in grey bracts. Dependable in light, well-drained soil.

SEDUM *(CRASSULACEAE)* – **stonecrop**

A large genus of succulent rock-growing plants of which only the familiar 'orpines' figure in gardens: sturdy plants with a broad, flattened inflorescence produced in late summer, they flourish in all garden soils when in the sun or semi-shade.

S. spectabile Z4–9 ↕ **45cm/18in** ● LSu–MA

This is the species which attracts so many butterflies. The small tortoiseshell butterfly is particularly fond of it. (The next species also attracts many insects but not butterflies.) Flowers are light pink. 'Stardust' has white flowers.

S. telephium Z4–9 ↕ **40–80cm/16–32in**   LSu–MA

Common orpine. A variable species which has been divided up into many subspecies. *S.t.* subsp. *maximum* grows large and has greenish flowers, *S.t.* subsp. *ruprechtii* is rather weak but has bluish leaves and yellowish flowers and *S.t.* subsp. *telephium* has dark red flowers. All of these subspecies have been vigorously crossed with each other. Therefore there are now greater numbers of cultivars worthy of the garden than naturally occurring species. 'Matrona' is an improvement on the over-familiar 'Herbstfreude', which always collapses so hopelessly. The plant grows extremely tall (80cm/32in), does not collapse, flowers in a somewhat paler pink and has a winter silhouette that is just as lovely. 'Möhrchen' is a little shorter and less robust but is completely dark red, even the leaves and stems. 'Munstead Red', an old favourite of Gertrude Jekyll's, is low-growing at 40cm/16in and has grey-green leaves on red stems and panicles of flowers which turn an elegant red-brown in autumn. 'Purple Emperor' (45cm/18in) has red-brown stems, red cabbage-coloured leaves and green-yellow flowers.

Top left: *Salvia nemorosa* 'Dear Anja'
Top right: *Scutellaria incana*
Bottom: *Sedum telephium* 'Munstead Red'

Silphium laciniatum

SENECIO (ASTERACEAE) – groundsel

Over the millennia this extremely varied and very ancient genus has passed through more or less every stage of evolution. There are remarkable, palm-like *Senecio* species in the mountains of East Africa, succulent species on the Canary Islands and unsightly, troublesome weeds. However, a phenomenon such as the marsh fleawort is also a species of *Senecio*: an excessively flowering annual which only likes to grow on reclaimed land and which therefore considers the Netherlands the centre of its universe. *Senecio* also includes some attractive garden plants, all of which behave differently. Consequently, we have spread them among the chapters of this book.

S. doria Z5–9 ↕ 1.5m/5ft MSu–EA

Golden ragwort. This grows into a robust clump and has oval leaves at the base and severely straight stems with few leaves. The top of the stem branches out to form an extremely abundant panicle of little yellow daisies. Has attractive, fluffy seed pods which you can leave alone without fear as the plant seeds itself only modestly. Grows well in good, moisture-retentive garden soil.

S. paludosus Z4–9 ↕ 1.8m/6ft ESu–LSu

Fen ragwort. Looks like the previous plant but grows even taller, has rather larger flowers but in slightly less floriferous panicles and more foliage on the stems, the leaves being narrow and covered in a white felt underneath. This plant also self-seeds very little. In the wild the plant often grows in places which are flooded during the winter. If you suffer from that, this is the plant for you. Otherwise, it will grow in any fertile, moisture-retentive soil.

SERRATULA (ASTERACEAE) – sawwort

S. seoanei Z5–8 ↕ 30cm/1ft MA–LA

A type of common sawwort (*S. tinctoria*) local to the Cantabrian mountains which appears to make an extremely good garden plant.

Produces slowly spreading hillocks of dark green, half-cut leaves and flowers very late in the year, but profusely, with lilac-pink thistles. A charming winter silhouette.

SIDA (MALVACEAE) – Indian mallow

S. hermaphrodita Z4–8 ↕ 1.6m/5¼ft MSu–LSu

Unknown, unloved. An unusual but effective and extremely respectable border plant with elegant, deeply cut, palm-shaped leaves and elongated racemes of white mallow flowers. Also grows well in poor soil.

SILPHIUM (ASTERACEAE) – cap plant

Giant plants from the North American tall grass prairie with large leaves and refined, bright yellow, daisy flowers. It is almost impossible to explain why the yellow daisies of *Heliopsis* are ugly whereas those of *Silphium* are attractive. You will just have to take our word for it. There are many species which are all very respectable but which can be bought virtually nowhere. For example, we know of a species with coarse leaves under the name of *S. gracile* which is always toppling over and so is completely unsuitable for the garden. However, when it blooms in October with wispy, light yellow, ray-florets, it produces such an elegant image in the decaying autumn garden that we have to give in. Another that is hard to find is *S. trifoliatum*: a strong plant with leaves in triple wreaths around the stems and which flowers at length on lightly branched panicles. Graham Stuart Thomas is enthusiastic about *S. terebinthinaceum*, which appears to have such large leaves that you can shelter beneath them on a hot summer's day. Too unkempt for us. The following are more accessible:

S. laciniatum Z5–8 ↕ 3m/10ft LSu–EA

Compass plant. Has large leaves, cut all the way to the central vein, which are always turned away from the sun (north–south). The yellow daisies open from the top of the tall stem as with hollyhocks.

S. perfoliatum *Z4–8* ↕ **2.5m/ 8ft**   *MSu–EA* ☼

Cap plant. Robust, square stems with opposite leaves which grow into one another at the base. The inflorescence becomes increasingly branched throughout the course of the summer, forming a 'cap'. Both species grow well in any moisture-retentive garden soil in full sun.

SMILACINA *(CONVALLARIACEAE)* – false Solomon's seal

S. racemosa *Z4–9* ↕ **70cm/ 28in**   *LSp–ESu* ☼ ◑

Looks just like ordinary Solomon's seal but has its flowers not beneath the leaves but in a tuft at the end of the stem. A woodland plant that is easy to grow even in dry, shaded locations.

SOLIDAGO *(ASTERACEAE)* – goldenrod

Although the goldenrods flower nicely, look very natural and are indestructible, they would never be our first choice. We agree completely with Graham Stuart Thomas: 'I seem to have a satisfying garden without them.' In fact, they flower for too short a time and grow too vigorously to be suitable garden plants (all of their neighbours will be swamped before you know it).

If, after all that, you still want to have goldenrod in your garden, 'Citronella' and 'Golden Mosa' are not unpleasant. We used to be enthusiastic about *S. caesia* but we have found that it does not do well after a hard winter. There is only one species which makes a real contribution to the garden:

S. rugosa 'Golden Rain' *Z3–8* ↕ **1.3m/ 4¼ft**   *EA–LA* ☼ ◑

A robust, eventually somewhat spreading, species with dark stems and a thinly spread inflorescence which from the middle of summer until the following spring is keenly present (as a winter silhouette). The flowers are yellow, as befits a goldenrod, and appear in mid-autumn when the rest of the garden has finished.

x SOLIDASTER *(ASTERACEAE)*

x S. luteus *Z4–9* ↕ **60cm–1.2m/ 2–4ft**   *MSu–LSu* ☼ ◑

A cross between *Solidago* and *Aster* which is neither invasive nor seed-bearing. It has eye-catching, luminous canary-yellow panicles of flowers. Pretty in a vase as well as in a garden. 'Lemore' is low-growing at 60cm/2ft. 'Super' grows to 1.2m/4ft.

STACHYS *(LAMIACEAE)*

A large and varied genus. The best species that are suitable for gardens have only recently come to attention. The long familiar, white, woolly-leaved *S. byzantina* usually looks dreadful in a wet climate, and by the time it turns into a disgusting heap of mush in the autumn we have had enough. So we shall skip that one. Much better garden plants are the species which belong to the subgenus *Betonica*, with attractive, regularly serrated leaves and compact, orchid-like flower spikes. Most of them do self-seed rather a lot and have been placed in the 'Playful' section. There are also various not unpleasant but quite troublesomely rampant species which are mentioned in the chapter 'Invasive plants'. The following, which belong to *Betonica*, are not self-seeding:

S. macrantha 'Superba' *Z4–8* ↕ **70cm/ 28in**   *ESu–MSu* ☼ ◑

Broad, ribbed, round-toothed leaves and large, light magenta lipped flowers in wreaths around the stem. Robust.

S. monieri *Z4–8* ↕ **25cm/ 10in**   *ESu–LSu* ☼ ◑

A low-lying species growing in neat clumps of healthy, fresh green leaves and countless compact flower spikes like sticks of rock. Rare but extremely strong.

Smilacina racemosa

Miscanthus sinensis 'Flamingo'

Winter
silhouettes

Winter is perhaps the best time of year for the gardener: the peace! You don't have to do anything, you don't have to think about anything and you don't have to worry about anything. You can just sit next to the fire reading gardening books and dreaming about how wonderful the garden will be next summer. Naturally, you will have to ensure that the garden has been prepared for winter: that is to say readied for winter without having cut back one plant or raked up one leaf. Silhouettes of *Eupatorium*, *Aster umbellatus*, *Veronicastrum virginicum* and the beautiful black spherical seed heads left by the monardas which even in the depths of winter smell like Earl Grey tea. Grasses, of course, especially *Miscanthus* with its amazing silver plumes, and a lot of *Calamagrostis* x *acutiflora* 'Karl Foerster' against the backdrop of a neatly clipped hedge or just against the chill winter wind: it is always sad when you have to cut it back again in spring. And in front, close to the house so you can see them from your armchair, the strong, fleshy shoots of hellebores, working their way through the fallen leaves and remains of last summer's border in tones of apple green, darkest purple, white and pale pink, exactly as you would see them in nature, in the Balkans. And, naturally, a specimen of *Viburnum* x *bodnantense* 'Dawn' next to the door so you can experience the delicious scent of its flowers every time you go in and out. A garden lovely enough to lift the spirits even on the most sombre and overcast days of winter. And when it has frozen and frost lies everywhere, or when it has snowed, it is so beautiful that you can sit, next to your cat, and stare outside for hours with your nose pressed against the window pane admiring the ghostly forms.

STROBILANTHES *(ACANTHACEAE)*

S. atropurpureus Z7–9   ↕ **1.5m/ 5ft** LSu–EA

It seems more like a labiate plant than an acanthus type. A robust plant with dense foliage and large, blue-purple lipped flowers which open in the morning and fade away in the afternoon. A decent plant for a warm, sunny spot out of the wind.

SYMPHYTUM *(BORAGINACEAE)* – **comfrey**

Comfreys are rough-textured plants with leaves like sandpaper but with attractive, pendent, tubular flowers. The majority, while attractive, are troublesome plants which run riot (see 'Invasive plants'). The following species are not like that:

S. caucasicum Z4–9   ↕ **1.25m/ 4ft** LSp–MSu

A large, slowly spreading plant, but not invasively so, with wonderfully pretty, azure-blue flowers which last for a long time in spring. It will not collapse and is extremely robust. It managed to survive in the Priona gardens for many years in a patch of stinging nettles, before it was given the prominent position it deserves.

S. x rubrum Z4–9   ↕ **50cm/ 20in** LSp–MSu

A cross between *S. officinale* and *S. ibericum*, with attractive, dark red, slightly blue-tinted, flowers. It is as persistent as *S. officinale*: any piece of root left in the ground will grow again. However, it is not invasive and does not seed itself. Consider carefully before planting.

S. tuberosum Z5–9   ↕ **30cm/ 1ft** LSp–ESu

Tuberous comfrey produces soft yellow flowers. Good for a sheltered position beneath shrubs. Disappears below ground after flowering.

TELLIMA *(SAXIFRAGACEAE)*

T. grandiflora Z4–9   ↕ **40cm/ 16in** LSp–ESu

A robust shade plant with a rosette of round, lobed, darkly veined leaves and elongated spikes of drooping green-white florets. Veins, stems and flowers are red-hued in the Rubra Group.

THALICTRUM *(RANUNCULACEAE)* – **meadow rue**

Species of meadow rue are recognizable by their much-divided foliage, the component parts of which are diamond-shaped, and large clusters of small florets mostly composed of anthers and stamens. They are perfect garden plants in any soil that is not too heavy. Evidently they think so, too, since they self-seed prodigiously; see the 'Playful' section in particular.

T. delavayi 'Hewitt's Double' Z5–9   ↕ **1.6m/ 5¼ft** MSu–EA

A double-flowered, sterile selection. Creates huge lilac sprays which have to be supported.

T. rochebruneanum Z5–9   ↕ **1.8m/ 6ft** ESu–MSu

An extremely robust species with thick, red-brown stems, blue-green leaves and open sprays of lilac flowers with yellow stamens. Will not topple over and self-seeds very little but will only grow in fertile, moisture-retentive soil.

T. 'Elin' Z5–9   ↕ **2.5m/ 8ft** ESu–MSu

A sterile hybrid, probably of *T. rochebrunianum* and *T. flavum* subsp. *glaucum*, discovered by Rune Bengtsson from Sweden and named after his mother. A plant with a great future. It appears in spring with virtually anthracite-coloured leaves which later turn grey-blue. The open sprays of light mauve florets on extremely tall, blue-grey stems are not at all likely to collapse. Takes up little space (the plant extends only upwards) and thus is perfect in a smaller garden.

Top: *Strobilanthes atropurpureus*
Centre: *Symphytum* x *rubrum*
Bottom: *Tellima grandiflora* Rubra Group with *Hosta* 'Moody Blues'

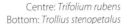

Top left: *Thermopsis villosa*
Top right: *Tricyrtis formosana*
Centre: *Trifolium rubens*
Bottom: *Trollius stenopetalus*

THERMOPSIS *(PAPILIONACEAE)*

An American genus of plants with yellow flowers like lupins. There are several quite seriously invasive species, the names of which are often confused. To prevent this, we mention only one species that we are certain about and which we know to be non-invasive.

T. villosa Z7–10 ↕ **1.2m/ 4ft** **ESu–MSu**

Syn. *T. caroliniana*. A robust, erect plant with trifoliate leaves like beans and large clusters of lemon-yellow flowers, followed by attractive pods. Good in dry soil.

TRICYRTIS *(CONVALLARIACEAE)* – **toad lily**

Delicate plants with strangely shaped, fringed and spotted flowers. It seems a little disloyal to call them after toads. They decorate shaded spots late in summer and would be used more if it were not for the fact that they are rarely very resilient. The strongest species seems to be:

T. formosana Z5–9 ↕ **60cm/ 2ft** **EA–MA**

This has nice, shiny green leaves and mauve-spotted flowers. Give it a good shaded spot with a humus-rich, moisture-retentive soil.

TRIFOLIUM *(PAPILIONACEAE)* – **clover**

Clover is not just food for horses. There are several very garden-worthy species as well. Unfortunately, it is not just horses but also rabbits that are completely crazy about clover. The following species will be fine in a rabbit-free garden whatever the soil type:

T. pannonicum Z6–9 ↕ **70cm/ 28in** **ESu–MSu**

Looks like red clover but the flowers are very large and a creamy green. Just like rabbit tails!

T. rubens Z5–9 ↕ **40cm/ 16in** **MSu–LSu**

Also looks like red clover but has long, narrow leaves and tall flower stems. In bud the flowers are silvery but open pinkish red.

TROLLIUS *(RANUNCULACEAE)* – **globe flower**

A genus closely related to *Ranunculus* which differs in that the flower parts are arranged in a spiral. The species *T. europaeus* is immediately recognizable by its globe-shaped flowers which makes them appear double, although they are typically single. Only *T. europaeus* looks like that. All the other species have flowers that bear a strong resemblance to the common buttercup.

T. europaeus Z4–8 ↕ **60cm/ 2ft** **LSp–ESu**

Mountain globe flower. A plant that loves cool places and will grow anywhere that is cold enough. In central and southern Europe, it grows only in the mountains in damp meadows where they are as commonplace as ordinary buttercups further north. An extremely long-lived plant in the garden given a cool spot in the shade where the soil never dries out. In full sun it is far prettier but it then needs a permanently damp soil. The rarely available species, with its relatively small, lemon-yellow, globular flowers (approximately 4cm/1½in wide), is much to be preferred above the countless number of cultivars. These have flowers that, although attractive in colour, are too large, causing the plants to topple over. Which is a shame. One good choice, however, is the pale yellow 'Cheddar'.

T. stenopetalus Z5–8 ↕ **60cm/ 2ft** **LSp–ESu**

Has widely separated, deep yellow (but attractive) 'buttercups' that are approximately 4cm/1½in in size. It makes more demands than *T. europaeus*, requiring a cool, damp, but well-drained spot in sun. That also applies to the other species sometimes on offer such as *T. chinensis*, *T. pumilus* and *T. yunnanensis*.

UVULARIA (CONVALLARIACEAE)

U. grandiflora Z5–9 ↕ 40cm/16in   MSp–ESu

This plant is closely related to *Polygonatum* but its leaves are more closely bundled together and it has larger, light yellow flowers hanging from beneath the leaves. It spreads slowly in humus-rich, moisture-retentive woodland loam. For enthusiasts, there are more species which look very like it.

VALERIANA (VALERIANACEAE) – valerian

The roots of ordinary valerian provide a relaxant when finely milled and placed in the medicine cabinet; not relaxing as a garden plant, however, for it is very invasive and really too unruly.

V. alliariifolia Z5–8 ↕ 1m/3½ft   ESu–LSu

Grows well in any garden soil, producing large, light green, heart-shaped leaves and dirty pink panicles of flowers. An uninspiring plant which self-seeds annoyingly. 'Sirene', on the contrary, is a marvellous discovery made by Brian Kabbes. It is sterile and produces pure white flowers.

VERATRUM (MELANTHIACEAE) – false hellebore

Stately plants which need to be left undisturbed for years before they will flower. They have wide, ovate leaves with ribbed veins giving them an almost pleated effect. When not in flower, they look just like *Gentiana lutea* and are often mistaken for it in their natural habitat, the Alps. Every few years, the plants produce long stems covered in star-like flowers which in turn change into wonderful seed capsules. They make few demands: any fertile, well-drained soil will do (the plant needs to be able to root deeply). The gardener must be patient and never transplant it. If in too much shade, or if the summer is very wet, the plants are sometimes eaten by snails.

V. californicum Z4–8 ↕ 1.75m/6ft   ESu–LSu

Every three or four years, it produces a gigantically branched flowering stem filled with white, green-veined flowers about 2cm/1in wide and fantastic seeds.

V. nigrum Z4–8 ↕ 1.5m/5ft   ESu–LSu

This plant has a less branching stem with smaller, mahogany brown flowers which produce seeds which are just as lovely. Flowers rather more regularly than the previous species and eventually grows into a hefty clump with several flowering stems at a time.

VERNONIA (ASTERACEAE) – iron weed

Large, rough plants which are extremely boring until they flower so showily in September, producing small, reddish purple thistle heads in panicles. Definitely a plant for the rear of the border! Various species are in circulation, some of which are too feeble and collapse before flowering. No good to you. This one is as strong as iron:

V. crinita 'Mammuth' Z5–9 ↕ 2.5m/8ft   EA–MA

Autumn flowering. Needs fertile, moisture-retentive soil.

VERONICA (SCROPHULARIACEAE) – speedwell

A large, varied genus which is immediately recognizable by its characteristic four-petalled flowers, the lowest petal of which is much smaller than the other three. Most species produce gorgeous blue flowers. Many species are rather unreliable, suddenly dying or getting mildew. Others seed themselves copiously. Given modest attention (they are small), the following two species will prove reliable:

V. austriaca subsp. teucrium Z5–8 ↕ 35cm/14in LSp–ESu

Forms creeping stems from which countless compact spires with deep blue flowers grow straight up. Many cultivars exist, each even more blue than the last.

Above: *Uvularia grandiflora*
Below: *Veratrum californicum* with *Angelica gigas*

***V. gentianoides* Z5–8** ↕ **35cm/ 14in** **LSp–ESu**

A slowly spreading plant with glossy green rosettes of leaves from which slender spikes of flowers ascend. The flowers are proportionally large and are pale blue with slightly darker blue veining.

VERONICASTRUM *(SCROPHULARIACEAE)*

Any plant lover will recognize these plants immediately as *Veronica*, but on closer inspection the characteristic four-petalled flowers are found to be absent. Thus another genus. The flowers are packed closely together on long spikes. The leaves grow in rosettes of five to eight around the base of the stem. All species have an attractive winter silhouette. Plant in soil that is not too dry.

***V. virginicum* Z4–8** ↕ **1.4–2m/ 4½–6½ft** **MSu–LSu**

Great Virginian speedwell. Both the leaves and flower spikes are narrower in this species than in its variety *sibiricum*. The spikes are borne in dense racemes along the stems and point stiffly upwards. Sturdy 'Diana' grows to 1.4m/4½ft and has white flowers, 'Fascination' produces lilac-blue flower spikes which branch out strangely: the plant, which shows fasciation, grows to 1.6m/5¼ft and tends to get top heavy and lean over. 'Lavendelturm' is pale lilac, 1.8m/6ft tall and does not collapse. *V.v.* var. *incarnatum* is 1.5m/5ft tall with pink flowers and sturdy. Finally, 'Temptation' is very different. The plant flowers earlier than the other varieties (at the beginning of summer), with lilac-blue spikes which point laterally rather than vertically. The plant does lean over but you should let that happen as it creates a 'hillock' of flower spikes pointing in all directions. Eye-catching and attractive until well into the winter.

***V. virginicum*
var. *sibiricum* Z4–8** ↕ **1.6m/ 5¼ft**   **ESu–MSu**

Robust, rather rough, plants with thick, somewhat unwieldy, crumpled flower spikes of up to 30cm/1ft long. 'Apollo' flowers in lilac, 'Spring Dew' in white, with its young shoots covered in a silvery dew. Like *V. virginicum* it provides a staple diet for bumblebees, bees and peacock butterflies.

VIOLA *(VIOLACEAE)*

Neither violets nor violas need an advocate. They are always welcome anywhere, of course. Perennial violets are mostly those known as woodland violets: welcome, spring-flowering gap fillers but too small for this book. Summer-flowering violas are generally very vulnerable plants and sometimes downright troublesome (how can violas be a nuisance?). They are mentioned in this book's other chapters. In our experience, only the following type is long-lived:

***V.* 'Belmont Blue' Z4–9** ↕ **30cm/ 1ft** **5–10**

Syn. *V. cornuta* 'Boughton Blue'. Produces an endless succession of light blue flowers. 'Milkmaid' is similarly profuse, but its flowers are white with a bluish tint. Now and then you will discover a seedling from these two but it is usually a different colour.

ZIGADENUS *(MELANTHIACEAE)*

**Z. elegans
subsp. *glaucus* Z5–9** ↕ **45cm/ 18in**   **MSu–LSu**

Grows into clumps of muted green, grassy leaves with grey-green stems and cream-coloured, green-speckled starry flowers. A celebration of subtleties. As strong as iron, it will tolerate years of neglect, but grows better given a little attention in fertile, well-drained garden soil.

Top: *Veronicastrum virginicum* 'Diana'
Centre left: *Veronicastrum virginicum* 'Fascination'
Centre right: *Veronicastrum virginicum* 'Lavendelturm'
Bottom: *Veronicastrum virginicum* 'Temptation'

Aralia californica with *Clematis* 'Perle d'Azur'

Giant plants

Giant plants. Everyone is well aware of them. Giant hogweed and Himalayan touch-me-not are the best known; you see them everywhere, not just in the garden but in the wild, too. Experienced gardeners speak of them with trepidation: 'Your whole garden will be swamped by them!' None the less, these people must have succumbed to their temptation at some point, or they would not be able to talk about them. Amazingly beautiful, they are not easy to resist.

The problem lies in the dizzying rapidity with which they grow or increase. Turn your back for a moment and the garden has literally grown up around your ears. Japanese knotweed (*Fallopia japonica*, syn. *Polygonum cuspidatum*), not described in this book because it is so fearsome, grows into impenetrable thickets which can colonize whole areas. Scarcely any other plants are able to survive among them; they can only be suppressed using the crudest, most poisonous of herbicides. Some species of bamboo are just as troublesome. Yet they remain fascinating to look at, just as fascinating as the question why they have not long ago conquered the whole world. Why is it that the whole of Japan has not been overgrown by the awful knotweed and the

oh-so-beautiful plume poppy (*Macleaya microcarpa*), the whole Himalayas with touch-me-not, the whole of the Caucasus with giant hogweed and the whole of the Netherlands with butterbur? In nature, the conditions for domination by a single species rarely occur. Human activities (pollution!) have contributed towards the enormous spread of such plants, but the doomsday scenarios sometimes projected of terrifying landscapes dominated only by giant plants have yet to materialize. Nature is too unruly to let that happen. You can continue to enjoy them in your garden as long as you remain the boss. But there is no denying that it will cost you a great deal of effort. If time and motivation fail you, it is better to go for giant plants which are not invasive, because they do exist. Butterbur can be replaced by *Darmera peltata*, which has large leaves and does not run rampant. Other non-invasive giants include: *Aralia californica*, *Eupatorium purpureum* subsp. *maculatum* 'Atropurpureum', *Filipendula camtschatica*, *Helianthus salicifolius*, *Miscanthus sinensis* cultivars, *Persicaria polymorpha*, *Rheum palmatum*, species of *Silphium*, *Thalictrum* 'Elin', *Verbesina alternifolia* and *Vernonia crinita* 'Mammuth'.

59

Persicaria amplexicaulis 'Firedance', *Miscanthus sinensis* 'Malepartus' and *Calamagrostis brachytricha*

Tough Grasses

Ornamental grasses are indispensable in a natural garden. Not only do they look natural, they are also terribly straightforward: they grow without protest in virtually all soil types and require almost no maintenance. Because of their open, airy appearance they lend a natural feeling to even the most deeply, brilliantly coloured flower combinations. The elegant winter silhouettes of many species contribute to the garden in winter. In our opinion, all this gives them a place in the top ten for a natural garden, if not the very first place: because of their dependable presence throughout a great part of the year, grasses often form the basis of a garden's design. A proper consideration of them would demand a long chapter with detailed plant descriptions. However, since we have just devoted a whole book to the subject (*Gardening with Grasses*, with Michael King), and considering that we have so many other plants to describe in this book, we will just take a very brief look at a few of the most useful.

ACHNATHERUM see **STIPA**

CALAMAGROSTIS (POACEAE) – **small reed**

C. x acutiflora
'Karl Foerster' Z5–9   1.75m/ 6ft   ESu–MSu
Grows in all soil types in sun. Indispensable for the winter garden.

C. brachytricha Z4–9   1.2m/ 4ft   LSu–MA
Grows everywhere and is always beautiful. Use it.

CAREX (CYPERACEAE) – **sedge**
Clump-forming, usually evergreen grass with a preference for damp soil and (semi-)shaded positions.

C. elata 'Aurea' Z5–9   65cm/ 26in   LSp–MSu
Bowles' golden sedge. Only in waterlogged soil. Has yellow leaves with a green margin.

C. grayi Z3–9   60cm/ 2ft   ESu–MSu
The eye-catching, round, prickly seed heads are long-lasting.

C. morrowii
'Variegata' Z7–9   45cm/ 18in   ESp–LSp
Grows in large clumps with lightly variegated leaves.

C. muskingumensis Z4–9   75cm/ 30in   ESu–MSu
Grows in clumps with tufts of leaves at the end of the stems, like palm trees in miniature. Not evergreen.

C. pendula Z5–9   1.1m/ 3½ft   LSp–ESu
Pendulous sedge. Flowers like hazel catkins. Grows into huge clumps.

C. plantaginea Z5–9   25cm/ 10in   MSp–LSp
Grows in small clumps with wide leaves. Tolerant of dry shade.

CHASMANTHIUM (POACEAE)

C. latifolium Z4–10   1m/ 3½ft   LSu–EA
Demands a good, moisture-retentive soil. Has an open growth habit with wide leaves and attractive, flattened flower heads.

DESCHAMPSIA (POACEAE) – **hair grass**

D. cespitosa Z4–9   1m/ 3½ft   ESu–LSu
Tufted hair grass. Clump-forming grass with a cloud of flowers, good in any moisture-retentive soil. 'Goldschleier' and the shorter 'Goldtau' flower profusely in gold. Does self-seed!

ERAGROSTIS (POACEAE) – **love grass**

E. curvula Z7–10   1m/ 3½ft   MSu–EA
African love-grass. Ornamental grass with thread-like leaves and wispy flowers. For dry, well-drained soil, especially in winter.

LUZULA (JUNCACEAE) – **woodrush**
Evergreen woodland grasses with 'true flowers'; good in any humus-rich soil.

L. nivea Z6–9   45cm/ 18in   LSp–ESu
Snowy woodrush. Produces small white panicles of flowers in the shade. 'Schattenkind' is lower-growing and with a more open inflorescence. 'Schneehäschen' is taller. Grows in dry shade as well.

L. sylvatica Z4–9   50cm/ 20in   MSp–ESu
Great woodrush. Grows everywhere in acid, dry soil with brown flower heads. 'Hohe Tatra' (Z5–9) has wider leaves than the species. 'Wäldler' (Z6–9) flowers profusely and has bright green leaves.

MISCANTHUS (POACEAE)

M. sinensis Z5–10   1.5–2.5m/ 5–8ft   MSu–MA
Grows well in any garden soil in full sunshine. Wonderful autumn colour, lovely winter silhouette. There are many cultivars available.

MOLINIA (POACEAE) – **moor grass**
Grows well in any garden soil that is not too dry. The inflorescence is slim and transparent, and will fit in anywhere. Lovely autumn colour.

M. caerulea Z5–9   60cm/ 2ft   MSu–MA
Purple moor grass. Has thin, stiffly erect flowers. 'Dauerstrahl' grows to 90cm/3ft in height, M.c. subsp. caerulea 'Heidebraut' to 1.2m/4ft and 'Moorhexe' to 60cm/2ft.

M. caerulea subsp.
arundinacea Z5–9   2–2.4m/ 6½–8ft   MSu–EA
Grows very tall and has a spread-out inflorescence. 'Fontäne' has overhanging flower heads. 'Karl Foerster' is more erect. 'Transparent' is one of the tallest types and has the most open growth habit. 'Windspiel' has robust flower heads which move with the wind.

PANICUM (POACEAE) – **panic grass**

P. virgatum Z5–9   1.25–1.5m/ 4–5ft   LSu–EA
This grass only starts to grow late in the season. It has an elongated, wispy inflorescence made up of tiny spikes and a beautiful autumn colour. Good in any garden soil given full sun. 'Rehbraun' is a robust selection, the leaves of which turn red as early as summer. 'Squaw' produces abundant flower heads.

SESLERIA (POACEAE) – **blue grass**
Clump-forming grasses with compact flowering spikes for dry soil.

S. autumnalis Z5–10   50cm/ 20in   LSu–MA
Late-flowering, green woodland grass, good in dry, shaded positions.

S. nitida Z5–10   60cm/ 2ft   MSp–LSp
Grows into hefty clumps with blue-grey leaves and whitish flower spikes. Sunny positions.

SPODIOPOGON (POACEAE)

S. sibiricus Z4–9   1.4m/ 4½ft   MSu–EA
Bamboo-like grass with an orange-red autumn colour. Grows in any moisture-retentive soil.

SPOROBOLUS (POACEAE)

S. heterolepis Z4–9   80cm/ 32in   MSu–LSu
Elegant grass for dry, stony soil that is not too deficient in nutrients.

STIPA (POACEAE) – **feather grass**
Grasses of the steppes, happiest in dry conditions. Not always reliable in a wet climate. Our best experiences have been with:

S. calamagrostis Z6–10   90cm/ 3ft   ESu–MA
Develops into arching plumes of grass in warm, dry locations. Will tolerate very little competition so you should plant it at the front of the border or allow it to hang over a low wall.

S. gigantea Z6–9   2.2m/ 7ft   ESu–LSu
Grows into broad, evergreen clumps with enormous stems and oat-like flowers. Only the very severest winters pose a problem for this plant.

S. turkestanica Z6–10   1.2m/ 4ft   MSu–LSu
Erect stems with open flowering plumes and fewer long glumes than most of the other (less reliable) species. A true Stipa: light and airy.

The caterpillar has just finished its meal: the whole plant is bare!

Food for all

One of the nicest things about a garden is the wildlife which you get with it for free. The wildlife in a natural garden will be much more varied than in a traditionally maintained garden: there is more to eat and there are more places to hide. Plant spiny bushes covered in berries for the birds to eat safely out of the cat's reach. Here and there, leave mounds of twigs and leaves under which hedgehogs and toads can hibernate. Seed heads left in the garden over winter for their attractive silhouettes will attract masses of greenfinches, blue tits, bullfinches and goldfinches. Spring will only really have come when the first bees start to hum around the snowdrops and crocuses and when you discover the first bumblebee in the lungwort. Summer has reached its zenith when the garden shimmers with butterflies and moths – you can make a study of which ones – and, if you are very lucky and have some water nearby, even dragonflies. What a delight, and all for free!

Naturally, there is also a downside to all this: the dense foliage of shrubs is an ideal hiding place for rabbits, which will dig up your new plantings and decapitate your precious violas. Dense foliage, leaf mould and humus-rich soil are a joy to snails which will leave only skeletal remains of your hostas. And never mind all the greenflies, grasshoppers, caterpillars, bugs and sgrubs of all sorts which come to join in the feast. What are you to do about all of that? Back to a traditional garden complete with insecticide and slug pellets only to wave goodbye to all the beneficial animal life which needs everything you

consider pests for food? Or else resign yourself to the fact that you can never be the absolute master of a garden?

We opt for the latter solution. Perfection is an unattainable illusion. If what you want is total control, you should tarmac your garden now and stick plastic trees in it. Moreover, the fauna in your garden do serve a useful purpose. Moles keep the grass healthy and the soil ventilated. Of course, trampling molehills is not quite our favourite job, but it rates higher than murdering moles. A fence will keep rabbits out – or, if the garden is too big to fence completely, you can set aside some special places with short grass for them. They will love it! Snails are just plain useful: they clean up anything that is weak or sick. In particular, snails eat algae, dying leaves and ailing plants which have been put in the wrong position. You should replant them in another location or, if they are eaten by snails again, just throw them away. Of course, snails eat young plants, too, before they have a chance to grow strong. That can be painful if the seedling concerned is particularly special to you. But if you really feel determined to succeed against all odds you can camp out next to it each night and, with your pocket torch, trap all the snails. Occasionally, catastrophes do happen, such as an extremely wet summer when snails can wreak real havoc in a garden. However, such instances pass and most plants have evolved to cope with such onslaughts.

This applies to plagues of other creatures too which can sometimes arise (not often, as a varied, natural garden is virtually never troubled by plagues of pests). The cause is always extreme weather conditions or something else equally beyond your control and this, too, passes in time. There is no reason at all to reach for the pesticide spray just out of nervousness. A garden was meant to be enjoyed, not worried about. Let there be food for all!

Royal ferns in the Thijssepark

Tough Ferns

Most ferns are extremely long-lived plants which, under favourable conditions, easily outlive the person who planted them. Favourable conditions for ferns are: shade, a moisture-retentive, humus-rich soil and, especially, constant high humidity. This explains why far and away the majority of species grow in the tropics. By comparison, there are only a few species found in temperate climates. They fare best in areas where it virtually never freezes and where it rains a great deal. Ireland is a true paradise for ferns, and so are Brittany, Cornwall, Wales and the Lowlands of Scotland. Outside these areas ferns are quite happy in sheltered, walled city gardens and on the old walls of bridges and quays. The list of species given here has been restricted to those which are hardy, and which are suitable for the average shaded garden. There are several cultivars from a number of species, mostly with rather sickly looking, strange pinnate or forked leaves. Such sophistications are unnecessary – ferns are attractive enough in themselves – and so we shall not mention them. In general, ferns demand little more from the soil than that it is rich in humus, and they are fiercely competitive: they do not easily allow themselves to be swamped by neighbouring plants. These plants are quite indispensable in a natural garden because of the characteristics of their leaves, which are unlike those of any other plant, and the marvellous way in which they unfurl like feathers in spring.

63

Above: *Blechnum spicant*
Below: *Dryopteris erythrosora* with *Hosta* 'Halycon'

ADIANTUM *(ADIANTACEAE)* – maidenhair fern

Ferns with almost transparent, light green, bipinnate or tripinnate fronds, the component parts (pinnae) being diamond-shaped. Fronds are up to 40cm/16in long. Three very similar species are commonly available: *A. capillus-veneris*, *A. pedatum* and *A. venustum*. All three need a sheltered spot where hard frost cannot damage them too badly.

ASPLENIUM *(ASPLENIACEAE)* – spleenwort

In general, spleenworts are small ferns which are usually found among rocks and in gaps in walls and not in garden soil. There is one larger species:

A. scolopendrium Z4–8 ↕ 60cm/ 2ft

Syn. *Phyllitis scolopendrium*. Hart's-tongue fern, with long, ribbed, tongue-like fronds which remain green in winter. For that reason, they are not able to cope with hard frost combined with sunshine. They prefer to grow in wall crevices but will also grow in other dark, chalky places, for example, against limestone walls facing away from the sun.

ATHYRIUM *(WOODSIACEAE)*

A. filix-femina Z4–9 ↕ 1.5m/ 5ft

Lady fern. A strong species with bipinnate fronds and finely divided pinnae. It dies back in autumn. The name 'lady fern' derives from the gracefulness of its fronds compared with the much more robust fronds of *Dryopteris filix-mas*, the 'male fern'.

BLECHNUM *(BLECHNACEAE)* – hard fern, deer fern

B. spicant Z4–8 ↕ 70cm/ 28in

An extremely attractive species with dark green, single pinnate fronds and entire pinnae which form a rosette at ground level. Fertile (that is, spore-bearing) fronds stand fully erect at the centre of the rosette and have extremely narrow pinnae making them look a little like fish bones. Acid, humus-rich soil and high humidity are important to these ferns.

CYSTOPTERIS *(WOODSIACEAE)* – bladder fern

C. bulbifera Z3–7 ↕ 90cm/ 3ft

Berry bladder fern. Light green, ornamental fern with bipinnate fronds. Thrives in shady, damp places. Quickly spreads from bulbils in the leaf axils.

DRYOPTERIS *(DRYOPTERIDACEAE)* – buckler fern

Large ferns with bipinnate or tripinnate leaves which are a little coarser than *Athyrium*. The fronds remain more or less green throughout the winter. There are many species and we shall just mention the most important.

D. affinis Z4–8 ↕ 1.5m/ 5ft

Syn. *D. pseudomas*. Looks like *D. filix-mas* but the frond stems are covered in bright orange bracts and the fronds are lighter green.

D. dilatata Z3–8 ↕ 1.5m/ 5ft

Broad buckler fern. The fronds are bipinnate while the pinnae are dentate. The whole frond is triangular. Not the most attractive species but certainly large and tolerant of very poor, dry soil as long as enough humus is mixed in with it. Is capable of self-seeding in abundance in between stones, for example, or on rotting tree stumps. *D. carthusiana* is similar but smaller.

D. erythrosora Z5–9 ↕ 80cm/ 32in

In late spring, this fern emerges an orange-brown and turns an attractive colour in autumn. In other words, not evergreen.

D. filix-mas Z4–8   ↑1m/ ↓3½ft

Male fern. Has bipinnate leaves with entire pinnae. A robust species which eventually forms gigantic clumps. Will tolerate sun in damp locations between stones or alongside a wall.

D. wallichiana Z6–8   ↑1m/ ↓3½ft

Not completely hardy, in fact, but definitely the most attractive in this family, especially in spring with its gold-green fronds against the black bracts of its stems. Plant in a sheltered position.

MATTEUCCIA (*WOODSIACEAE*) – **ostrich plume fern, shuttlecock fern**

M. struthiopteris Z2–8   ↑1.5m/ ↓5ft

Grows quite rampantly into a bowl shape. Later in the summer, the fronds fall back to reveal the stiffly erect stolons (which bear the spores). Tolerates more sun than the other ferns (but not dry conditions) and does not like deep shade. These ferns will create a weed-suppressing carpet. For difficult corners of the garden.

OSMUNDA (*OSMUNDACEAE*)

O. regalis Z3–9   ↑2m/ ↓6½ft

Royal fern. Gigantic ferns which only like growing in acid, damp to boggy soil. The hairless fronds are bipinnate with the stolons pointing proudly above the fronds, looking like an astilbe after flowering. Beautiful autumn colour.

POLYPODIUM (*POLYPODIACEAE*) – **polypody**

P. vulgare Z5–8   ↑25cm/ ↓10in

Common polypody. An evergreen species with pinnate fronds which slowly but surely spreads via rootlets. Grows well in dry soil poor in humus, for example at the base of trees where fallen leaves are blown away by the wind, but also in walls and on old, pollarded willows. *P. interjectum* is closely related and has serrated fronds, grows a little larger and requires a rather more fertile soil.

POLYSTICHUM (*DRYOPTERIDACEAE*) – **shield fern**

Evergreen ferns with pinnate or bipinnate fronds which are severely dentate. If planted out in the open without protection they will succumb to a cold winter. Given a sheltered position, however, they will thrive in any soil type.

P. aculeatum Z4–8   ↑60cm/ ↓2ft

Hard shield fern. Has bipinnate, leathery, glossy, dark green fronds.

P. setiferum Z5–8   ↑1m/ ↓3½ft

Soft shield fern. This fern has bipinnate, and sometimes tripinnate, fronds which are somewhat softer and lighter than in the previous species. It looks beautiful on emergence in spring, with its brown-flecked stems. 'Herrenhausen' is even more attractive.

PTERIDIUM (*DENNSTAEDTIACEAE*) – **bracken**

P. aquilinum Z3–9   ↑2m/ ↓6½ft

We only mention this fern as a warning. Terribly invasive and almost impossible to eradicate. Moreover, it will not tolerate any other plant in its vicinity. To be avoided.

Polystichum setiferum 'Herrenhausen'

Narcissus poeticus in the Pyrenees

Tough
Bulbs

Bulbs add an extra dimension to your garden. They form a sort of underground army (with unusually good manners). For most of the year they are invisible. Early in spring they emerge in force, only to make way politely for the perennials when they get the urge to start growing. Managing not to compete with one another, they live side by side in almost perfect harmony.

Even the summer-flowering alliums produce their leaves in spring to store energy for the following season. They have already shed their leaves by the time the perennials are growing up. Either that, or else they are hanging from the plant all yellowed and withered, in which case you can just cut them off. Afterwards, all that is left is their long-stemmed flowers raised high above ground level.

Many bulbs appear to have eternal life; they don't need a male to procreate. They clone themselves by producing smaller bulbs around the mother bulb. As the central bulb dies, the smaller bulbs themselves grow into mother bulbs which also produce smaller bulbs around them; and so it goes on *ad infinitum*. Under ideal conditions, that is. For most bulbs, ideal conditions mean a strong, chalky soil (with a high pH), enough moisture in spring – even waterlogging does not jeopardize them – followed by a warm and dry-as-dust summer. Few areas offer precisely this combination. The conditions closest to the ideal are to be found along the inland side of the dunes in Holland, where extremely lime-rich and well-drained sand comes together with desiccating sea winds and high light levels. No wonder bulb growers have claimed this area as their own!

However, there are enough species of bulbs which have proved able to establish themselves under less favourable conditions. These are the stars which will be allowed to shine in this book, along with a number of species which probably do not look as though they would be able to thrive for long but which, with a little assistance (not too much), can still cope in ordinary garden soil for quite a long time. It is worth remembering, though, that you will be able to achieve much more in a sandy area or on dry clay or loam. If you have a wet and acid soil, you can labour and spray all you like but despite your efforts almost nothing will work (except *Leucojum aestivum*). Of course, we are not talking about real enthusiasts here: they will always find some way or other to encourage their bulbs and keep them flourishing.

We are proud to announce that in compiling the following entries we have had the help of the renowned bulb authority Rita van der Zalm.

ALLIUM *(ALLIACEAE)* – onion

Allium is the largest genus of all bulbous plants, containing hundreds of species, including, for our food and health, the indispensable onion, leek, garlic and chives. In general, they appreciate – as steppe plants – a dry, lime-rich, sunny location, although there are exceptions. Their spherical flowers are stunning: they should not be left out of any summer border with well-drained soil.

A. carinatum subsp. *pulchellum* Z6–9 40cm/16in MSu–LSu

A decorative species. At the end of summer, its hanging bunches of dusky mauve-pink, bell-shaped flowers burst from intriguing pointed caps. *A.c.* subsp. *p.* f. *album* has white flowers.

A. cernuum Z3–8 30cm/1ft ESu–EA

Produces a panicle of pendent, dusky mauve-pink bell flowers. Less of a bulb than an evergreen leek. Unlike most other *Allium* species, this grows best in moisture-retentive soil where it seeds itself abundantly.

A. cristophii Z4–10 40cm/16in LSp–MSu

An eye-catching, straightforward species with huge, spherical flower heads filled with silvery lilac, star-shaped florets which remain attractive long after they have faded.

'Firmament' is a cross with *A. atropurpureum* and has a slightly smaller inflorescence (10–12cm/4–4½in in diameter) with aubergine-coloured stems. 'Globemaster' is a cross with *A. macleanii.* 80cm/32in tall, it has an extremely compact, spherical inflorescence, 20–25cm/8–10in in diameter, which can contain hundreds of individual florets.

A. fistulosum Z6–9 40cm/16in MSp–ESu

Welsh onion. Not a bulbous plant but a clump-forming one with thick, hollow, tubular leaves and compact greenish white flower heads ending in a point. Seeds itself nicely.

A. flavum Z5–9 30cm/1ft ESu–MSu

Thin, blue-green leaves and small, sulphur-yellow flowers. For growing in sunny, dry places and allowing to run wild; and that is no problem as it self-seeds copiously.

A. hollandicum Z4–10 80cm/32in LSp–ESu

An extremely vigorous species with large, mauve, rounded flower heads which sets seed abundantly. *A.h.* 'Purple Sensation' has deeper, red-purple flowers.

A. karataviense Z3–9 20cm/8in LSp

This species produces two broad leaves, blue-grey above, purple below and grey-pink, spherical flower heads about 10cm/4in in diameter. Long-lived in barren, dry spots, alongside a path (or in it) or between stones. Self-seeds copiously.

A. nutans Z6–9 50cm/20in ESu–MSu

A species with many long, wide, rather flapping, grey leaves which appear as early as winter, and subtle grey-pink panicles of flowers.

A. obliquum Z4–9 80cm/32in ESu–MSu

A fabulous species with subtle lemon-yellow flowers on long grey stems. Vigorous and grows well in any well-drained garden soil. Self-seeds well, too.

A. paradoxum Z4–9 30cm/1ft MSp–ESu

A not particularly eye-catching species with just one leaf and between one and five hanging white flowers with bulbils in their midst. Will spread far in shady gardens.

A. schoenoprasum Z3–9 40cm/16in LSp–ESu

Chives are, of course, again not bulbs but rather clump-forming

Top: *Allium carinatum* subsp. *pulchellum*
Centre: *Allium* 'Globemaster'
Bottom: *Allium obliquum*

plants. They produce an abundance of lilac-pink flowers, spread freely and will seed themselves on any available plot of ground. 'Forescate' develops into a hefty plant with purplish red flowers.

A. sphaerocephalon Z6–10 ↕ 60cm/2ft ❋ MSu–LSu
Round-headed leek. You really should try buying a large sackful. It'll brighten up the whole garden in summer. The dark reddish purple globes, each about 5cm/2in in diameter, should be spread out *en masse* throughout your border. And they are cheap, too!

A. ursinum Z5–9 ↕ 30cm/1ft ❋ MSp–LSp
Wild garlic's white umbels bear light green leaves on which dew-drops come so prettily to rest. This familiar woodland plant will spread unstoppably in shaded, rich, peaty soils.

A. vineale Z5–9 ↕ 70cm/28in ❋ ESu–LSu
Crow garlic. Unremarkable, with greenish purple flower heads which often contain more bulbils than flowers but which are fun when planted as a large group. Grows everywhere and naturalizes freely.

A. zebdanense Z4–10 ↕ 40cm/16in ❋ MSp–LSp
Produces from five to fifteen white flowers in a bunch. Naturalizes freely.

ANEMONE *(RANUNCULACEAE)* – **windflower**

As well as the perennial anemones, there are also species which behave like bulbous plants even though they are not strictly bulbs (they form rhizomes). The well-known and beautiful *A. blanda* may stay with you for years, but it is not truly dependable. The following species are extremely dependable, all of them easily grown in shaded, humus-rich soils:

A. x lipsiensis Z4–8 ↕ 20cm/8in ❋ MSp–LSp
A cross between the following species, with pale yellow flowers on delicate stems that are flushed red.

A. nemorosa Z4–8 ↕ 30cm/1ft ❋ MSp–LSp
Wood anemone. Has white flowers and, after a slow start, spreads to form whole carpets, even among clumps of perennials. There are many cultivars. The most important of these are 'Robinsoniana', with large lavender-blue flowers, and 'Vestal' which produces jolly, double, white flowers somewhat later.

A. ranunculoides Z4–8 ↕ 15cm/6in ❋ ESp–MSp
Produces a profusion of small, buttercup yellow flowers. Those of *A.r.* subsp. *wockeana* are even smaller. Deep in her heart, Rita van der Zalm thinks it has a 'sweeter' appearance because it grows in little circular clumps.

ARUM *(ARACEAE)*

Shade-loving plants with large, arrow-shaped leaves which appear above ground in winter and disappear after flowering in late spring/early summer. The great club-like spadix bearing bright orange (poisonous) berries emerges from the ground in late summer/early autumn. They grow everywhere but only flower well in moist, chalky soils.

A. maculatum Z7–9 ↕ 30cm/1ft ❋ LSp–ESu
Lords and ladies. Has glossy green leaves, sometimes with dark spots, and a pale green spathe (the modified leaf which sheaths the flowers attached to the brownish purple spadix within).

A. italicum Z7–9 ↕ 40cm/16in ❋ LSp–ESu
The white-marbled leaves of this species appear as early as autumn. The spathe is whitish, the spadix yellow.

Top: *Allium ursinum* with *Fritillaria meleagris*
Centre: *Anemone x lipsiensis* with *Jeffersonia dubia*
Bottom: *Anemone nemorosa* 'Robinsoniana'

CAMASSIA *(HYACINTHACEAE)* **– quamash**

It is difficult to understand why these beautiful bulbs, which are so suited to naturalizing, are still so unfamiliar. They grow best in moisture-retentive soils but will also tolerate drier conditions. Our advice is to dig up the plants every four years to separate the bulbs. This will ensure better flower production. Moreover, the mass of leaves will eventually become so large that it will be a great temptation to slugs and snails.

C. cusickii Z3–10 ↕ 70cm/28in LSp–ESu ☼

Produces an oblong spike of large, silver-blue, star-like flowers.

C. leichtlinii Z4–10 ↕ 80cm/32in LSp–ESu ☼

Produces hefty spires of flowers. 'Alba' is pale blue-white, *C.l.* subsp. *suksdorfii* Caerulea Group is deep blue.

C. quamash Z4–10 ↕ 30cm/1ft LSp–ESu ☼

Looks like the previous species but is in all respects smaller and more ornamental. It is ideal for a flower meadow with its deep blue flowers. 'Blue Melody' is an even more intense blue and has white variegation running the length of the leaf.

C. scilloides Z5–10 ↕ 40cm/16in ESu–MSu ☼

Looks just like a wood hyacinth, has light blue flowers and attractive seed pods and self seeds well.

CHIONODOXA *(HYACINTHACEAE)* **– glory of the snow**

Small bulbs, suitable for naturalizing in grass or in light shade. All species self seed.

C. forbesii Z4–9 ↕ 15cm/6in ❀ ESp–MSp ☼ ☼

Has large, lavender-blue flowers with white centres.

C. luciliae 'Alba' Z4–9 ↕ 25cm/10in ❀ ESp–MSp ☼ ☼

Has large white flowers with yellow stamens. 'Pink Giant' has larger, pink flowers.

C. sardensis Z4–9 ↕ 10cm/4in ❀ ESp–MSp ☼ ☼

If you are ever at some old country estate in springtime and see fields of blue, it is most likely this species. This small, deep blue species not only seeds itself abundantly but the parent bulb pushes the bulblets out of its way so it cannot be stifled by them. After a few years you can have a field of them of your own.

COLCHICUM *(COLCHICACEAE)* **– meadow saffron**

Produces large goblet-like flowers in autumn with plentiful, rather large leaves in the spring. If you place *Colchicum* species among perennials you must remember to find a place where they will not be obscured by the leaves of neighbours in late summer. Otherwise the flowers, which emerge direct from ground level, will be hidden from view and become the target of slugs and snails. The following two species can manage well with colder climates:

C. autumnale Z5–9 ↕ 15cm/6in LSu–EA ☼

The common meadow saffron with relatively small lilac flowers. In the wild, it grows in boggy meadows, often near springs. In gardens, therefore, it should not be planted in too dry a position and will tolerate some shade. There are many cultivars. 'Album' is a pretty white variety. The double varieties are too sophisticated for our taste.

C. speciosum Z6–9 ↕ 25cm/10in EA–MA ☼

Looks just like the previous species, but grows much larger, flowers later and tolerates drier conditions. There is a good white variety of this, also called 'Album'.

Above: *Camassia leichtlinii* 'Alba'
Below: *Colchicum autumnale*

Some snapshots from the wealth of variety to be found in *Corydalis solida*

CORYDALIS (PAPAVERACEAE)

C. cava Z6–8 ↕ 30cm/ 1ft   ESp–MSp

Produces large racemes of spurred, red-purple, sometimes white flowers above a tuft of finely divided foliage. Breathtaking, but only in fertile, humus-rich soil.

C. solida Z6–8 ↕ 20cm/ 8in  ESp–MSp

Looks very much like the previous species but is a little smaller, flowers in lilac-pink and is less demanding as to soil type. The seeds are dispersed by ants and seedlings turn up in various parts of the garden as a result. The species has a wide range of naturally occurring forms and in Asia virtually every range of hills has a type that is different from the next.

CRINUM (AMARYLLIDACEAE)

C. x powellii Z7–10 ↕ 1.5m/ 5ft   MSu–EA

This large bulbous plant from South Africa is, of course, not hardy but experience has taught us that it will survive the severest winters if you plant the (huge) bulbs deep enough. The top of the bulb should be placed at least 40cm/16in below ground (and only in places that are above ground-water levels even in wet years). The plant produces a large, somewhat spreading forest of grassy leaves and long stems with a spray of large pink lily-like flowers at the top. The sunnier the position, the better it will flower.

CROCUS (IRIDACEAE)

Crocuses require no introduction. In theory they will grow everywhere. However, in practice that can lead to disappointment. In poor, acid, sandy soil they will grow but will hardly multiply at all. Eventually, you will lose them all because crocuses have a number of natural adversaries: voles eat the bulbs, hares and rabbits eat the leaves (and the flowers *en passant*), and birds peck at the flowers. In more fertile soil they multiply so quickly that they are able to run ahead of their adversaries. Many more species will grow in such conditions than we have mentioned below. The very strongest which are pretty much dependable everywhere are:

C. chrysanthus Z4–9 ↕ 10cm/ 4in   MW–ESp

The smallest and one of the earliest to flower. There are many hybrids in soft, pastel colours. 'Cream Beauty' is cream-coloured. 'Goldilocks' is golden-yellow, 'Prinses Beatrix' lavender-blue.

C. speciosus Z6–9 ↕ 10cm/ 4in   EA–MA

The most robust autumn crocus with lilac-pink flowers emerging above ground level without leaves. The leaves appear only in spring and are unsightly but should only be cut back once they have yellowed and withered.

C. sieberi Z7–9 ↕ 10cm/ 4in   EW–LW

The earliest crocus to flower; in mild conditions, mid-winter or even earlier. It is lavender-blue with a yellow throat. *C.s.* subsp. *sublimis* 'Tricolor', the best-known cultivar, has an apricot-coloured throat.

C. tommasinianus Z5–9 ↕ 15cm/ 6in   MW–ESp

A slim crocus in soft lilac-pink with a silvery exterior. Spreads explosively. 'Ruby Giant' is purple, 'Barr's Purple' amethyst-violet with a silvery sheen on the outside.

C. vernus Z4–9 ↕ 10–25cm/ 4–10in MW–ESp

The species, in white or pale lilac, is seldom available. We shall not trouble you with naming all the many cultivars. There are some very attractive ones among them, but some hideous ones too, such as the crocuses with over-large petals you see planted so nicely on roundabouts. Once you have them in the garden and you see how outsize they are, it is too late to get rid of them.

CYCLAMEN *(PRIMULACEAE)*

Extremely long-lived, tuberous plants which will brighten up a shady garden outside of the normal growing season, as long as the following condition is met: shade combined with a chalky soil. Cyclamens adore a lime-rich environment. Give them agricultural lime, marl, bonemeal or eggshells. There are many species but only the following two are completely hardy:

C. coum Z6–10   ↕ 10cm/4in   EW–ESp

A winter-flowering species with small, round, marbled leaves and little magenta flowers in the depths of winter. Unbelievable colour in the middle of a dreary season.

C. hederifolium Z5–10   ↕ 15cm/6in   LSu–MA

The light pink flowers with dark centres start to appear from mid-summer onwards. The slightly lobed, marbled leaves follow and remain a feature all winter. *C.h.* f. *albiflorum* produces pure white flowers.

ERANTHIS *(RANUNCULACEAE)* – **winter aconite**

E. hyemalis Z5–9   ↕ 10cm/4in   LW–ESp

Happily runs wild in fertile, moisture-retentive soil where it creates carpets of bright yellow flowers just above ground level. It will barely grow at all in a sandy soil. There is a variety on the market under the name *E.h.* Cilicica Group which tolerates drier summer conditions and has more deeply cut leaves and larger flowers.

ERYTHRONIUM *(LILIACEAE)*

This genus has nodding flowers with reflexed petals that make them look like cyclamens. There are many species, few of them reliable.

E. dens-canis Z3–8   ↕ 15cm/6in   ESp–MSp

Dog's-tooth violet. A jolly plant with prettily speckled leaves and gorgeous pink flowers which is quite fussy about where it will grow: a cool, fertile spot with sun and space in spring and shade in summer. If it is closed in among other plants in spring, the snails will get at it.

E. 'Pagoda' Z5–9   ↕ 25cm/10in   MSp–LSp

After a few years, this grows into sturdy clumps of large, fresh green, sometimes darkly marbled leaves and produces quantities of pale yellow, bell-like flowers. This is a robust cultivar that is just as much at home in acid, dry soil.

E. californicum 'White Beauty' Z5–9   ↕ 20cm/8in   MSp–LSp

Marbled leaves and ivory white, bell-like flowers with a light brown ring in the centre. Just as vigorous as the previous species.

FRITILLARIA *(LILIACEAE)* – **fritillary**

A large genus with subtly coloured (striped, chequered or marbled) bell-shaped flowers which any gardener falls for instantly. Unfortunately, most of the species are not very reliable in the garden. Just why is not completely clear. Probably, as one often finds with such subtle beauties, they have very specific requirements for where they are planted – requirements the average garden finds it hard to meet.

F. imperialis Z5–9   ↕ 80cm/32in   MSp

Crown imperial. A familiar plant with large, orange flowers in a rosette at the top of the stem (the 'crown'). 'Lutea' is bright yellow, 'Aureo-marginata' is red-orange and has leaves with yellow margins. Reliable when planted in a warm, sunny spot in well-drained, chalky soil.

F. meleagris Z4–9   ↕ 30cm/1ft   MSp–LSp

Snake's-head fritillary. A favourite fritillary with its purple-and-white chequered flowers (sometimes completely white). In the wild it is

Top: Crocus speciosus
Centre: Crocus tommasinianus
Bottom left: Cyclamen coum
Bottom right: Erythronium dens-canis

Hyacinthoides hispanica 'Alba'

extremely choosy: it will grow only in boggy ground which is flooded annually to leave a fine layer of silt behind. It doesn't survive very long in gardens with heavy clay or peat soil, but does seed itself considerably: in this way it 'strolls' through the garden.

F. uva-vulpis Z7–9 ↕ **25cm/ 10in** **MSp–LSp** ☼
Is happiest and will increase in fertile, well-drained soil in full sun. The flowers are grey speckled purple and yellow within.

GALANTHUS (AMARYLLIDACEAE) – snowdrop
The reliability of snowdrops is not in question. They would appear to have eternal life. If you want to have lots of them in your garden you should not wait for them to seed themselves. You could wait for ever. Once they have finished flowering, dig up the clumps and pull them apart. It works miracles and within a few years your garden will be filled with them. It is a little like the story of the loaves and the fishes. There are many species and cultivars. The most important are:

G. elwesii Z6–9 ↕ **25cm/ 10in** **EW–LW** ☼ ☼ ☼
Just like a common snowdrop but earlier-flowering with broader leaves and larger flowers.

G. ikariae Z6–9 ↕ **30cm/ 1ft** **LW–MSp** ☼ ☼ ☼
Has wide leaves which are much greener than those of the common snowdrop, with larger flowers. Grows into robust clumps and spreads out considerably.

G. nivalis Z4–9 ↕ **20cm/ 8in** **MW–MSp** ☼ ☼ ☼
We are not going to describe the common snowdrop. There are an awful lot of cultivars which all perform well. Whether they are all as attractive is another matter.

HYACINTHOIDES (HYACINTHACEAE) – bluebell
Produces a large clump of leaves with large spikes of pendent, bell-shaped flowers, usually blue. There are two separate species which like growing in any soil that is not too saturated with moisture:

H. hispanica Z4–9 ↕ **30cm/ 1ft**  **LSp-ESu** ☼ ☼ ☼
Spanish bluebell. The flowers grow in a regular pattern all around the spike and are usually blue, although there are many cultivars in light blue, pink and white.

H. non-scripta Z5–9 ↕ **25cm/ 10in** **LSp-ESu** ☼ ☼
The true bluebell so commonly found in the wild in Britain: the sky-blue flowers all face from one side of the stem. Is virtually never available as the true type. Nursery specimens all have some *H. hispanica* genes in them.

IPHEION (ALLIACEAE)

I. uniflorum Z6–10 ↕ **10cm/ 4in** ● **ESP–ESu** ☼
The ideal bulb for beginners. *Ipheion* does well in any location, so long as it is dry and sunny: in pots, between stones and steps, between grape hyacinths or tulips, in clumps and as edging, in school gardens or country estates. Pale blue, star-like flowers which smell of soap, amid plentiful leaves.

LEUCOJUM (AMARYLLIDACEAE) – snowflake
A close relative of *Galanthus*, but these plants grow larger and the bell-shaped flowers are fatter. They only grow well in soil which never dries out.

L. aestivum Z4–9 ↕ **50cm/ 20in** **MSp–LSp** ☼ ☼
Summer snowflake. A bog plant which must have waterlogged soil and which produces tall stems topped by clusters of small, white, bell-shaped flowers. 'Gravetye Giant' has more and larger flowers.

L. vernum Z5–9 ↕ 25cm/10in   ESp–MSp

This species looks like a snowdrop but is much more robust with wide-open white flowers. For moisture-retentive woodland loam.

LILIUM (LILIACEAE) – lily

Lilies are difficult garden plants, requiring a lot of attention and food and cannot remain in the same spot for years without running into problems. One problem that all lilies have in common is the beautiful, bright red lily beetle which can frequently be found pairing in the leaf axils. Their larvae can eat the entire plant before it ever comes into flower. If you want to see any flowers you have to pick off the beetles every day.

Lilies are most reliable if planted in well-drained soil that has been dressed with compost or wood chips (lilies do not like to have warm roots). A selection: 'Apollo', white, 'Connecticut King', yellow, 'Gibraltar' (syn.'Elite'), orange, 'Roma', white and 'Sterling Star', white with brown speckles. Another extremely reliable candidate is:

L. martagon Z4–8 ↕ 1m/3½ft   ESu–MSu

Martagon lily. Has pink, brown-speckled flowers with the petals curling back like a turban to form a rosette at the top of the stem. *L.m.* var. *album* is white. For humus-rich soil in semi-shaded positions.

MUSCARI (HYACINTHACEAE) – grape hyacinth

However familiar they may be, grape hyacinths are in no way permanent bulbs. After a few years the flowering diminishes and then suddenly stops almost altogether. Most species in the wild are agricultural weeds which need to be disturbed by ploughing at regular intervals in order to be able to flower properly. So the solution is to dig them up and separate the offsets regularly. However, that is not something that this book should be recommending. Without turning over the soil, the longest flowering you can expect in dry and sunny spots will be from:

M. latifolium Z4–10 ↕ 25cm/10in   MSp–LSp

Produces just one wide leaf. The flower spike is dark blue, light blue at the tip.

M. neglectum Z4–10 ↕ 20cm/8in   MSp–LSp

Produces few leaves and the flowers are composed of black-blue florets with a white margin.

NARCISSUS (AMARYLLIDACEAE) – daffodil

When you really think about it, daffodils have very strange flowers indeed. The flower is composed of two parts: half of it is made of protective petals which are proudly separated in a kind of star shape; in the other half, these petals have merged to form a kind of trumpet, the corona. You knew that of course, but it is still very odd. And the effect is lovely enough for them to fall in love with themselves (as *Narcissus* they would).

The following species are all very reliable and go on flowering for ever in any soil that is not too acid or too dry, even if they do not always flower equally well every year. To give a complete picture, we should add that many of the larger cultivars, which crash to the ground so hopelessly after the first shower of rain, are also very reliable.

N. cyclamineus Z6–9 ↕ 10–40cm/4–16in   LW–MSp

The cyclamen-flowered daffodil. The species is a diminutive plant with small, deep yellow flowers which have outer petals that are sharply reflexed. Jolly plants which run wild in heavier soils. The cultivars grow well virtually anywhere. 'February Gold' is 40cm/16in tall with bright yellow cups. 'Tête-à-Tête' (not classed as a Cyclamineus cultivar but with some *N. cyclamineus* blood in its parentage) is 20cm/8in tall with several flowers per stem.

Top: *Leucojum vernum*
Bottom: *Lilium* x *dalhansonii*, a martagon type

N. poeticus Z4–9 ↕ **50cm/ 20in**   LSp

The poet's narcissus. White flowers with small green-yellow cups which smell wonderful. Sadly, the species itself, which can brighten entire mountainside meadows in southern Europe, is not widely cultivated. There are, however, several varieties. *N.p.* var. *recurvus* is the one most similar to the species. The cup has a slightly red tinge but this is not too noticeable. Does not like soil that is too dry.

N. pseudonarcissus Z4–9 ↕ **15–30cm/ 6in–1ft**   LW–MSp

Wild daffodil or lent lily. The grandfather of all the large-cupped daffodils has a relatively small flower with a light yellow cup and even paler outer petals. It grows wild throughout western Europe. Dozens of local subspecies have been described; every mountain valley in the Pyrenees seems to have its own. Particularly pretty examples are 'Lobularis' from Belgium, which is pale yellow, and the Tenby daffodil, *N.p.* subsp. *obvallaris*. The origin of this is not known but it is naturalized in Wales and has nicely shaped, golden yellow flowers.

N. triandrus Z4–9 ↕ **20–40cm/ 8–16in**   MSp–LSp

Compared to other species, this narcissus has more flowers per stem and the 'trumpet' is shorter and more rounded. The hybrid 'Hawera' is short and its flowers are long-lasting, light lemon yellow and smell delicious. 'Thalia' is a taller hybrid and has cream-white flowers.

NECTAROSCORDUM *(ALLIACEAE)* – honey garlic

N. siculum Z4–10 ↕ **1m/ 3½ft**   LSp–MSu

Still far too little appreciated as it is an extremely respectable and extraordinarily lovely species with long stems and large clusters of pendent, beige, bell-shaped flowers with brown-green stripes and dark red within. The flowering stems straighten after flowering so that the seeds eventually point upwards. Likes all soil types. Not too dry.

ORNITHOGALUM *(HYACINTHACEAE)* – star of Bethlehem

A large genus with white, star-shaped flowers. Many species are not hardy. The 'lilies of the field' referred to in the Bible may have been a species of *Ornithogalum*. Guaranteed hardy species are:

O. nutans Z6–10 ↕ **40cm/ 16in**   MSp–LSp

Produces a spike of hanging, bell-shaped flowers, translucent in silver-white with clear blue-green veins. Good in any soil that is not too dry; tolerant of shade too.

O. pyramidale Z7–10 ↕ **70cm/ 28in**   ESu–MSu

Produces an elongated spike covered in small, white, star-shaped flowers which persist for a long time. Drapes itself nicely between and over neighbouring perennials.

O. umbellatum Z5–10 ↕ **25cm/ 10in**   MSp–LSp

Star of Bethlehem. A low-growing species which produces a flat-topped cluster of pure white, star-shaped flowers which are green underneath. It happily seeds itself in shady spots but the flowers open only in sunshine.

PUSCHKINIA *(HYACINTHACEAE)*

P. scilloides var. libanotica Z5–9 ↕ **15cm/ 6in** ESp–MSp

An easy plant for soil that is not too wet or too poor. It produces compact clusters of white, star-shaped flowers veined light blue. There is also a pure white variety.

SCILLA *(HYACINTHACEAE)* – squill

Small bulbs with mostly blue, star-shaped flowers in clusters. They naturalize easily.

Top: *Narcissus cyclamineus*
Bottom: *Ornithogalum nutans*

S. bifolia Z6–9 10cm/4in ESp
This species produces clusters of deep blue, star-shaped flowers. It increases easily in soils which are not too dry. 'Rosea', in baby pink, flowers more abundantly with even smaller star-shaped flowers.

S. litardierei Z6–9 15cm/6in LSp–ESu
Only in moisture-retentive soil does this species reveal the fragile beauty of its violet-blue, compact flower clusters.

S. mischtschenkoana Z6–9 10cm/4in MW–ESp
This species is particularly strong, with white stars with light blue veins. It will grow anywhere. It looks like *Puschkinia*, but blooms earlier and has larger flowers.

S. siberica Z3–9  10cm/4in ESp–MSp
This species' flowers are a truly brilliant blue and are carried on red stems. They grow everywhere but naturalize best in soils with a little more moisture. 'Alba' is pure white.

TRILLIUM *(TRILLIACEAE)* – **Trinity flower, wood lily**

Trilliums are not true bulbs; they produce short rhizomes but otherwise behave just like bulbs. They grow slowly but consistently and can live to a ripe age in humus-rich, woodland loam. Three leaves are produced per stem, with one three-petalled flower. There are many (specialist) species and the best-known are:

T. sessile Z5–9 30cm/1ft MSp–ESu
This species has delicately marbled leaves. Flowers may be dark red, green or bronze. The similar *T. luteum* produces an attractive green-yellow flower.

T. grandiflorum Z4–9 30cm/1ft MSp–ESu
Wake robin. The leaves are not marbled and it has large, white flowers.

TULIPA *(LILIACEAE)* – **tulip** Z5–9

Large, goblet-shaped tulips do not belong in a natural garden. And of the many lovely species available on the market, the question is whether you could really call them permanent in your garden. In dry, lime-rich soil some species may well carry on for up to ten years, but, unless you have really dry summers, eventually the quality of the flowers will diminish.

There is one species, *T. sylvestris*, the woodland tulip, which has survived for centuries in country gardens with good clay soil. However, it seldom flowers. No good for a garden, then.

So as not to discourage you entirely, we shall mention a few species which seem to be fairly reliable, even so. In the end, there is nothing more lovely than a field of wild tulips in a spring garden!

T. aucheriana (5–10cm/2–4in) is a deep pink, *T. linifolia* Batalinii Group (5–10cm/2–4in) has blue-green leaves and small, pale yellow flowers which turn a caramel colour in warm weather. *T. hageri* 'Splendens' (10cm/4in) is deep red. *T. orphanidea* (30cm/1ft) is staggeringly lovely: orange with a broad, green central stripe and a brown centre, *T.o.* 'Flava' is lemon-yellow, topped off in red. *T.o.* Whittallii Group (30cm/1ft) has small flowers which are cinnamon-orange and green-brown outside. *T. tarda* (10cm/4in) produces several flowers and is white with a large yellow centre. *T. turkestanica* (20cm/8in) is a svelte, robust, white tulip with a golden centre and dark stamens. *T. urumiensis* (10cm/4in) has buttercup-yellow flowers and is extremely vigorous. Once again, they prefer a sunny position and dry, lime-rich soil (mix in some ground eggshells).

Right: *Trillium sessile*
Below: *Tulipa aucheriana*
Bottom: *Tulipa hageri* 'Splendens'

Shrubs combined with perennials. *Perovskia atriplicifolia* in front of *Tamarix ramosissima* (on the left) and a purple-leaved smoke bush

Tough **Shrubs**

In this section we shall be discussing a number of shrubs that stay small enough or can be pruned to an appropriate size for inclusion within a mixed border. They are principally summer- and autumn-flowering shrubs which contribute towards a border. One attractive complementary aspect of shrubs is that they are still there in early spring after the perennials have been cut down, allowing you to maintain some structure in the border. Slightly less satisfactory is the fact that you cannot plant perennials immediately beneath shrubs. As a result, you get bare patches. On the other hand, bare patches like this are the very place to put spring bulbs, and later in the summer, when the perennials have grown tall enough, the bare patches will not be noticeable anyway. We have omitted all rhododendrons, which require a very specific environment (acid and moist) and which take up too much room in the end. While doubtless they can be pruned, they are not made any more attractive as a result. Of course, there are several smaller species which would fit well in borders (with an acid soil). However, since most of them flower in spring, and the group is in any case too large to discuss in this book, we prefer to refer you to the specialist literature which has been published on the subject.

AMORPHA *(PAPILIONACEAE)* – **bastard indigo**

A. canescens Z3–9   ↕ 1.2m/ 4ft   LSu–EA

A small shrub with very delicate, unevenly pinnate leaves and, late in summer, svelte spikes of pink flowers with dark, eye-catching anthers. Grows well in dry, sandy soil.

ARTEMISIA *(ASTERACEAE)*

A. abrotanum Z5–8   ↕ 1m/ 3½ft

Southernwood, lad's love. A compact bush with finely pinnate, grey-green leaves which smell strongly of lemon. The flowers are of no consequence. Will grow in any well-drained soil. Keep compact by hard pruning in spring.

BUDDLEJA *(BUDDLEJACEAE)*

B. davidii Z6–9   ↕ 2m/ 6½ft   MSu–EA

Butterfly bush. A favourite shrub which attracts masses of butterflies when in flower and which will grow anywhere, even in heavy clay and peat soil. However, because the shrub likes to root deeply, it can be frozen to death in such situations. In dry, well-drained soil, where deep rooting is possible, the chance of this happening is less. Narrow leaves, dark green above and grey-green underneath, and compact, heavily scented spikes of flowers. There are many cultivars which range from white to a deep, dark purple. We shall not go into these: you can choose your own favourite. The butterflies won't care: they find all varieties equally delectable. The shrub can reach heights (and widths) of 4–5 metres (13–16 feet): too large for a border. This is why you should prune back hard in spring, encouraging better flowering. *B.d.* var. *nanhoensis* has grey leaves and does not grow as tall (to a maximum of 1.5m/5ft) but is not as hardy.

CARYOPTERIS *(VERBENACEAE)*

C. x clandonensis Z6–9   ↕ 1m/ 3½ft   LSu–EA

A lovely shrub for a sunny, dry spot with small grey-green leaves; it is

swamped in lavender-blue plumes of flowers in the summer. A hard winter will cut it back to ground level. You should prune it back in spring after a mild winter.

CEPHALANTHUS *(RUBIACEAE)*

C. occidentalis Z6–10   ↕ 1.5m/ 5ft   MSu–LSu

In the wild this species grows on marshy ground and reaches 6m/20ft. In dry, not too rich, soil it makes a slow-growing bush of manageable dimensions with glossy leaves and red stems with a profusion of scented, white, rounded flowers about 1.5cm/½in across that are attractive to butterflies.

CLEMATIS *(RANUNCULACEAE)*

With the exception of a number of perennials, most clematis are climbing plants, of course: we shall not be discussing these in this book. However, a few species are so humble in terms of size that you can let them trail freely in between perennials in a border.

C. x durandii Z6–9   ↕ 1.8m/ 6ft   ESu–LSu

A cross between *C. integrifolia* and *C.* 'Jackmanii'. Not woody. Every year it produces tender shoots with round, undivided leaves and long-lasting flowers which are large and pendulous and coloured a deep, velvety blue with a cream-coloured centre of anthers. A superb border plant. Try it between tall perennials or on a trellis.

C. heracleifolia Z4–9   ↕ 1.2m/ 4ft   LSu–EA

This species has an open, bushy habit. It is woody at the base, with robust, composite leaves and small blue flowers. 'Côte d'Azur' produces deep blue flowers with a lighter coloured centre.

C. x jouiniana Z5–9   ↕ 2m/ 6½ft   MSu–MA

Forms a woody base and a confusion of stems. Good for allowing to sprawl between shrubs or taller perennials. It can also be used as ground cover. It has many composite leaves and a mass of scented, milky blue flowers at the end of the season. 'Praecox' flowers from mid-summer.

Clematis x *durandii* with *Euphorbia corallioides*

Above: *Clematis* x *jouiniana* 'Praecox'
Below: *Hibiscus syriacus* 'Oiseau Bleu'

CLERODENDRUM (VERBENACEAE)

C. trichotomum **2m/**
var. *fargesii* Z7–9 **6½ft** MSu–EA
Produces hefty branches with large leaves (which smell like peanut butter) and broad clusters of small white flowers which afterwards turn into dark blue berries held in eye-catching red calyces. Theoretically, it grows too large for a border. However, the plant dies right back when it freezes. Alternatively, you can prune it hard back anyway. It will always shoot from the base. It is a little problematic, but so lovely!

FUCHSIA (ONAGRACEAE)

F. magellanica Z8–10 **1.5m/**
5ft MSu–MA
The only hardy fuchsia species, this originates from Tierra del Fuego and not, as many people believe, from Ireland, where the shrub has run wild along roadsides. Grows well in moist, humus-rich soil and produces a profusion of small, bright red flowers. Will usually die back to ground level when frosted but reappears again from the base in spring. There are many variants for the enthusiast, *F.m.* var. *molinae*, with its pale blush-pink flowers, being the most important.

HEDYSARUM (PAPILIONACEAE)

H. multijugum Z6–9 **50cm/**
20in MSu–EA
Should be pruned back to ground level in spring. Produces large branches with pinnate leaves. The pinnae (the leaflets that make up the whole leaf) are rounded. Clusters of large, red-purple flowers appear in the leaf axils and persist for a long period. An attractive bush for a warm spot in well-drained soil.

HIBISCUS (MALVACEAE)

H. syriacus Z6–9 **3m/** **10ft** LSu–EA
Somewhat stiff-looking shrubs with angular cut leaves and extremely large, loose, mallow flowers at the end of summer. There are many cultivars in white, pink and blue and all shades in between. When the shrub is employed in isolation as a specimen it can be a slap in the face, because of the profusion of flowers that it produces. However, in a border, half obscured between large perennials reaching the end of flowering, this hibiscus is a spectacular surprise. Light spring pruning will keep the shrub at the height desired. It flowers on the newly formed wood.

HYDRANGEA (HYDRANGEACEAE)

'Mophead' hydrangeas are familiar shrubs, growing into compact shapes, with large, oval leaves and cauliflower-like clusters (corymbs) of pink, white or blue flowers which are composed entirely of sterile flowers. They are attractive in a cottage garden or alongside a driveway but are slightly more difficult to incorporate in a natural garden, although you can find creative ways around this. We shall concentrate on the other types, which have fertile flowers and are a little closer to nature: mostly flat corymbs of flowers with small, true flowers in the centre enclosed by rings of sterile ray flowers. All hydrangeas need a lot of water during the hot days of summer, so moisture-retentive soil is essential. Several species produce their flower buds in spring. As a result, a late frost can occasionally destroy all of the summer's flowers.

H. arborescens **1.25m/**
'Annabelle' Z4–9 **4ft** MSu–LSu
Severe spring pruning is a precondition to producing the large, white corymbs (about 20cm/8in across) composed mostly of many sterile florets and only a few fertile ones. The corymbs become ever smaller if you desist from pruning. Only for extremely fertile soil.

H. aspera Z7–9 **2.5m/**
8ft MSu–LSu
A gaunt shrub with red-brown, peeling bark, leaves which are

oblong, pointed and slightly grey-haired, as well as lilac corymbs with white marginal florets. Will tolerate relatively dry conditions as long as it is planted in not too sunny a position. *H.a.* subsp. *sargentiana* is in all respects larger and more coarsely haired, with larger, woolly corymbs.

H. involucrata Z2–9 ↕ 70cm/ 28in   MSu–LSu

A coarse-haired smaller shrub with dark green leaves and lilac-blue flowers with white marginal florets in half-open, dome-shaped flower heads. 'Hortensis' has pale pink, double, begonia-like flowers.

H. macrophylla Z6–9 ↕ 1m/ 3½ft   MSu–LSu

This is the parent of all the 'mophead' hydrangeas with hairless, glossy leaves. 'Mariesii Perfecta' (syn. 'Blue Wave') produces corymbs of blue, fertile florets (bluest in acid soil, whereas in alkaline soil the flowers will turn pink; this is typical of many hydrangeas). 'Maréchal Foch' is pink, 'Veitchii' is ice-blue, only in acid soil, and is less compact, 'White Wave' is white.

H. paniculata Z4–8 ↕ 2.5m/ 8ft   ESu–MSu

A hydrangea with large, white, tapering panicles of flowers. It needs fertile soil. 'Kyushu' has very open flowers with many fertile flowers; 'Unique' also has very open flowers although they are somewhat flatter.

H. quercifolia Z5–9 ↕ 2m/ 6½ft   MSu–LSu

This species is of particular interest for its remarkable leaves, cut like an oak's, which turn a beautiful orange-brown in autumn. It only grows well in moisture-retentive, acid soil and only flowers in warm summers, producing cream panicles which age pink.

H. serrata Z6–8 ↕ 1.5m/ 5ft   MSu–LSu

A small, compact shrub with almost black branches and smallish, flattened corymbs. 'Bluebird' is blue with pink marginal florets. The hybrid 'Preziosa' is pink, later turning dark red.

HYSSOPUS *(LAMIACEAE)* – hyssop

H. officinalis Z6–9 ↕ 50cm/ 20in   MSu–LSu

A shrubby plant with narrow leaves and truly blue spikes of lipped flowers which attract great numbers of butterflies. Extremely reliable in dry, chalky soil. Must be pruned back in spring.

INDIGOFERA *(PAPILIONACEAE)*

Shrubs with pinnate leaves and spikes of lilac-pink flowers growing from the leaf axils. In sunny positions, the flowers persist for a long period.

I. amblyantha Z7–9 ↕ 2m/ 6½ft   LSp–EA

Given a warm spot in well-drained but moisture-retentive soil, this flowers throughout the summer. It produces fairly small, pure pink flower spikes.

I. heterantha Z7–9 ↕ 1.5m/ 5ft MSu–EA

Must be pruned back to ground level in spring. When given a sunny position in any type of soil, produces long, drooping branches with long, tapering flower spikes.

I. kirilowii Z5–8 ↕ 1.5m/ 5ft   LSp–MSu

Freely produces arching branches with wide leaves and compact spikes of light pink flowers about 2cm/1in across. Given a sunny position, performs well in any soil type.

LAVANDULA *(LAMIACEAE)* – lavender

L. angustifolia Z6–10 ↕ 30cm–1m/ 1–3½ft   MSu–LSu

Succumbs only in the very bitterest of winters. Therefore, we shall treat it as hardy. The other species of lavender (of which there are

Above: *Hydrangea involucrata* 'Hortensis'
Below: *Hydrangea aspera*

Top: *Paeonia delavayi* var. *lutea*
Centre: *Paeonia rockii*
Bottom: *Viburnum nudum*

---

many) are noticeably less hardy. It scarcely needs to be described: a small shrub with extremely aromatic, needle-like leaves and small spikes of purple, lipped flowers which attract butterflies. To keep the plants in shape, you need to prune fairly severely in spring (nearly back to the old wood). There are masses of cultivars which also have pink and white flowers. The most important is 'Hidcote', with a profusion of deep lavender flowers and compact at 40cm/16in.

LESPEDEZA (PAPILIONACEAE)

L. thunbergii Z6–8   2m/6½ft   LSu–MA

Looks like *Indigofera* but at the end of summer produces panicles, rather than spikes, of pink flowers at the tips of long, arching branches. An autumn-flowering spectacle which should be pruned back to ground level in spring.

LIGUSTRUM (APIACEAE) – privet

L. quihoui Z6–9   2m/6½ft   LSu–EA

A deciduous privet of reasonable dimensions with gigantic, thinly branched, panicles of cream flowers which afterwards turn to black berries. Will grow in any soil type but does need to be sheltered (it cannot endure hard frost for any length of time).

PAEONIA (PAEONIACEAE) – peony

Tree peonies are extremely hardy and long-lived shrubs with ternate pinnate leaves which often have a bluish tint beneath. For a short period each summer they produce heartbreakingly beautiful flowers. They grow well in any reasonable garden soil. As to be expected from such lovely plants, there exists an endless selection of cultivars, each one more gorgeous than the last. We shall limit ourselves to three from which you can expect everything you would hope for in a peony:

P. delavayi var. lutea Z5–8   2.2m/7ft   LSp–ESu

Produces velvet-red flowers with yellow centres. The seed pods, which remain on the plant for ages, spring open to reveal black seeds.

P. lutea Z5–8   2.2m/7ft   LSp–ESu

Produces yellow flowers, about 9cm/3½in across, and also has attractive seed pods.

P. suffruticosa Z5–8   1.5m/5ft   LSp–ESu

The species has disappeared virtually without trace beneath a deluge of cultivars from China and Japan. *P. rockii* (syn. *P.* 'Rock's Variety') is a wild species with large white flowers, blotched dark purple in the centres. 'You should beggar yourself for this one!', says Graham Stuart Thomas.

PEROVSKIA (LAMIACEAE)

P. atriplicifolia Z6–9   1.2m/4ft   MSu–EA

This shrub from Kashmir revels in dry conditions. It has felted grey branches and narrow, serrated leaves which are grey underneath. Its lavender-blue flowers are clustered in long spikes at the end of the branches. Tends to collapse outwards. An improvement on this is 'Blue Spire', a hybrid of *P. atriplicifolia* and *P. abrotanoides*, which is more robust. It is at its best in dry, well-drained and fertile soil. It gets into a very sorry state in poor, sandy soil. Severe spring pruning needed.

POTENTILLA (ROSACEAE) – cinquefoil

P. fruticosa Z3–7   1m/3½ft   LSp–EA

Shrubby potentilla is a living fossil which was a widespread feature of the northern hemisphere long before the last ice age, but which is now restricted to a small number of locations separated far from one another. In Europe, for example, it grows only in the Burren in Ireland, in the north of England, in one spot in the Pyrenees and in the Rhodope mountains in Bulgaria. As often happens with such living fossils, the shrub has outlived all of its natural adversaries and is as good as disease-resistant. It is consequently a very easy garden plant indeed, and it will grow anywhere. Unfortunately, this has made it ideal for wide-scale uninspiring abuse on roadsides and traffic islands, especially in the urban sprawl of the 1960s and 1970s. In fact it is just a nice, unpretentious bush with red-brown, peeling branches and small, deeply cut leaves, which combines well with perennials and will bloom almost continuously all summer long. You can prune the shrub back hard once it starts to look a little slovenly. There are many cultivars, such as 'Abbotswood', with white flowers in red calyces, 'Klondike', golden-yellow, 'Red Ace', orange-red, and 'Tangerine', orange-yellow.

ROSA (ROSACEAE) – rose

It would be attempting too much if we were to indicate which roses were suitable in a natural garden. All wild roses can be included, of course, as long as they do not grow too large. However, even forgetting the countless numbers of cultivars, you can still make an infinite number of combinations if you do not find it too much trouble to weed in between painfully thorny rose bushes. Consult the many specialist books on this subject. Just one comment: you can only expect roses to contribute to your garden in any kind of disease-free fashion if the soil is rich and moisture-retentive. In poor and dry soil, roses become so sickly that they will be unable to form any part of a natural garden.

RUTA (RUTACEAE) – rue

R. graveolens Z5–9 ↕ 80cm/32in   ESu–LSu

Common rue. A shrub with small, deeply divided, blue-green leaves and sulphur-yellow, four-petalled flowers, followed by attractive seed pods. The young shoots are purple-blue. 'Jackman's Blue' has grey-blue leaves. It is reliably hardy in well-drained, chalky soil as long as the shrub is pruned back hard in spring. If not, the branches will become too woody, the whole shrub will become messy and it will eventually suffer frost damage. It seeds itself keenly.

SALVIA (LAMIACEAE) – sage

S. officinalis Z6–9 ↕ 1m/3½ft   ESu–MSu

True sage is not only an indispensable herb in ossobuco and other Italian dishes, or effective for a sore throat when gargled, it is also an attractive garden plant with its ovate, wrinkled, grey-green leaves and large clusters of lavender-blue, lipped flowers held within red-brown calyces. It keeps its leaves over winter and is completely hardy in dry, well-drained soil. Hard pruning immediately after flowering will keep the shrub in shape. Does slightly run wild because of self-layering where the branches touch the ground and take root. There are too many cultivars to mention them all, which is why we have made a selection: 'Albiflora' has white flowers, 'Berggarten' is low-growing and has wide, grey leaves and hardly flowers, if at all, much like the purple-leaved 'Purpurascens'. 'Rosea' has pink flowers and 'Würzburg' is a robust, medium-sized selection (60cm/2ft high) with felted grey leaves and purple-blue flowers.

SPIRAEA (ROSACEAE)

S. japonica Z4–9 ↕ 80cm/32in   MSu–LSu

A strong little shrub with small, wrinkled leaves and flattened heads of usually pink flowers. Traditionally planted to fill a single border, but much more fun when put between perennials. Seeing how strong the shrub is, it should be used in places where almost nothing else will grow or flower (dry semi-shade). Pruning back hard in spring will guarantee a profusion of flowers and a more attractive shape.

SYRINGA (OLEACEAE) – lilac

There are several lilacs with small leaves and quite small, compact panicles of flowers. By pruning (after flowering), you can keep them compact and in this way make them completely suitable for inclusion in a border.

S. meyeri var. **spontanea** 'Palibin' Z4–8 ↕ 1.5m/5ft 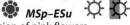 MSp–ESu

A compact lilac which produces a profusion of pink flowers, although they do smell a little of cheap soap.

S. pubescens subsp. **microphylla** 'Superba' Z5–8 ↕ 2m/6½ft   LSp–ESu

Looks very much like the previous lilac but grows rather faster. However, with some pruning it can be kept under control with no problem. If it is not pruned, the shrub sometimes flowers a second time in autumn.

S. x persica Z3–7 ↕ 2m/6½ft   LSp–ESu

Persian lilac. This species has small, lance-shaped leaves, sometimes pinnate, and lilac flowers. The white-flowering cultivar, 'Alba', is the most attractive.

TAMARIX (TAMARICACEAE) – tamarisk

T. ramosissima 'Rubra' Z3–8 ↕ 2.5m/8ft   LSp–ESu

A heather-like shrub with long, arching branches covered in needle-like leaves. Produces an abundance of flowers in spring with open plumes of dark pink flowers. Needs well-drained soil.

VIBURNUM (CAPRIFOLIACEAE)

A large genus of profusely flowering shrubs with rather uninspiring foliage but with all the more inspirational flat or rounded clusters of flowers which are usually fragrant. A few are suitable for combining with perennials:

V. x bodnantense 'Dawn' Z7–8 ↕ 2m/6½ft   MA–MSp

A cross between V. farreri and V. grandiflorum. Not a very stimulating plant in summer, but it should be placed in a prominent position anyway so you can smell its deliciously scented clusters of pink flowers daily in winter. They are in force from mid-autumn until well into spring, as long as it does not freeze. 'Deben' produces paler pink flowers.

V. x burkwoodii Z5–8 ↕ 2m/6½ft   MSp–LSp

A cross between V. carlesii and V. utile. In spring it produces scented, domed clusters of light pink flowers held in darker coloured calyces. The parent species, V. carlesii, has similar flowers but is shorter (1.5m/5ft).

V. nudum Z6–9 ↕ 1.5m/5ft   LSp–ESu

A small shrub with oblong, glossy, leathery leaves and rather sallow flowers. However, the flowers are followed later in the summer by fine berries on red stems: first white, then pink and finally blue-black.

VITEX (VERBENACEAE) – chaste tree

V. agnus-castus Z7–9 ↕ 1.5m/5ft   MSu–MA

Chaste tree. This species was formerly planted in cloisters because the leaves were supposed to have a chastening effect on lustful feelings, agnus-castus meaning chaste lamb! It is an attractive shrub which can sometimes reach 4m/13ft in height but which usually dies back (sometimes to ground level) in winter. As a result, it is a candidate for a border. It has dark green leaves which are grey underneath. The leaves, placed two by two, are cut like fingers. The clusters of flowers are lavender-blue.

Echinops ritro 'Veitch's Blue' in front of *Telekia speciosa* and *Thalictrum aquilegiifolium* in seed

Stachys officinalis 'Alba'

At this point the book becomes exciting, since it is now about plants that can be trusted to come back just as reliably as the plants in the previous section – only you never know precisely where! It is in fact all about self-seeding perennials, annuals and biennials. Using such plants does not exactly make garden maintenance more laborious, but it does demand more attention: you must be constantly aware of what is going on. You have to decide again and again which seedlings you want to keep and which you will discard. The great advantage of plants that seed themselves is that the planting gradually begins to look more natural: plants wander through the garden, choose the spot that suits them best, and so a natural zoning starts. One great disadvantage is that during the process they swamp many other plants, and if you don't take action, you end up only having a few species left. The job is not so much knowing what you want (you did not want so many spontaneous seedlings, that is obvious), but to know what you definitely don't want, so that you can act in time.

Playful
Self-seeding perennials

These are actually the most reliable plants there are: not only are they perennial, but they are also self-seeding, so if you are not careful they will go on increasing for ever! When such a plant is not quite in the right spot, it lets you know by seeding itself where it would rather grow. However, if it is in completely the wrong place, then of course you will find no seedlings: they are not magic.

ACHILLEA (ASTERACEAE) – milfoil

A. grandifolia Z4–8 1.5m/5ft ESu–MSu

A giant form of the common milfoil with fine grey-green, deeply cut foliage and clear white umbelliferous flower heads. Perhaps not so spectacular in colour as the many *A. millefolium* cultivars, but far more reliable, and very useful because of its great height and early flowering. If the flowers are cut regularly, they will bloom right through the summer – and not seed themselves around so much.

AGRIMONIA (ROSACEAE) – agrimony

A. eupatoria Z6–9 1.4m/4½ft ESu–MSu

A commonly occurring wild plant, whose distinguished appearance can make a real contribution to the perennial border. Tall upright stems, covered with compound leaves, and slender spikes full of small yellow flowers, looking like a slender *Verbascum*, are succeeded by beautiful seed burrs. These prickly seed cases easily fasten themselves to clothing and animal skins, which is why seedlings sprout up anywhere in the garden. *A. odorata*, which prefers rather more shade and moisture, is similar.

ALCHEMILLA (ROSACEAE) – lady's mantle

Lady's mantle, with its pretty pleated leaves that collect dew drops like pearls, and with airy sprays of small greenish-yellow flowers, is, of course, familiar to every gardener. Everyone also knows that it seeds itself around in every nook and cranny. All species are apomictic; in other words, they reproduce asexually: all the descendants are identical to the mother plant and crosses between the different species do not occur. All species grow best in reliably moist soil in light shade.

A. epipsila Z5–8 35cm/14in LSp–MSu

Has rather angular pointed leaf lobes and is generally lower in height.

A. mollis Z4–8 60cm/2ft LSp–MSu

The best-known species, originally from the Caucasus – and also the most beautiful.

A. vulgaris Z4–8  45cm/18in LSp–MSu

The collective name for a large number of species, differing from each other in minor details. The flower heads tend in general to be slightly greener than *A. mollis*.

ANTHRISCUS (APIACEAE) – cow parsley

A. sylvestris Z4–9 1.5m/5ft LSp

Queen Anne's lace, fairy lace, lovely names for a sublime plant, though not everyone wants to use such a superlative for a plant that turns every roadside, wood margin or moist pasture throughout the country white in May. A delightful plant in a spring garden, too, although it seeds around indiscriminately. However, the seedlings are quite easy to remove. There is a particularly lovely cultivar, 'Ravenswing', with a purplish red leaf, but it has a short life and does not come true from seed.

ARTEMISIA (ASTERACEAE)

A. absinthium Z4–9 80cm/32in MSu–LSu

Wormwood. Fully hardy sub-shrub with blue-grey leaves and a slightly unpleasant smell. It was at one time used to make the poisonous drink absinthe, which contributed to the death of Toulouse-Lautrec. A fine, profusely seeding plant for dry areas.

A. vulgaris Z4–9 1.5cm/5ft MSu–LSu

Mugwort is a weed on made-up ground, industrial areas and neglected gardens, and is therefore seldom used as a garden plant. It is, however, a delicate grey-green border plant, ideal for linking various sections of a garden together, provided you can keep the number of seedlings under control.

ASPARAGUS (ASPARAGACEAE)

A. officinalis Z2–9 1.2m/4ft LSp–ESu

If you allow asparagus to bolt, it forms tall, waving branches with needle-fine leaves and small greenish yellow flowers, followed in the autumn by red berries (on female plants), while the foliage turns a fine yellow-orange colour. Attractive as a linking element in borders (not just in old-fashioned bouquets with freesias). Sometimes it is stripped completely bare by the asparagus beetle, a close relation of the lily beetle; just as troublesome and just as beautiful (with red and black stripes).

ASTRANTIA (APIACEAE) – masterwort

A. major Z4–8 70cm/28in LSp–EA

Decorative plants with five-lobed leaves and a 3cm/1¼in flower head with smooth-edged involucral bracts in white, tinged with green and pink. Grows easily in any garden soil that does not dry out. After the main flowering in May and June there is a second flowering in the autumn. 'Claret' is a cultivar with deep red flowers of varying shades; every seedling is a surprise. For this reason the following cultivars are vegetatively reproduced; when they seed themselves the result is unpredictable. 'Lars' has small flowers and is dark red and 'Ruby Wedding' has rather larger flowers and is a deep dark red. 'Sunningdale Variegated' has greenish white flowers and leaves that are margined with creamy yellow in spring.

A. major subsp. involucrata Z4–8 80cm/32in LSp–EA

A subspecies with larger flowers and fringed involucral bracts. 'Canneman' starts red and in full flower is green or white, and often has a second flowering; 'Shaggy' has white, elongated and pointed involucral bracts, green at the tips.

BRUNNERA (BORAGINACEAE)

B. macrophylla Z4–8 50cm/20in MSp–LSp

A fine woodland plant from the Caucasus, with large tufts of sky-blue forget-me-not flowers in the spring, and large heart-shaped leaves after flowering. The plant seeds itself profusely if it is in a position that suits it, in moisture-retaining, humus-rich soil in shade.

BUPLEURUM (APIACEAE)

Closely related to *Astrantia*. Here, too, the involucral bracts are the most striking part of the flower. *Bupleurum* species often have five involucral bracts, rather like 'real' flowers. Most species are too small or not fully hardy for general garden use. A suitable one is:

B. longifolium Z3–9 50cm/20in ESu–MSu

Grows easily and seeds itself profusely on well-drained soil, with blue-green perfoliate leaves; brown involucral bracts enclose the small, yellow 'real' flowers, creating an overall golden effect.

CALAMINTHA (LAMIACEAE) – rock thyme

C. grandiflora Z5–9 35cm/14in LSp–EA

This unpretentious species forms woody clumps with serrated aromatic leaves and attractive pink-lipped flowers about 1cm/½in across. It flowers throughout the summer, although not very abundantly, and seeds itself prettily between other plants, without becoming a nuisance. An ideal plant for the front of borders.

CAMPANULA (CAMPANULACEAE) – bellflower

C. alliariifolia Z4–8 60cm/2ft ESu–LSu

Clump-forming, with beautiful, heart-shaped, fresh green leaves and rather untidy or, better, unconstrained curved stems full of drooping, milk-white bells. Graham Stuart Thomas calls them 'balanced', and Brian Kabbes 'pleasantly informal'. An all-rounder.

C. latifolia
var. macrantha Z4–8   ↕ 1m/3½ft

Rather coarse plants, dense foliage with broad leaves and a generous cluster of plump purple-blue bells about 5cm/2in across. Grows and seeds itself freely on any good garden soil in shade. As with most campanulas, it only flowers for a short time, and after flowering the plant disappears under ground. Not really a very good plant for the garden, in contrast to the pure white-flowering form, *C.l.* var. *m. alba*, which, even if it is short-lived, draws attention to itself.

C. rotundifolia Z3–8   ↕ 25cm/10in   LSp–EA

The familiar harebell is a delightful plant for the margins of dry areas, long-flowering with graceful blue bells, on tall, upright, sparsely leaved stems. Seeds itself about, particularly in gravel and among stones.

C. trachelium Z4–8   ↕ 80cm/32in    MSu–LSu

Nettle-leaved bellflower. This rough-haired plant has dense foliage with serrated, pointed leaves, and pale purple-blue bells about 4cm/1½in across held in hairy calyces. Grows, flowers and seeds itself in the stoniest spots of a shady garden, where in full summer nothing else will flower. *C.t.* var. *alba* has off-white flowers.

CARDAMINE (*BRASSICACEAE*) – bitter cress

C. pratensis Z3–9   ↕ 40cm/16in   ESp–LSp

The cuckoo flower or lady's smock needs no description. Everyone knows this harbinger of spring, growing profusely in damp pastures. Not everyone knows that it is also a woodland plant. Left to grow wild in damp shady grass or in the shade garden it does very well. On heavier clay soils it can sometimes be difficult to keep its countless seedlings under control, but on lighter soils you can never have too many of them.

CENTAUREA (*ASTERACEAE*) – knapweed

C. scabiosa Z4–9   ↕ 80cm/32in   LSp–EA

On not-too-rich soil this good border plant goes on producing its large lilac-pink cornflowers seemingly for ever. The plant seeds itself profusely and is somewhat lax, but that can be an advantage among rather sturdier border plants. Butterflies love it. The same goes for the common knapweed, *C. jacea*, but this is smaller and so the flowers are less showy.

CEPHALARIA (*DIPSACACEAE*)

C. gigantea Z3–8   ↕ 2.5m/8ft   ESu–MSu

Huge plants with large, pale yellow scabious flowers on lightly branched stems, so light that in spite of its height the plant also fits into the front of a border. Almost indispensable for its colour, habit and the length of time it flowers. However, there is little left of the plant after it has finished flowering, so it should not be used in large clumps, but scattered lightly throughout the border. In a recently planted border it may become a nuisance by seeding itself. If you don't deal with it in time, it can very quickly swamp other plants, but once the border is established it will behave itself beautifully.

CHELIDONIUM (*PAPAVERACEAE*) – celandine

C. majus Z5–8   ↕ 60cm/2ft   MSp–EA

Greater celandine. A notorious weed, which we mention mainly to warn you against it: before you realize it, the whole garden is full of it. Quite pretty, of course, with its small yellow poppy-like flowers, typical compound grey-green leaves, and bright orange sap, which is said to be useful for curing warts. Only suitable for the periphery of a garden, under the hedge, or better still, in your neighbour's garden. There is a charming double cultivar, 'Flore Pleno', which you will instantly fall for, but you have been warned!

Top: *Anthriscus sylvestris*
Centre: *Astrantia major* 'Claret' in front of *Geranium psilostemon*
Bottom: *Campanula latifolia* var. *macrantha*

Persicaria amplexicaulis 'Firedance' with *P.a.* 'Alba'

Colour schemes

Some time ago the idea of the colour wheel was introduced as an aid to garden design, so that from then on it would be in everyone's power to put together a suitable colour scheme. We find this rather patronizing – and in any case we thoroughly dislike 'suitable' colour schemes. We want to decide for ourselves what we consider suitable. And we don't find the theory about 'complementary' colours at all helpful: do colours situated exactly opposite each other in the wheel, such as red and green, yellow and purple, blue and orange, complement each other perfectly? This may well be so, but in the garden we can't quite picture it. And, to tell the truth, whenever we try it out, it sends shivers down the spine. We think, too, that it is absurd to regard the colour of the flowers as the prime consideration when putting plants together. The shape of the bloom, the height of the plants, the leaf shape, the flowering season and, last but not least, their appearance after they have finished flowering, are all equally important. A garden should, if at all possible, be beautiful the whole year round, even if most people (not us!) think that it is at its peak during the usually short period when everything is in bloom.

It is, of course, a bonus if the colours do not clash too much. In a natural garden this is what happens anyway. Nature itself cheerfully scatters all the colours of the rainbow around without ever clashing: nature does not need a colour wheel. This is not only because there is a great deal of neutralizing grass between the flowers, but because the way the plants grow and the shape of the flowers (usually small) also play an important part. In a natural garden it is the same, though it may be rather more complicated because the flowering plants in a garden are rather closer together; a mismatch is easily made. But a colour wheel? No way.

CIRSIUM *(ASTERACEAE)* – **plumed thistle**

C. oleraceum Z3–9   ↕ 1.5m/ 5ft   MSu–EA

Cabbage thistles are eye-catching plants in moist soil, with a wealth of fine, divided, pinnate leaves, without prickles, and large, pale yellow thistle flowers, half masked by yellow-green prickly bracts. Rarely available, but beautiful.

C. rivulare Z4–8   ↕ 1.5m/ 5ft   ESu–MSu

Equally rarely available, a wild and therefore profusely seeding form of the sterile *C. rivulare* 'Atropurpureum'. See the section on 'Tough' plants. Also has large red-purple flowers, but grows much taller, stays upright and definitely needs moist soil.

CORYDALIS see PSEUDOFUMARIA

DIANTHUS *(CARYOPHYLLACEAE)* – **pink**

D. carthusianorum Z3–9   ↕ 60cm/ 2ft   ESu–LSu

In dry, sunny spots this plant forms long-lasting rosettes of narrow grassy leaves from which tall, blue-grey, almost leafless stems arise, bearing at their tips a little tuft of reddish brown calyces that open into small, toothed, rose-red flowers. Seeds itself into nooks and crannies to hover airily everywhere.

ECHINOPS *(ASTERACEAE)* – **globe thistle**

E. sphaerocephalus Z3–8   ↕ 1.6m/ 5¼ft   MSu–LSu

Globe thistles are sold under all kinds of fancy names, but they usually turn out to be the liberally seeding *E. sphaerocephalus*; a rather coarse plant with a viciously prickly leaf and a well-branched inflorescence of white globes with dark blue stamens, buzzing with bees, bumblebees and butterflies. Beautiful even after it has finished flowering, but the birds have usually emptied the seed pods well before the winter. But that is how it should be in a natural garden!

ERYNGIUM *(APIACEAE)*

E. planum Z5–9   ↕ 90cm/ 3ft   ESu–LSu

Above a small rosette of shiny oval leaves, well-branched flower stems rise full of small, light to dark blue thistle flowers. The colour varies from seedling to seedling. Likes sunny, open, cultivated ground, not too dry.

EUPHORBIA *(EUPHORBIACEAE)* – **milkweed, spurge**

E. dulcis 'Chameleon' Z4–9   ↕ 45cm/ 18in   LSp–ESu

Forms a tidy tuft of purple-brown foliage, fading to green in shade, but keeping its colour in full sun. The flower heads are an inconspicuous green. The deep red seedlings are easy to recognize.

FILIPENDULA *(ROSACEAE)* – **meadowsweet**

F. ulmaria Z3–9   ↕ 1.25m/ 4ft   MSu–LSu

A familiar sight, meadowsweet draws its cream-coloured stripes along ditches and paths in sandy and peaty soil. It also grows well in ordinary moisture-retaining garden soil, and will seed like mad. 'Aurea' is in our opinion a yellow-leaved freak, but according to Graham Stuart Thomas 'one of the most attractive of foliage plants in spring'. We think it looks as if it has just been sprayed with weedkiller, particularly in summer, when the yellow fades to white. Seedlings of 'Aurea' generally revert to plain green.

Top left: *Dianthus carthusianorum*
Top right: *Echinops sphaerocephalus*
Centre: *Eryngium planum*
Bottom: *Euphorbia dulcis* 'Chameleon'

Top: *Geranium phaeum* 'Samobor'
Centre: *Geranium pratense* 'Mrs Kendall Clarke'
Bottom: *Lamium orvala* 'Album'

GERANIUM (GERANIACEAE) – cranesbill

G. himalayense Z4–8   ↕ 40cm/16in   LSp–ESu

A vigorously spreading species with deeply toothed leaves, changing to an attractive colour in the autumn and with large, deep blue flowers up to 6cm/2¼in across. Does not bloom very profusely but will grow anywhere and seeds freely.

G. maculatum Z4–8   ↕ 50cm/20in   MSp–LSp

Early-flowering species, with five- to seven-lobed leaves and delicate mauve flowers with a white centre. Vigorous, spreads abundantly, and being self-seeding maintains itself in grass.

G. phaeum Z4–8   ↕ 70cm/28in   LSp–ESu

The dark cranesbill or mourning widow is a prolific seeder, which can overrun whole sections of a garden in no time. So watch this charming widow, with her drooping, purple-black flowers. There are several cultivars, which seed true for colour if they are not too close together. They are all very rewarding.

G.p. 'Album' Z4–8   ↕ 80cm/32in   LSp–MSu

A long-flowering geranium with large, clear white flowers and light-green leaves.

G.p. 'Lily Lovell' Z4–8   ↕ 1m/3½ft   LSp–ESu

This is a vigorous plant with violet-blue flowers.

G.p. 'Rose Madder' Z4–8   ↕ 50cm/20in   LSp–ESu

Grows slowly, with curious brownish rose-red flowers.

G.p. 'Samobor' Z4–8   ↕ 70cm/28in   LSp–ESu

Similar to the species, but with a striking brownish black ring on the leaf.

G. pratense Z4–8   ↕ 1m/3½ft   ESu–MSu

A wild species with sharply toothed leaves and tall, well-branched stems full of large, bright blue flowers. Seeds itself profusely, and is perhaps a little too wild for the average garden: the plant is inclined to collapse. On the other hand, it does very well in long grass. That is how you have to use it – as if it were in the wild. The same applies to 'Mrs Kendall Clarke', a form with fine white-veined flowers, which looks quite cultivated, but behaves with just as little restraint as the wild species. Seedlings come true for colour. 'White Lady' has white flowers, stays much lower and consequently does not fall over.

G. sylvaticum Z4–8   ↕ 60cm/2ft   LSp–ESu

This is pretty in the wild, in damp meadows and along the edges of woods throughout Europe, but disappointing in gardens. The soft lavender-blue flowers, about 3cm/1¼in across, are very short-lived. There are several cultivars that flower better and do not seed themselves so profusely: 'Amy Doncaster' is very attractive, and has bright blue flowers with white centres, 'Baker's Pink' is a form found in the wild in Switzerland. It grows a metre high (3½ft) and produces bright pink blooms.

LAMIUM (LAMIACEAE) – dead-nettle

L. orvala Z4–8   ↕ 60cm/2ft   MSp–LSp

This absolutely non-invasive dead-nettle comes up purple-red in the spring, and forms a sturdy clump with dark green leaves and large, beautifully marked, deep pink flowers. Can grow in deep shade, but its seedlings search out where it most wants to be. 'Album', with light green leaves and muted white flowers, must be propagated vegetatively, since it does not come true from seed.

LAVATERA (MALVACEAE) – **mallow**

L. cachemiriana Z6–8   ↕ 1.6m/ 5¼ft   MSu–EA

The plant produces only a few stems, but these are remarkably sturdy. The silky mauve petals do not overlap each other, as in other lavateras. Extremely decorative. We have the impression that the plant, although perennial, does not have a long life, but it compensates for this by producing ample descendants.

LEONURUS (LAMIACEAE) – **motherwort**

L. cardiaca Z5–9   ↕ 1.5m/ 5ft   MSu–EA

A plant with dark green palmate leaves, light green underneath, and long ascending flower stems, covered from top to bottom with whorls of small, pink, downy-haired flowers. Towards the tip the leaves become progressively smaller and trefoil. After flowering the calyces are viciously prickly. An excellent border plant by virtue of its upright habit, but seeds itself out madly.

LOBELIA (CAMPANULACEAE)

It is hard to accept that with their typical two-lipped flowers, of which the two top petals are much smaller than the bottom three, lobelias belong to the family of bellflowers. As botanical ignoramuses, all we can say is that Linnaeus' methods are unfathomable. There are many exceptionally pretty varieties which, however, are also all exceptionally unreliable. There is only one variety which is reasonably hardy, and in any case, it seeds itself so freely that you will never be without it!

L. siphilitica Z5–9   ↕ 1m/ 3½ft   MSu–EA

Forms sturdy stems, densely leaved at the bottom, and a long spike-like cluster of sky-blue flowers, all facing more or less the same way. Grows in any normal garden soil; best in moist ground.

LUNARIA (BRASSICACEAE) – **honesty**

Honesty is generally known and loved for its striking flowers in the spring and its even more striking papery seed pods the size of coins. Like many other spring-flowering crucifers it is an important food plant for the orange-tip butterfly. There is a perennial species.

L. rediviva Z3–9   ↕ 70cm/ 28in   MSp–ESu

A lovely plant for the shade garden, with large, heart-shaped, dark green leaves, turning into olive green, and large clusters of pale lilac flowers. The papery seed pods are elliptical and adorn the plant throughout the winter. Seeds itself less aggressively than the ordinary biennial honesty.

LYCHNIS (CARYOPHYLLACEAE)

A genus of plants with brightly coloured carnation-like flowers, with various cultivation requirements. A good perennial is:

L. chalcedonica Z4–8   ↕ 1.5m/ 5ft    ESu–MSu

Jerusalem cross, Maltese cross. This plant definitely needs moisture-retaining soil to thrive. It will grow on drier ground, but the leaves quickly turn yellow and begin to look unsightly. Because of its vibrant red flowers it is difficult to place. We once saw it in a ditch combined with yellow flags, and that was very beautiful. If you want to let such a brightly coloured plant seed itself in a rather wilder garden, it can have surprising results. If you want more control, *L.c.* var. *albiflora* with white flowers, and *L.c.* 'Carnea' with flesh-pink ones, are more obvious choices.

Top left: *Lavatera cachemiriana*   Centre: *Lunaria rediviva*
Top right: *Lobelia siphilitica* 'Alba'   Bottom: *Lychnis chalcedonica* 'Carnea'

Origanum laevigatum 'Herrenhausen'

LYTHRUM *(LYTHRACEAE)* – **purple loosestrife**

L. salicaria Z4–9 ↕ 1.2m/ 4ft MSu-EA

The wild species grows in any moisture-retaining garden soil, but seeds itself aggressively, and should therefore only be considered for wilder gardens. For the cultivars, see the section on 'Tough' plants.

MECONOPSIS *(PAPAVERACEAE)*

Alas, none of these sublime sky-blue Himalayan poppies are reliable. You need pine-forest soil, high humidity and very green fingers just to attempt to cultivate these miracles of nature. Not a miracle, but still very pretty and reliable, is the west European species:

M. cambrica Z6–8 ↕ 45cm/ 18in LSp-MSu

Welsh poppy. Bright yellow poppy flowers in deep shade: there isn't much to beat it. The plant seeds itself enthusiastically, if you can put up with it. The one thing we will not put up with is the ugly bright orange form.

MEUM *(APIACEAE)* – **spignel, baldmoney**

M. athamanticum Z5–8 ↕ 45cm/ 18in LSp-ESu

If you lie down in an alpine meadow in France, a strong scent of fennel rises. If you look around you, then you see *M. athamanticum* growing as a kind of ground cover among the grass. On normal, not too dry garden soil it is a pleasant clump-forming plant, seeding itself happily, with cream-coloured umbels and that delicious smell of fennel.

MYRRHIS *(APIACEAE)* – **sweet cicely, myrrh**

M. odorata Z4–8 ↕ 1.2m/ 4ft MSp-ESu

A plant closely resembling cow parsley, but with a paler green leaf, larger flower heads and smelling strongly of aniseed. An ingredient of some rather bizarre-tasting old-fashioned stews. The umbels of large shiny black seeds formed after flowering are attractive, but take care. The seedlings will become very large in no time. Particularly suitable for allowing to grow wild in moist half-shade.

ORIGANUM *(LAMIACEAE)* – **marjoram**

O. vulgare Z4–8 ↕ 50cm/ 20in MSu-EA

Oregano, wild marjoram. A dry sunny spot, preferably on limy soil, with wild marjoram in flower: what greater feast could you imagine for summer. One heaving, buzzing mass of mauve, alive with insects of all kinds: hoverflies, bumblebees, moths and all kinds of butterflies, they all love it. And then a lovely scented leaf that can, of course, be used for cooking. However, a warning is not out of place, since it spreads appreciably and seeds freely enough to become a decided nuisance. This also goes for the following cultivars, of which you can only retain the true colour by division: *O. laevigatum* 'Herrenhausen', a vigorous plant with mauve flowers in dark calyces, *O.* 'Ingolstadt', with a light green leaf and white flowers, and *O.* 'Rosenkuppel', the best form, with large mauve flower heads.

OXALIS *(OXALIDACEAE)*

O. acetosella Z3–9 ↕ 5cm/ 2in MSp-LSp

Wood sorrel. Evergreen woodland plants with light green double trefoil leaves and delicate blossoms in late spring. We really should not mention such small plants; indeed we don't list other kinds of wood sorrel, but we make an exception for this because it will grow in the darkest places, even under rhododendrons.

PENTAGLOTTIS *(BORAGINACEAE)*

P. sempervirens Z3–8 ↕ 1m/ 3½ft   LSp–LSu

Green alkanet. A coarse, hairy plant with abundant foliage and a few sky-blue forget-me-not flowers. It flowers for a long time and is extremely vigorous. For neglected gardens.

PERSICARIA *(POLYGONACEAE)* – **knotweed**

P. virginiana Z3–9 ↕ 80cm/ 32in   MSu–EA

Syn. *P. filiformis*. A decorative plant with rather coarse, ovate, pointed leaves with a darker area in the centre (as in redshank) and pinhead-sized red flowers on tall, thread-like stems. Seeds itself enthusiastically.

PHYTOLACCA *(PHYTOLACCACEAE)*

P. americana Z4–9 ↕ 1.5m/ 5ft  MSu–LSu

Virginian pokeweed. A large, coarse plant with a rather subdued inflorescence followed by magnificent bunches of purple-black berries on red stalks. If the plant enjoys the right conditions, on fertile moisture-retaining peat and clay soils, it can make a nuisance of itself, by seeding profusely.

PIMPINELLA *(APIACEAE)* – **burnet saxifrage**

P. major 'Rosea' Z5–9 ↕ 1.2m/ 4ft   ESu–MSu

The plant stands high, as it flowers with an abundance of pink umbels, and reaches its greatest height as it sets its seed. An airy plant with dainty pinnate leaves, which will seed freely and so becomes a linking element in borders on moisture-retaining soil. Also pretty growing wild between shrubs.

POLEMONIUM *(POLEMONIACEAE)* – **Jacob's ladder**

P. caeruleum Z4–8 ↕ 80cm/ 32in   LSp–MSu

In most of the northern hemisphere the common Jacob's ladder is a wild plant, and that is also obvious: in gardens the plant seeds itself indiscriminately. In a tidy border this is a nuisance, but it is ideal for a wildflower meadow. The flowers above the delicate pinnate leaves are usually purplish blue, but can also be sky-blue or white. These colour variants are offered by nurserymen under all kinds of fancy names, but seedlings usually tend to revert to the common species. There are, of course, other species of *Polemonium*, but they are rarely available and mostly prove to be short-lived.

POTENTILLA *(ROSACEAE)* – **cinquefoil**

P. recta Z4–8 ↕ 50cm/ 20in MSu–EA

Plant with palmate, toothed, strawberry-like leaves and lightly branching stems with pretty yellow flowers, about 3cm/1¼in across, which are never obtrusive, although the plant sets seed freely. Even nicer are the lemon-yellow flowers of *P.r.* var. *sulphurea*. Grows easily on any well-drained soil.

PSEUDOFUMARIA *(PAPAVERACEAE)*

P. lutea Z5–8 ↕ 30cm/ 1ft

Syn. *Corydalis lutea*. This is easy to spot. In sheltered places, as long as it does not freeze, this plant can flower all through the year. It forms tidy clumps with delicate compound leaves and bright yellow 'bird flowers', and it seeds itself like one possessed, but only in places that never dry out, between stones and in cracks in walls. In average garden soil it is no trouble at all (provided it wants to grow there). A plant with an interesting history: in the wild it grew only in a limited part of the southern Alps (Monte Baldo) but from the Middle Ages on was spread, possibly deliberately, throughout Europe and later over the whole world, and now grows on all old city walls and quays. *P. ochroleuca* closely resembles it, but has cream-coloured flowers.

Top: *Persicaria virginiana*
Centre: *Phytolacca americana*
Bottom: *Pimpinella major* 'Rosea'

PULMONARIA (BORAGINACEAE) – lungwort

Spring-flowering shade plants with prominent, usually spotted, downy leaves that – provided it is not too dry – remain effective throughout the summer. Most species seed themselves and cross with each other freely, which is why there are many cultivars that do not belong clearly to one species or another. At first most seedlings of a cultivar are reasonably true to colour, but in the course of time the seedlings degenerate to a mishmash. We therefore describe most of the cultivars separately from the species.

P. longifolia Z5–8 ↕ 30cm/ ↓ 1ft 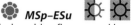 MSp–ESu

Flowers later than the other species, with deep blue flowers and has an elongated, sometimes spotted leaf. 'Bertram Anderson' has a very pretty leaf with white spots.

P. mollis Z4–8 ↕ 50cm/ ↓ 20in   LW–MSp

Has rather insignificant, small blue flowers quite early in spring, but afterwards develops strikingly large and hairy unspotted leaves, 40cm/16in long by 10cm/4in wide.

P. officinalis Z4–8 ↕ 25cm/ ↓ 10in   ESp–LSp

The common lungwort has a rather randomly spotted leaf and pink flowers ageing to pale blue. Very variable; some of the seedlings are very beautiful and some quite ordinary.

P. rubra Z5–8 ↕ 30cm/ ↓ 1ft   LW–MSp

Flowers early with bright pink, almost red flowers above velvety light green leaves.

P. saccharata Z4–8 ↕ 30cm/ ↓ 1ft   ESp–LSp

Strongly resembles *P. officinalis*, but has a larger leaf which is more clearly spotted and sometimes completely grey, and larger pink flowers ageing to pale blue. Most cultivars are described as belonging to this species, but as these usually result from crossings with other 'minor' species not described here, such as *P. vallarsae* and *P. affinis*, we list them separately.

Cultivars Z5–8

There are far too many to list all of them, particularly since some hardly differ from each other. You have to see them to make your own personal choice. Of our own favourites, 'Dora Bielefeld' has soft green, lightly spotted leaves and pure pink flowers. 'Majesté' flowers blue and has leaves that turn completely silver; this is better than the familiar 'Margery Fish', whose almost completely grey leaf for some reason clashes with the muted pink flowers. 'Opal' has a heavily spotted, silver-white leaf and flowers abundantly, from light pink to pale blue, 'Pink Dawn' has pink flowers and speckled leaves, 'Reginald Kaye' has a strongly marked leaf with a green edge and bright blue flowers with a red tube, and the familiar 'Sissinghurst White' has leaves clearly spotted white, and pure white flowers. Seedlings tend to revert to *P. officinalis*.

RANUNCULUS (RANUNCULACEAE) – buttercup

R. acris 'Sulphureus' Z4–8 ↕ 60cm/ ↓ 2ft   LSp–ESu

This sulphur-yellow cultivar of the common buttercup grows reasonably well from seed. There is sometimes a bright yellow seedling mixed up with it (you can't really identify it by its unspotted leaf, as is sometimes suggested: you must wait until the plant flowers), but it is easy to remove, provided, of course, you do so in time. A nearby meadow with common buttercups is not a good idea either, but far removed from all these, in an isolated border, you can expect to have wonderfully beautiful clouds of sulphurous yellow.

Top: Ranunculus acris 'Sulphureus'
Bottom: Salvia glutinosa

SALVIA (LAMIACEAE) – sage

S. glutinosa Z5–8   90cm/3ft MSu–EA

Jupiter's distaff. A marvel for the shade garden, flowering in late summer when hardly anything else is still in flower, and yet also a true sage: sticky and hairy, with a slightly unpleasant smell, but with handsomely large, three-cornered leaves and large pale yellow lipped flowers. Not just for 'rough places', as G. S. Thomas advises, but for any shade garden. Seeds itself in moderation.

S. verticillata Z5–9   50cm/20in ESu–MA

This plant, with dense, grey-green, hairy leaves, flowers profusely with small, lavender-blue florets in whorls round the stems all through the summer. 'Alba' is a dirty white variant not worth mentioning. 'Purple Rain', on the other hand, is a beauty, with spikes of purple flowers and mauve-purple calyces, and 'Smouldering Torches' is a more upright form, which after flowering has a purple glow. Seedlings of the cultivars revert to the common species.

SANGUISORBA (ROSACEAE) – burnet

S. officinalis Z4–8   1.5m/5ft ESu–MSu

Great burnet. A slender plant with a richly branching inflorescence full of dark red knots of flowers. Prettiest on moist ground, where it seeds itself profusely.

SCORZONERA (ASTERACEAE) – viper's grass

S. hispanica Z6–10   80cm/32in LSp–MSu

Common viper's grass. It may seem odd to include these in a book on ornamental plants, but they are reliable perennials, which seed themselves modestly. Narrow leaves clasp the tall stems, which have a sparsely branched inflorescence of large, bright yellow 'dandelion' flowers, followed by large, brown, fluffy seed heads. Usually only available from dealers in vegetable seeds. You may also find there *S. purpurea*, which flowers a wonderful pinkish purple.

SEDUM (CRASSULACEAE) – stonecrop

S. altum Z6–10   60cm/2ft MSu–EA

Deviant, rather stiffly erect species with greenish yellow flowers in wreaths on brownish red stems.

S. telephium Z4–9   50cm/20in LSu

The wild orpine is very different from the many sterile cultivars (see the 'Tough' section). Rather lax stems with small blue-green leaves and a high inflorescence instead of a flat one, deep dark red with blue-grey buds in the centre. Flowers in late summer. Seeds itself modestly, but in the strangest places, for instance in roof guttering. Can stand quite a lot of shade.

S. telephium subsp. maximum Z4–9   80cm/32in MSu–EA

Large subspecies with panicles of wide greenish flowers that seeds itself profusely. Must definitely be kept in a very dry place if it is to stay reasonably compact. The cultivars of this subspecies are decidedly more beautiful.

SENECIO (ASTERACEAE) – ragwort

S. nemorensis subsp. fuchsii Z5–9   1.8m/6ft MSu–EA

Syn. *S. ovatus*. Wood ragwort. A vigorously spreading plant with long arching stems and curious yellow daisy flowers whose butterfly-like ray-florets fail to develop completely. A splendid plant to have growing wild among trees and shrubs in moisture-retaining soil.

SILENE (CARYOPHYLLACEAE) – campion

A genus of fragile plants with opposite leaves and ephemeral five-petalled flowers. Most species are rather unreliable annuals and rock plants. The species formerly classed as *Melandrium* (see the 'Biennials' section) are reliable, as are the following species:

S. vulgaris Z5–9   60cm/2ft LSp–LSu

Bladder campion provides the basis of every alpine meadow, and can also do so in a rather wilder garden, since it seeds itself everywhere and dominates the garden for a long time. The inflated, green-veined white calyces are more striking than the rather crumpled white flowers that open only at night. The long fleshy roots resent disturbance. *S. fimbriata* has heavily fringed flowers, but is rather weak. *S. uniflora* (syn. *S. maritima*) is a compact plant with blue-green leaves and distinctly larger flowers, but is actually only suitable for the rock garden.

SIUM (APIACEAE)

S. suave Z4–9   1.2m/4ft ESu–MSu

Water parsnip. We have not known this plant for long, so we dare not stake our lives on its reliability yet. It appears to be perennial and

Top: *Stachys officinalis* surrounded by *Silene vulgaris*
Bottom: *Sium suave*

seeds itself profusely, but it is rather susceptible to slug damage. It is, however, one of the most beautiful members of its family, with firm blue-grey stems turning to red-brown at the tips, feathery blue-grey leaves, and creamy flower heads. If in the long run it proves reliable, it will be an absolute winner.

SONCHUS (ASTERACEAE) – sow thistle

S. palustris Z4–9 ↕ **3m/ 10ft**   **MSu–EA**

Marsh sow thistle. A gigantic, slender plant of upright habit, with fine, sharply toothed, wedge-shaped leaves and – right at the top – a richly branched inflorescence of pale yellow dandelion flowers on scaly black stems. Stands high above everything else and shows a fine silhouette, particularly in cloudy weather. In the wild it grows on alluvial soil; in the garden it likes fertile soil with plenty of bulky organic matter.

STACHYS (LAMIACEAE)

S. officinalis Z4–9 ↕ **90cm/ 3ft**   **ESu–MSu**

Betony is a sturdy upright plant with typically blunt, ribbed leaves and a flower head rising in spikes, which from a distance resembles a reed orchid (O. praetermissa); at least this is true for the best, compact-flowering, red-purple form, 'Hummelo', which can only be reproduced vegetatively. Seedlings of this and other cultivars are rather variable, usually with indeterminate mauve flowers. Flower colour also depends on their location: in poor but mineral-rich soil in full sun they have the deepest colour and in fertile soil or in shade the palest – but that is true of many plants. The species and its cultivars are also sold as S. monieri, but that is a much smaller species (see the 'Tough' section). 'Alba' is a beautiful, tall, pure white form; 'Nivea' also has white flowers, but stays much lower (50cm/20in) and may be a hybrid. 'Rosea' is a pretty pink form.

STYLOPHORUM (PAPAVERACEAE)

Bears a striking resemblance to a very large celandine, with a larger, more blue-grey leaf and fewer, but much larger, poppy-like yellow flowers. Also seeds itself freely, but it is not nearly so troublesome as the celandine. For fertile soil in shade.

S. diphyllum Z5–8 ↕ **45cm/ 18in**   **MSp–ESu**

Bushy, the large yellow flowers rising just above the leaves. Later it has oval seed pods with a pointed 'beak'.

S. lasiocarpum Z6–9 ↕ **30cm/ 1ft**   **LSp–ESu**

Grows rather more freely, has angular leaves and narrow upright seed pods.

SUCCISA (DIPSACACEAE) – devil's bit scabious

S. pratensis Z3–9 ↕ **90cm/ 3ft**   **MSu–LSu** ☼

Resembles a scabious, but the leaf is elongated, not divided, and it has pincushion-like flowers, formed in large masses on tall stems. Grows well in any moisture-retentive garden soil. The colour of the flowers varies from seedling to seedling, from light to deep blue, rarely pink or white. The species has only recently been recognized as a usable garden plant, but selection based on a good colour, such as deep dark blue or soft mauve-pink, has yet to be done.

TANACETUM (ASTERACEAE) – tansy

Common tansy is quite unsuitable as a garden plant. It is far too invasive, and also collapses hopelessly. The two species listed below are much more suitable, although they hardly look like tansy, or like each other. In times gone by, when a plantsman's life was still simple, all species that looked anything like a daisy were lumped together in the single, rather variable genus of Chrysanthemum. Today this genus has been ripped apart into a large number of

different genera for reasons that may undoubtedly be botanically correct, but are incomprehensible to the average plant watcher. So be it.

T. corymbosum Z6–9 ↕ **1m/ 3½ft**   **ESu–MSu**

Forms a rosette of finely divided, sharply toothed leaves and stiff woody stems, with branching heads (corymbs) of single daisy-like flowers, each about 4cm/1½in across, white with a yellow centre. Beautiful on a sunny spot on dry, limy soil. 'Festtafel' has rather larger flowers.

T. macrophyllum Z5–8 ↕ **1m/ 3½ft**   **ESu–MSu**

Resembles a giant form of the common milfoil with pale green, deeply cut (but not divided) leaves and flat, rather dirty white umbels of flowers. Not fashionable, but can be impressive in a damp shady spot.

TELEKIA (ASTERACEAE) – oxeye

T. speciosa Z4–9 ↕ **1.5m/ 5ft**   **MSu–LSu** ☼ ◫

Enormous plants with large, toothed, heart-shaped leaves and large, yellow daisy flowers with a round brown centre (the 'eye'); very popular with butterflies. Grows best on well-drained soil which has been well manured and contains little lime. In the wild, in the Balkans, it often grows near farms. A striking plant that forces itself into the foreground and can seed itself generously.

THALICTRUM (RANUNCULACEAE) – meadow rue

T. aquilegiifolium Z5–9 ↕ **1.5m/ 5ft** ◉ **MSp–ESu** ☼ ◫

A robust plant with coarser leaves than the other species; a large, wide, fluffy umbel that seems to consist entirely of stamens, followed by large clusters of sublime 'shivering' seeds. Be sure you know what you are doing when you leave them on the plant; under the weight of the heavy seeds the plant will collapse, and you can expect thousands of seedlings the following year. The colour of the flower varies from very pale lilac, almost white, to deep purple. Because of these variations in colour and its tendency to collapse there are 'improved' selections on the market. T.a. var. album forms white powder puffs on purple stems, 'Thundercloud' has deep purple flowers on purple stems, keeps low (70cm/28in) and so does not fall over. At its best on moisture-retaining soil in half-shade, also on heavier soil types.

T. delavayi Z5–9 ↕ **1.8m/ 6ft** ◉ **MSu–EA** ☼ ◫

Syn. T. dipterocarpum. Forms only a few stems and so takes up little space: you can (and should) plant plenty. Enormous, airily branched clouds of small lilac flowers with yellow stamens, which can be put anywhere in the border, including the front (you can see through them). On heavy clay soil the plant will not grow at all, but it will thrive on well-drained, peaty and sandy soil. There it seeds itself enthusiastically, even in dry shade. The plants, which on hot summer days smell of incense, need to be discreetly staked.

T. flavum subsp. glaucum Z6–9 ↕ **2.5m/ 8ft** ◉ **ESu–MSu** ☼

Syn. T. speciosissimum, is in theory one of the loveliest of all plants: it forms a magnificent tuft of waxy blue-grey foliage in the spring and produces enormous clusters of fluffy, lemon-yellow flowers. But the plant can't carry all that luxuriance; it falls hopelessly to the ground in a jumble of stems. Only to be used behind a shrub, over which it can drape itself, or on arid, poor, sandy soil; then it grows less tall and is less untidy. Seeds itself unrestrainedly.

T. lucidum Z6–9 ↕ **2m/ 6½ft**   **ESu–MSu**

Grows best on rather heavier, moisture-retaining soil, where it forms a large sturdy clump with a rather unusual leaf: the segments are

Top left: *Thalictrum aquilegiifolium*
Top centre: *Thalictrum lucidum*
Top right: *Thalictrum delavayi* 'Album'
Above: *Thalictrum rochebruneanum*
Left: *Thalictrum polygamum*

narrow and triangular, not diamond-shaped. It produces large, pale yellow plumes of flowers. On poor, loose soil the plant forms one or two wispy flower stems that promptly fall over.

T. polygamum Z3–9   ↕ **1.8m/ 6ft**   **ESu–MSu**

A vigorous, fast-growing plant with large cream-coloured flower heads and fine clusters of seeds. Does not collapse. Because it grows so airily you can (and should) have plenty of it. That is quite easy to achieve, because it readily seeds itself.

TRADESCANTIA (COMMELINACEAE) – spiderwort

T. virginiana Z5–9   ↕ **60cm/ 2ft**   **LSp–LSu**

Compact plants with grassy foliage and three-petalled flowers hidden among the leaves ('Moses in the bulrushes') in blue, white, purple, white with a blue centre, you name it. This may sound nice, but in practice it just looks untidy. Graham Stuart Thomas puts it like this: 'the presentation of their charming three-petalled blooms among the untidy and prolific greenery leaves much to be desired'. Quite right! And if for this reason you decide to banish the plant from your garden, you will find it is almost impossible to do so. Any piece of root left behind will keep coming up. Moreover, the plant seeds itself only in places where you really don't want it. Our advice is to leave well alone.

VERBESINA (ASTERACEAE)

V. alternifolia Z4–10   ↕ **2.4m/ 8ft**   **LSu–EA**

A giant plant from the tall grass prairie, with sturdy, strikingly winged stems, rough lance-shaped foliage, and a large cluster of bright yellow daisy flowers. The flowers don't seem to develop properly: often they only have a few ray-florets, but that gives the plant a specially charming appearance. This plant doesn't know how to fall over (even if that was what you wanted) and grows everywhere, even on poor sandy soil. Seeds itself modestly. After flowering the plants quickly die back.

VERONICA (SCROPHULARIACEAE) – speedwell

V. longifolia Z4–8   ↕ **80cm/ 32in**   **ESu–LSu**

In the wild a fairly rare species, growing in reed beds along streams. In the garden almost a weed, also on dry soil, but not unpleasing with its long blue (sometimes white) flower spikes. Should be allowed to grow wild in nooks and crannies, between paving stones and alongside a pond, but not in the border.

VIOLA (VIOLACEAE)

V. cornuta Z5–8   ↕ **25cm/ 10in**   **LSp–MA**

Horned viola. Anyone who has ever seen a Pyrenean mountain meadow blue with *cornuta* violas is smitten: you must have it in your garden, too. All right, no problem. The plant flowers for ever with fairly large, lilac-blue violets, and seeds itself happily in nooks and crannies. Alba Group does the same in white.

V. elatior Z4–8   ↕ **50cm/ 20in**   **LSp–ESu**

Although ordinary woodland violets are reliable and profusely self-seeding plants, we do not deal with most of them in this book: they are too small. We make an exception for *V. elatior*, which grows tall, displaying sky-blue flowers with a white centre above striking, elongated leaves. It only flowers for a short time, but there is always room in the garden for such a modest, decorative plant. If you can't find room, it will do so for itself: it seeds itself very well.

Digitalis ferruginea, Agastache foeniculum and *Monarda* 'Fishes'

The rhythm section

Assembling plants for a garden is sometimes called 'composing', as if you were putting together a piece of music. An odd comparison really. A garden is after all primarily a visual experience; the aural aspect of it – birdsong, the wind, the ever-present background noises of modern times – is of secondary importance. It adds just as little as the formal dress of a symphony orchestra does to a musical performance. Admittedly, a garden without sound is as hard to imagine as a symphony orchestra in jeans, unshaven, or with curlers – still, sound only comes second. But anyway, let us carry on the metaphor: the notes are the colours; the changes of pitch are represented by shades of colour; the musical instruments are the plants; the rhythm – what actually represents the rhythm in a garden? Rhythm is an absolutely essential part of a musical composition, however slow or atonal it may be. But rhythm in a garden? You could possibly imagine something like it in a repetitive border: the kind of border in which the same groups of plants are constantly repeated, at regular distances from each other. But translating it back to music, you could liken a repetitive border to a music hall song with a constantly repeated refrain, or at best with a folk song. But a

symphony? That is a different kettle of fish! Nevertheless, a good garden should have a rhythm section.

When you create a planting plan the first thing to decide on is the rhythm: plants that determine its appearance are scattered throughout the borders: plants you can count on for a long time – *Miscanthus* and *Eupatorium purpureum* subsp. *maculatum* 'Atropurpureum' for the autumn and winter; a single variety, such as *Thalictrum aquilegiifolium*, setting the tone from late spring through to the end of summer; and some bulbs, such as *Narcissus* 'February Gold', to hide the bareness of early spring. These will provide a rhythm around which you can compose your melody. Normally in landscape architecture this is called the skeleton (that's it – the rhythm is the skeleton!). Both of us work mostly with an extensive rhythm section: spiky, flat, rounded, plumed and clustered flower shapes together make a complex rhythm, within which the melody, the colour composition, emerges seemingly of its own accord. So for a garden the rhythm is just as important as it is for a piece of music. Whether it is the rhythm of an oompah band or a Beethoven piano sonata is a matter of personal taste.

The kitchen garden of the Priona gardens in flower

Alcea rosea 'Nigra' in front of flowering leeks and parsnips running to seed

Playful
Biennials and tender perennials

Biennials thrive above all in an environment where the soil is occasionally disturbed. Not disturbed systematically as in arable farming, which is turned over every year: biennials would never flower there. They are seen at their best in places where a wood has just been cleared; two years after clearance you find great tracts of foxgloves. Other familiar places where many biennials grow are road verges, railway embankments and industrial sites: all places where the soil is regularly disturbed, without the whole lot being ploughed up every year. It will be obvious that gardens, where you are always rummaging about somewhere, are ideal places to grow biennials. And the evidence is quite plain, since they sow themselves about in all holes and corners, and right into the middle of perennials. If you know how tall most species may become, you also realize that they must be thoroughly weeded, so that you only keep those specimens that don't get in the way of the rest of your planting. This may seem rather negative publicity for biennials, but they flower so abundantly, and they contribute so much to the feast that a summer garden can provide, that you will never want to be without them once you have them. Moreover, because they also bloom in a different place every year, they liven things up.

'Tender perennials' is a rather strange concept. It applies to plants which are in theory perennials, but in practice usually have a short life in a cool temperate climate, because they cannot reliably stand up to the winter, or for some other reason. They compensate for their shortcomings by seeding themselves about profusely, behaving just like biennials, in fact.

Above: *Alcea rugosa*
Below: *Anchusa officinalis*

AGASTACHE *(LAMIACEAE)* – giant hyssop

Sun-loving plants, with aromatic leaves, that will grow on any well-drained garden soil. They are relatively short-lived, but seed themselves profusely. In winter the fine seed heads are an almost inexhaustible food source for blue-tits. In recent years a number of species other than the two listed here have been introduced, but at the moment we still have serious doubts, not about their hardiness in cold winters, but about their ability to withstand mild wet ones.

A. foeniculum Z7–10 1m/ 3½ft MSu–LSu

Anise hyssop. A slender, upright plant with glossy foliage and dark blue flower spikes. It lives longer than the next species and also seeds itself less profusely.

A. rugosa Z8–10 1m/ 3½ft MSu–EA

This most familiar species is short-lived. At first sight it looks very like a stinging nettle, but it does not sting and smells deliciously of fennel. The lilac-purple flower spikes seem rather 'dustier' than the previous species, because the calyces are a little larger and the flowers rather smaller. Flowers for a long time and provides a feast for insects and butterflies. Seeds itself true to colour.

ALCEA *(MALVACEAE)* – hollyhock

Hollyhocks need no description, everyone knows them. They are not biennial, as is so often wrongly claimed, but short-lived: they will keep going four or five years before they give up. That is long enough to seed themselves in moderation in the garden. They seed better between paving stones or in gravel.

A. rosea Z3–9 1.8m/ 6ft MSu–EA

The familiar hollyhock, with single or double flowers, in all colours of the rainbow. Very often it is impossible to buy the prettiest colours anywhere; you have to find them in someone's garden, screw up your courage, and ring the doorbell to ask for seed. 'Nigra' with its dark red, almost black flowers, is regularly available.

A. rugosa Z3–9 1.8m/ 6ft MSu–EA

Has rather more deeply indented leaves and pale yellow flowers. Several other pale yellow species are marketed under a variety of names, but as far as we are concerned they are all the same.

ALLIARIA *(BRASSICACEAE)* – garlic mustard

A. petiolata Z2–9 1m/ 3½ft MSp–LSp

This can be a troublesome weed, but we list it because in the year before flowering it forms a beautiful rosette of fine, round, glossy, serrated leaves, smelling of onions. The start of its flowering (white) is also pretty, particularly in very dark spots, but as it goes on flowering over time, its appeal is lost, and it all gets very untidy. Only for wild, shady corners. An important food plant for the orange-tip butterfly.

ANCHUSA *(BORAGINACEAE)* – alkanet

A. officinalis Z6–10 60cm/ 2ft LSp–MA

Forms long stems, liable to fall over, full of rough-haired leaves. Because new stems keep rising in the heart of the plant, during the course of the summer a 'mound' is created. Flowers richly and endlessly with large, gentian-blue flowers about 1.5cm/½in across. Does best on barren and dry soil, as it is then more compact, although the plant will also do well in ordinary garden soil. It is then rather untidy, but still always beautiful. Seeds itself freely.

ANGELICA *(APIACEAE)* – angelica

A stately plant with characteristic domed flower heads. The most popular species in recent years, *A. gigas*, with domed, claret-coloured flower heads, does not always set enough seed and so tends to vanish from the garden again. Reliable self-seeders are:

A. archangelica Z4–9   ↕ 1.8m/6ft   LSp–MSu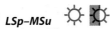

The familiar species, with large luminous green, domed flower heads. Grows anywhere, but the more fertile the soil, the more stately the plants become and the more freely they seed themselves.

A. sylvestris 'Vicar's Mead' Z4–9   ↕ 1.4m/4½ft   MSu–LSu

A form of the common angelica with dark brown leaves and flower heads turning pink. Some of the seedlings keep their darker colour. Needs moisture-retentive soil.

ANTHEMIS *(ASTERACEAE)* – chamomile

A. tinctoria Z4–8   ↕ 80cm/32in   ESu–MA

The yellow chamomile is a short-lived plant for dry sunny places, which grows shrubby with small, divided, feather-like leaves, with plenty of bright yellow daisy flowers throughout the summer. Rigorously cutting back the plant in early autumn – when it is still in full bloom – prolongs its life. If you are reluctant to do this – and it is a pity – don't worry, it seeds itself excessively in any case. There are a number of cultivars with more usable colours; however, their seed reverts to bright yellow. The plant has a tendency to fall apart. 'E.C. Buxton' flowers yellow, but stays low and does not therefore fall over, 'Sauce Hollandaise' flowers a light creamy yellow and 'Wargrave Variety' is pale yellow with a rather darker yellow centre.

AQUILEGIA *(RANUNCULACEAE)* – columbine

The spurred flowers of the columbine are indescribably peculiar, so we will not try to describe them: you know what they look like. The foliage, too, is very strange, and not like that of any other plant: compound with small diamond-shaped leaf sections; you know that, too. What may surprise you is that we have put the genus in this chapter at all. After all, columbines are perennial, aren't they? In practice, they appear to thrive for a few 'fat' years, either to disappear completely, or to drag out their existence for a few more years, but only with a few lean flowers. Usually by then they have been elbowed out by young, vigorous seedlings. There are many species, many of them so delicate that they can only be kept alive by very industrious gardeners with the utmost difficulty. The really reliable ones are:

A. flabellata Z4–9   ↕ 30cm/1ft   LSp–ESu

A low-growing species with waxy blue-grey foliage and large blue-and-white flowers. Exceptionally pretty. The plant seeds itself modestly, but reasonably true to type.

A. vulgaris Z5–9   ↕ 70 cm/28in   LSp–ESu

This beautiful plant has been cultivated since time immemorial and the original wild species, with purple-blue flowers, has now almost disappeared, even in the wild. People talk of a swarm of hybrids, which means that you never really know what colour a seedling will be; we have come across only one pink form, with almost spurless flowers, *A.v.* f. *rosea*, which breeds true to colour. In the long run the following cultivars all degenerate; sometimes for the better, so let it happen. 'Adelaide Addison' is double and blue and white, 'Nora Barlow' is spurless and fully double, greenish white with pink, and 'Ruby Port' is double, also spurless, and a warm dark red.

ARCTIUM *(ASTERACEAE)* – burdock

Burdocks are large, coarse, rubbish-tip plants, with coarse foliage and small, unsightly, purple thistle flowers. The prickly seed heads attach themselves to pullovers, trouser legs and the coats of cats and dogs, and so spread everywhere. The seedlings with their deep tap roots are troublesome to get rid of. So, not in the garden, with one splendid exception:

A. tomentosum Z3–8   ↕ 1.5m/5ft   MSu–LSu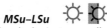

Just as coarse and troublesome as the other burdocks, just as small a

Top: *Angelica sylvestris* 'Vicar's Mead'
Centre: *Anthemis tinctoria* 'E.C. Buxton'
Bottom: *Aquilegia flabellata*

flower, but with striking, large, white, downy bracts. Irresistible to most people.

BORAGO (BORAGINACEAE) – borage

The familiar rough-haired borage is an annual (see the chapter on 'Annuals'). There is also a perennial species, which, however, is not hardy, but seeds itself adequately.

B. pygmaea Z5–9 ↕ 30cm/1ft   LSp–EA

Syn. *B. laxiflora*. A lovely little thing that creeps over the ground with long stems and wriggles its way up between other plants. Scattered over the stems, a few sky-blue, small, five-pointed stars in coarse calyces appear throughout the summer, looking downwards.

CAMPANULA (CAMPANULACEAE) – bellflower

C. patula Z5–9 ↕ 45cm/18in   LSp–EA

The meadow campanula is a slender, pretty, blue-flowering plant for dry, not too acid soil. Considered by many to be 'the most beautiful of all'.

C. rapunculus Z4–9 ↕ 90cm/3ft ESu–LSu

The rampion bellflower is a tall, spindly species, with a long cluster of small purple-blue bells; it seeds itself everywhere on dry soil.

CARDUUS (ASTERACEAE) – thistle

Thistles are, of course, not garden plants; they are much too prickly. But the following species has such a beautiful flower, that we gladly make an exception:

C. nutans Z3–9 ↕ 1.5m/5ft   ESu–MSu

Musk thistle. From top to bottom a prickly plant with lilac-pink thistle flowers, 7cm/2¾in across, bent downwards: bumblebees sleep below them in the evening, not only in picture books but in the garden, too. Also very popular with brimstone butterflies. It usually forms only one tall flowering stem, but in an area grazed by Highland cattle we have seen low, very heavily flowering plants with several stems. This could possibly be achieved in a garden too: pretend to be a cow and nip off the young stems in the spring!

CENTRANTHUS (VALERIANACEAE)

C. ruber Z5–9 ↕ 80cm/32in   LSp–EA

Red valerian. A perennial plant that is not fully hardy in ordinary garden soil, but seeds itself adequately, particularly among stones and gravel. Quite hardy on sunny walls. Airy plants with glaucous leaves with a shimmer of blue and bright pinkish red flower plumes. In spite of its colour it fits in almost anywhere, particularly in a hot, sunny spot. *C.r.* 'Albus' flowers white and is therefore easier to combine with other flowers, but it is not as captivating.

CICHORIUM (ASTERACEAE) – chicory

C. intybus Z4–8 ↕ 1.2m/4ft   MSu–LSu

The wild ancestor of vegetable chicory. A rather untidy, sparsely branched plant with splendid sky-blue, sometimes pink or white dandelion flowers. Only grows on very heavy kinds of soil.

CONIUM (APIACEAE) – hemlock

C. maculatum Z3–9 ↕ 2.5m/8ft   ESu–MSu

The spotted hemlock is a very large, almost spine-chilling plant with a leaf like that of cow parsley, striking dark red spotted stems, and small white flower heads high at the top of the plant. Spine-chilling also because it is one of the most poisonous of plants (if you eat it). The poisonous draught with which Socrates was executed contained hemlock. Plant it (if you dare!)

Top: Campanula patula with Persicaria milletii
Bottom: Centranthus ruber with Salvia nemorosa

COREOPSIS *(ASTERACEAE)* – **tickseed**

C. grandiflora Z4–9 ↕ 1m/ 3½ft   ESu–LSu ☼

We never expected to find this plant beautiful, with its large, glaringly yellow daisy flowers with broad, toothed petals and a small brown heart. The tall, almost leafless stems fall apart gracefully, and that is what makes the plant just acceptable. It is short-lived, but seeds itself well.

CORYDALIS *(PAPAVERACEAE)*

C. cheilanthifolia Z5–8 ↕ 50cm/ 20in   LSp–MSu ☼ ◐

Biennial. Forms a dense mass of fresh green, ferny foliage, and elongated spikes of bright yellow bird-like flowers. Seeds itself arbitrarily only where it wants to be, in nooks and crannies, among stones and gravel. The comparable *C. ophiocarpa*, with grey-blue foliage and small, very pale yellow flowers, behaves the same way.

CYNOGLOSSUM *(BORAGINACEAE)* – **hound's tongue**

C. officinale Z3–8 ↕ 80cm/ 32in   LSp–ESu ☼

A plant covered in grey hairs. In the first year it forms a tidy rosette of elongated ovate leaves and in the second it flowers, with grey cymes providing a particularly effective background for the small deep dark red flowers (1cm/½in). The prickly seeds, characteristic of the genus, appear after flowering, always in clusters of four, and attach themselves to everything. In this way the plant infiltrates all the dry and sunny spots in the garden.

DAUCUS *(APIACEAE)* – **carrot**

D. carota Z3–10 ↕ 1m/ 3½ft   MSu–LSu ☼

We don't need to describe the foliage: carrot leaves. But not everyone knows the flowers: a large cluster of flat white umbels with a small red flower at their centre. When the seed has formed the flower heads close together like a fist. One of the most beautiful and most effective umbelliferous plants known, but it seeds itself so freely that it will give you a great deal of work to do. If in the spring you plant out carrots left over from the winter, these sometimes produce deviant flowers: lavender-grey, domed flower heads.

DIGITALIS *(SCROPHULARIACEAE)* – **foxglove**

Mostly biennials that can seed themselves profusely. They hardly ever fall over, and the tall flower spike is very characteristic with its thimble-like drooping flowers: bumblebee bedrooms.

D. ferruginea Z7–9 ↕ 1.2m/ 4ft   MSu–LSu ☼

On good moisture-retaining soil this forms rosettes of glossy dark green leaves and in the second year produces a tall spike, thickly covered with honey-brown flowers with red-brown veining. Spectacularly beautiful.

D. grandiflora Z4–8 ↕ 60cm/ 2ft   MSu–LSu ☼ ◐

Syn. *D. ambigua*. Flowers with 'real' thimbles about 5cm/2in long, in pale yellow. Has the reputation of being perennial, but in our experience is short-lived and seeds itself sparsely, and only on fertile, well-drained, lime-free soil.

D. lanata Z5–9 ↕ 80cm/ 32in ⊛ MSu–LSu ☼

Rather resembles *D. ferruginea*, but stays a little lower and has rather larger white flowers with reddish brown veining and a clearly protruding white lower lip.

D. lutea Z4–8 ↕ 1m/ 3½ft   MSu–LSu ☼ ◐

A short-lived plant with narrow leaves and a tall spike with small, pale yellow flowers. Likes limy soil. Its many seedlings can vary rather in colour.

Top: *Digitalis ferruginea* with *Persicaria amplexicaulis*
Bottom: *Digitalis grandiflora*

D. parviflora Z5–8   ↕ 60cm/ 2ft   ESu–MSu

The slender spikes are covered over their whole length with small, chocolate-coloured flowers. Let it grow wild *en masse* between grasses that flower at the same time, such as *Deschampsia*.

D. purpurea Z5–9   ↕ 1.5m/ 5ft   ESu–LSu

The common foxglove needs no description; everyone with a garden on well-drained soil is troubled with them. The flowers are mostly pink, sometimes white. The white form, *D.p. f. albiflora* may be sold separately, but usually does not succeed in keeping all its seedlings white, because there is always a bumblebee around who has just visited a pink form elsewhere.

DIPSACUS (DIPSACACEAE) – teasel

Everyone knows teasels: enormous plants with opposite leaves, joined at the base, with a little pool of water at the base of each one. Large, ovate, prickly inflorescence flowering from bottom to top with successive rings of small lilac flowers, which look so good indoors in winter. Outside too, in fact, since with a little luck they attract goldfinches. They seed themselves abundantly, but the rosettes of foliage with their prickly, 'quilted' leaves are easy to recognize. This description applies only to the following species.

D. fullonum Z4–9   ↕ 2m/ 6½ft   MSu–LSu

The common teasel. There is another kind, which looks completely different.

D. pilosus Z4–9   ↕ 2m/ 6½ft   LSu–EA

Small teasel. This has soft, rounded leaves without prickles and with an enormous, widely branched plume full of small, round, cream-coloured flowers about 2cm/1in across. It seeds itself just as fanatically as *D. fullonum*, preferably on fertile soil in the shade. Despite its height it does not fall over.

ECHIUM (BORAGINACEAE) – viper's bugloss

Plants for dry, stony, preferably lime-rich soil with torch-shaped inflorescences full of flowers that look like the open mouth of a snake, with stamens protruding a long way.

E. russicum Z5–9   ↕ 70cm/ 28in   ESu–MSu

Forms a rosette of narrow, dark green foliage, and a torch-shaped inflorescence with tightly packed dark red flowers. A steppe plant from the Ukraine and therefore fully hardy. Prefers a dry position.

E. vulgare Z7–10   ↕ 1m/ 3½ft   LSp–EA

From a rosette of elongated, rough-haired leaves rise tall, equally hairy stems covered over almost their whole length with a plume-like inflorescence, consisting of numerous short sprays of first reddish, then purple, and finally blue flowers.

ERIGERON (ASTERACEAE) – fleabane

Genus of mainly small-flowered weeds on arable land with aster-like flowers displaying many thread-like rays. There are a number of large-flowered cultivars, which are, however, not particularly reliable (see the chapter on 'Capricious plants'). One of these field weeds can make a material – if troublesome – contribution to the garden:

E. annuus   ↕ 1.5m/ 5ft   ESu–MA

The plant flowers endlessly, and forms an enormous cloud of white until late in the autumn. To see it is to want it, but the plant seeds itself at an impossible rate. It flits through the borders almost unnoticed. Only for zealous gardeners.

ERYNGIUM (APIACEAE) – sea holly

E. giganteum Z6–9   ↕ 60cm/ 2ft   ESu–LSu

A fantastic plant: from a rosette of ordinary, green, rounded leaves

arises a sturdy, grey, tightly branched stem with broad, silver-grey, prickly leaves and tall, greenish blue cones of flowers, surrounded by equally silvery involucral bracts. Dies after flowering, but seeds itself abundantly. It is sometimes called Miss Willmott's ghost because Miss Willmott, the eccentric nineteenth-century plantswoman, scattered the seed of this plant in the gardens of everyone she went to visit. A good idea!

EUPHORBIA (EUPHORBIACEAE) – spurge

E. amygdaloides Z6–9   ↕ 45cm/ 18in   MSp–LSp

A perennial plant that is in fact short-lived. It degenerates after a few years, and then, when a hard winter comes, that's it. But by that time the garden is full of seedlings. The plant forms yellow-green clusters of flowers on densely leaved stems. *E.a.* 'Purpurea' is prettier, with red-purple leaves and virulent green flowers. Seeds itself true to colour.

E. characias Z7–10   ↕ 1m/ 3½ft   MSp–ESu

Without doubt one of the most desirable euphorbias. Forms tall, densely leaved branches, growing woody from below, and has large clusters of yellow-green flowers with a striking black eye. It is perennial and reasonably hardy, but if a north-easter blows and the temperature falls below -15°C (8°F) within a few hours, you will be too late with your protective covering. If you have not cut off the flower heads immediately after they have finished flowering, as some garden books advise, you can at least expect to have seedlings, since it seeds itself enthusiastically. *E.c.* subsp. *wulfenii* from the eastern Mediterranean grows even taller and has larger clusters of flowers of a brighter yellow, but is even less hardy.

E. corallioides Z6–10   ↕ 45cm/ 18in   LSp–LSu

Forms densely leaved stems with green leaves with a plain white central rib, and flowers throughout the summer with widely branched clusters of yellow-green flowers. Then dies, but seeds itself well.

E. lathyris Z6–10   ↕ 1.5m/ 5ft   ESu–MSu

Caper spurge. A pretty weed, which also behaves like a weed in the garden, but . . . It has stiffly rising blue-grey stems with blue-green leaves in crosswise pairs, and a wide-branched flower head, remarkable for the large round seeds. Is supposed to drive away moles, but they just go round it, so you end up with more damage.

E. stricta Z6–10   ↕ 50cm/ 20in   ESu–LSu

A pretty plant, flowering yellow-green and turning red to red-brown as it dies. Seeds itself well.

FOENICULUM (APIACEAE) – fennel

F. vulgare Z4–9   ↕ 1.8m/ 6ft   MSu–EA

Perennial, but not fully hardy. However, the plant seeds itself so freely that you will never lose it. Flowers from the first year, so it is effective from the start, and after a mild winter you have enormous fluffy plumes, very finely divided, with a lovely smell of liquorice, light green leaves and delicate yellow-green flower heads. Always fits in anywhere, as does 'Purpureum' with its bronze-coloured leaves.

GERANIUM (GERANIACEAE) – cranesbill

G. pyrenaicum Z7–10   ↕ 60cm/ 2ft   LSp–MSu

Forms round, shallow-lobed leaves and many small, lilac-pink flowers, about 1.5cm/½in across, with deeply indented petals. After the main flowering in late spring through early summer, the plant carries on flowering a little. Very beautiful, particularly when they are massed together in a spring garden. In this chapter we should in fact also describe herb Robert, *G. robertianum*, but it is such a nuisance, we dare not. It certainly looks pretty if you have a spot for it, for instance on a flat roof. Brian Kabbes tolerates the white-flowering form 'Celtic White' in his nursery.

Top: *Euphorbia characias*   Bottom: *Foeniculum vulgare* 'Purpureum' with *Verbena bonariensis*

GLAUCIUM (PAPAVERACEAE) – horned poppy

G. corniculatum Z7–10 ↕ 50cm/ 20in ESu–EA

A beauty for hot arid areas, with silver-grey, fragile, indented leaves and orange-red poppy flowers, followed by pods shaped like broadswords, 10cm/4in long, full of seed, also grey of course.

HELLEBORUS (RANUNCULACEAE) – hellebore

H. foetidus Z6–9 ↕ 50cm/ 20in EW–ESp

Stinking hellebore. A short-lived species with fine, dark green leaves, indented like fingers, and large tufts of bell-shaped, vivid green flowers with a mahogany-coloured edge. Within a few years it forms an enormous clump and then gives up, but by that time it has seeded itself about liberally. Depending on the temperature in winter, the plant can start flowering in December, lies flat on the ground during a frost, and when it thaws, cheerfully gets up to flower again. Grows anywhere, but best in limy soil.

HERACLEUM (APIACEAE) – hogweed, cow parsnip

H. mantegazzianum Z3–9 ↕ 3m/ 10ft ESu–MSu

Familiar gigantic plant that can easily grow to more than 4m/14ft high if it rains heavily in early summer, its growing season. Huge, deeply indented leaves, and enormous domed white flower heads. If you allow the plant to run to seed, you will never get rid of it. Not suitable for small gardens, and planting in the wild is illegal. If you damage part of the plant while weeding, the sap spurting out causes sinister-looking dark red burns on the skin, which can last for months. Brushing against its hairs can cause burns too. They are not always painful but can be agonizing, and, of course, they are a gruesome sight! Not suitable for children's play areas or where you want to do your gardening in a bathing costume, but otherwise – very impressive.

HESPERIS (BRASSICACEAE)

Short-lived brassica with striking violet-coloured flowers.

H. matronalis Z4–9 ↕ 1m/ 3½ft LSp–MSu

Dame's violet or sweet rocket. A rather untidy plant with inconspicuous foliage and large clusters of bright pinkish red flowers, sweet-scented, particularly in the evening, a treat for butterflies by day and a feast for moths by night. Very robust, it grows everywhere and seeds itself all over the place, even in deep shade and among stinging nettles. The common form is not often seen; a much more frequent sight (and more beautiful) is *H.m.* var. *albiflora*, with white flowers.

H. steveniana Z5–9 ↕ 70cm/ 28in LSp–EA

Slimmer, more graceful and more choosy than the previous species, with grey, hairy foliage and soft lilac-purple flowers. A beauty for a favoured spot on good garden soil in the full sun; there it will seed itself nicely.

HYPERICUM (CLUSIACEAE) – St John's wort

There are, of course, many reasonably reliable shrubs which we find so boring and uninteresting that we just would not know what to write about them. So we miss them out. Several species of hypericum fall into this category. However, worth listing is:

H. perforatum Z3–9 ↕ 60cm/ 2ft ESu–MA

A short-lived plant that can behave like a true weed, particularly on dry sandy soil. But the plant flowers without stopping with large plumes of yellow flowers, with thick stamens at their centre, and has fine orange-brown seeds that have a strong medicinal effect. Very useful therefore, but only suitable for very wild gardens and/or very industrious gardeners.

Above: *Helleborus foetidus*
Below: *Hesperis steveniana*

ISATIS *(BRASSICACEAE)* – **woad**

I. tinctoria Z7–10   ↕ **1.2m/ 4ft**   **MSp–LSp**

Woad is an old dye plant and was cultivated in monastery gardens for this reason. We consider the not insubstantial decorative value of the plant much more interesting. In the first year it forms a small rosette of waxy grey-blue foliage and in the second an enormous fluffy plume full of small, pale yellow flowers, succeeded by fine, elongated shiny black seeds. Grows on any kind of soil in sun.

KNAUTIA *(DIPSACACEAE)* – **scabious**

Knautia and *Scabiosa* are as alike as two drops of water, but differ in the flower receptacle, which in *Scabiosa* is scale-like, but not in *Knautia*. Now you know. Gardeners can go on the fact that *Knautia* generally has coarser foliage. The plants are busily sought after by everything that flies and buzzes.

K. arvensis Z6–9   ↕ **60cm/ 2ft**   **ESu–EA**

Field scabious. This is an untidy plant with coarse foliage and wispy flower stems, with lilac flowers about 4cm/1½in across. Best (and least untidy) on poorish but not acid soil, or even better in grass. Officially a perennial, but in practice short-lived, though it seeds itself about lavishly.

K. macedonica Z5–9   ↕ **60cm/ 2ft**   **MSu–EA**

Short-lived plant, rather less untidy than *K. arvensis*, but it needs some brushwood to keep it in shape, and it can then also be grown on fertile garden soil, which is good, because the flowers are brilliant: a dark claret colour. Seeds itself modestly. There is also a sterile variety available with slightly larger flowers, but it does not seed itself, so you lose it after a few years.

LAPSANA *(ASTERACEAE)* – **nipplewort**

L. communis Z3–9   ↕ **1.5m/ 5ft**   **ESu–LSu**

A very common wild plant which will grow anywhere; along roads and ditches, but also on industrial sites and in deciduous woods. Obviously very troublesome and not in fact a garden plant, if it were not that the airy, thinly branched inflorescence with small yellow dandelion flowers, which only open in the morning, gives an overwhelmingly delicate effect in darker corners of the garden. In the first year it forms a rosette of coarse-toothed foliage.

LINARIA *(SCROPHULARIACEAE)* – **toad flax**

Genus of rock plants and small field weeds with exceptionally fine small flowers: spurred and two-lipped with a 'mask', usually in another colour, which closes the mouth of the flower. This, particularly in warm climates, can lead to the oddest combinations: purple with orange, for example. In cooler parts only one species is sufficiently reliable for gardens:

L. purpurea Z5–8   ↕ **80cm/ 32in**   **ESu–EA**

A tall, slender plant that seeds itself extensively, with small, narrow, grey leaves and a long spike of small purple flowers with a white mask. Always and everywhere a welcome sight. There are cultivars: 'Canon Went' flowers pink and 'Springside White' is pure white, but unless they are grown in isolation they do not breed true to colour.

LUNARIA *(BRASSICACEAE)* – **honesty**

L. annua Z8–10   ↕ **1m/ 3½ft**   **MSp–LSp**

The familiar honesty, which can magically transform shady spring gardens into a red-purple sea of flowers and in the following winter into a silver sea of seeds. It seeds itself excessively, but experience teaches that you never, or hardly ever, have to weed out the seedlings, because the plants broaden at a time when other shade plants are still below ground (and if they are already above ground,

Right: *Isatis tinctoria*
Below: *Knautia macedonica*
Bottom: *Nepeta clarkei*

a little extra shade can often do no harm). There is no reason at all to panic: enjoy them. The white-flowering variety, *L.a.* var. *albiflora*, is even more beautiful, and grows well from seed if the common form is not around.

LUPINUS (PAPILIONACEAE) – lupin

L. polyphyllus Z3–6 ↕ 1.2m/4ft   LSp–MSu ☼

This is the only species of lupin that is reliable in cool temperate climates; even so you have to give it the opportunity to seed itself, since the plant is short-lived. Do we have to describe the lupin, with its typical, fan-shaped, compound leaves and large spikes of purple-blue flowers? The enormous clusters with their dense seed pods, turning purplish, make the plant top-heavy, so that it tends to fall apart. It is not a good plant for the garden and is only a good idea in poor grassland. If you do not let the plant run to seed, it lives rather longer and is less untidy, but then you lose it entirely in the end. The same applies to the many attractively coloured cultivars.

LYCHNIS (CARYOPHYLLACEAE)

L. coronaria Z4–8 ↕ 80cm/32in 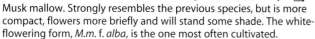 LSp–MSu ☼

Rose campion. A short-lived plant with a rosette of flannel-like grey foliage and sturdy, straight-branched stems with large, glaringly red-purple flowers that fit in hardly anywhere. Only if you allow the plant to go its own way in a large, wild garden can this produce a spectacular effect. Much more usable is *L.c.* 'Alba', with white flowers, which seeds itself true to colour provided the red form is not around. Likes dry soil.

MALVA (MALVACEAE) – mallow

With their five-petalled flowers with a remarkable 'stamen tree' at their centre, and palmate, more or less deeply divided, foliage, mallows are unmistakable. Most species are biennial, and those known as 'perennial' are short-lived.

M. alcea Z4–8 ↕ 1.2m/4ft   ESu–EA ☼

Greater musk mallow. A sizeable plant that needs supporting, with deeply indented foliage; it flowers very profusely with pale pink flowers, about 5cm/2in across, with dark pink veining. Often has a full second flowering in early autumn.

M. moschata Z4–8 ↕ 60cm/2ft   ESu–MSu ☼ ☼

Musk mallow. Strongly resembles the previous species, but is more compact, flowers more briefly and will stand some shade. The white-flowering form, *M.m.* f. *alba*, is the one most often cultivated.

M. sylvestris Z5–9 ↕ 1.5m/5ft   ESu–EA ☼ ☼

Common mallow. A rather lanky plant with many broad-lobed leaves and pale purple flowers with darker veining, about 3cm/1¼in across. Inconspicuous, but still pretty for a rough spot. Seeds itself liberally. *M.s.* var. *mauritiana* has much larger, deep purple flowers, but seeds itself about less reliably.

MELILOTUS (PAPILIONACEAE) – melilot

Melilot is widely known, since it grows everywhere in sandy soil: along roads, railway embankments and on industrial sites, but if it is in a garden everyone wants to know what it is. Large, strongly branched plants with small trifoliate leaves and countless narrow yellow or white flowering spikes. Goes on flowering for ever and is extraordinarily effective in the border, but beware: the plants seed themselves so profusely they will drive you up the wall!

M. albus ↕ 2m/6½ft ESu–MA

White melilot. Flowers white.

M. altissimus ↕ 2m/6½ft   ESu–MA ☼

Tall melilot. Flowers pale yellow and has a strong scent of coumarin.

MYOSOTIS (BORAGINACEAE) – forget-me-not

M. sylvatica Z4–10 ↕ 40cm/16in   MSp–LSp

This is the familiar garden forget-me-not that runs wild so delightfully and colours whole expanses sky-blue in spring. Seeds itself everywhere, but only flowers in sheltered places where the plants cannot be damaged by frosts.

NEPETA (LAMIACEAE) – catmint

N. clarkei Z3–9 ↕ 50cm/20in ESu–MSu ☼

A fine plant with blue-lilac two-lipped flowers with a white lower lip in whorls on the stem. Short-lived, but seeds itself well. Classically combined with the oriental poppy 'Karine'.

OENOTHERA (ONAGRACEAE) – evening primrose

There are several more or less perennial evening primroses (for dry, sunny places) that flower so showily, not to say glaringly, yellow, that we have, in our wisdom, ignored them. We make an exception, with some reluctance, for the common biennial evening primrose:

O. biennis Z4–10 ↕ 1.75m/6ft   ESu–EA ☼

Everyone falls for the luminous yellow, four-petalled flowers that open in the evenings. We can find no other reason for the popularity of the evening primrose. The plants grow and flower throughout the summer, and eventually become so large that they inevitably fall to the ground. They seed themselves shamelessly and the seedlings with their long taproots are difficult to remove. Oh well, it's up to you! *O. glaziouana* (syn. *O. erythrosepala*), with larger flowers of a paler yellow, is more beautiful, but just as troublesome.

ONOPORDUM (ASTERACEAE) – cotton thistle

O. acanthium Z6–10 ↕ 2.5m/8ft MSu–LSu ☼

The cotton thistle, also known as the Scottish thistle, is a huge plant with strongly branched, slightly prickly stems and large, floppy leaves with tremendous prickles on which you can hurt yourself badly, and large, typically purple thistle flowers, beloved by butterflies. The whole plant is covered by woolly grey hairs. Monumental; you only need one or two.

PAPAVER (PAPAVERACEAE) – poppy

P. rupifragum Z8–9 ↕ 40cm/16in LSp–EA ☼

A short-lived species with grey, hairy leaves and delicate soft orange flowers that seeds itself everywhere. But don't panic, the seedlings survive only in places where they are not overshadowed by other plants, in other words right in the front of the border, between stones and along walls. As befits a poppy, it flowers only in the morning.

PASTINACA (APIACEAE) – parsnip

P. sativa Z7–10 ↕ 1.5m/5ft ESu–MSu ☼

Before the arrival of the potato in Europe, parsnips were the most important vegetable for the common people. Boiled, they provide a mealy, tasteless pap: their replacement by potatoes was quite justified. Stir-fried or baked parsnips, on the other hand, are quite tasty. We consider their formidable value in the garden much more important. They are large, richly branched plants, which stay upright, with deeply indented leaves and wide umbels full of greenish yellow flowers, alive with insects, just like fennel and dill, but earlier in the year. Dies off handsomely, gradually changing colour via orange-brown to beige. They will give you plenty of work, because they seed themselves liberally. On clay soil they will also do well in grass.

Pastinaca sativa with *Papaver somniferum.*'Danebrog'

Papaver orientale 'Aglaja'

Soap bubbles

garden, are desert or steppe plants which once a year, or sometimes once in several years, after a period of rain or sometimes a few heavy showers, suddenly shoot out of the ground, flower and set seed, before they are scorched by the searing heat of the sun again. They bloom in bright colours, because in their short life it is imperative that they attract attention in order to be pollinated in time.

There are gardeners who have made a life's work of 'blowing bubbles'. Every year they work like mad in the spring and early summer. First they sow seed in little pots in the cold frame, then they pot on into more little pots – the frame can now be opened if the weather is fine – and then, one by one, they plant them out in beds in the open and weed, weed, and weed again, for that single short explosion of colour in mid-summer. Single because such annuals don't return of their own accord in a changeable climate.

Sometimes the soap bubbles are to be found among the perennials: peonies often flower so briefly that you can completely miss their flowering if you are away from home for a few days. Perennial poppies by nature flower very briefly, and there are also spring flowers, such as the very lovely *Jeffersonia dubia*, that bloom for such a short time that they are over before you realize it. Such plants should be introduced with discretion, or you will have little pleasure from your perennial garden. This does not apply to spring bulbs, which you can scatter liberally. They mostly flower for quite a long time, but if there is a spring heat wave, they behave like soap bubbles and are gone very quickly.

But all soap bubbles, annual or perennial, have one thing in common: they are absolutely enchanting.

Once you are grown up you no longer blow bubbles, except perhaps occasionally for your children or grandchildren, using one of those little clay pipes. But no one can forget the enchantment of those fleeting multicoloured soap bubbles that burst again in a fraction of a second. You have no time for such flights of fancy any more. But in the garden you may enjoy them with impunity, like the Reverend Wilks, who in the late nineteenth century bred a whole strain of remarkable coloured poppies (Shirley poppies). In this book we list only annuals that are big and strong enough to be able to compete with perennials, but there are, of course, many more, in the most fantastic colours, which you may like to try some time when you happen to have a bare spot of earth, or when the perennial flower border has been newly planted to give colour in the first year. Most annuals, and certainly the ones we like to see in the

PETRORHAGIA *(CARYOPHYLLACEAE)*

P. saxifraga Z4–9 ↕ 1.5m/5ft ESu–EA ☼

Forms clouds of endlessly branched wiry stems, covered throughout the summer with small, pale pink flowers. Short-lived, but seeds itself generously in dry corners.

PETROSELINUM *(APIACEAE)* – **parsley**

P. crispum Z5–10 ↕ 90cm/3ft MSu–LSu ☼

Parsley is notoriously hard to grow from seed. You have to water it for weeks before it eventually sprouts. Just leave a plant to bolt, once in a while. It becomes a strong, widely branched plant, chock-full of small, greenish yellow flower heads, that will seed itself spontaneously and looks well in every border.

PEUCEDANUM *(APIACEAE)* – **hog's fennel**

P. verticillare Z4–8 ↕ 2m/6½ft MSu–LSu ☼

Tall, umbelliferous plant with lovely, compound, grey-green foliage on leaf-stems turning purple, and greenish white flower heads on a long, sturdy stalk. Seeds itself nicely in borders on good moisture-retaining soil or between stones.

PLANTAGO *(PLANTAGINACEAE)* – **plantain**

P. major Z4–9 ↕ 25cm/10in ✹ LSp–EA ☼

Greater plantain. We don't have to plant greater plantains, they come of their own accord, as weeds on the garden paths. The following cultivars are short-lived, but grow well from seed. 'Rosularis' is a freak: the spike-shaped inflorescence is replaced by a tuft of small green leaves, like a little green rose. 'Rubrifolia' has purple-red foliage and looks best in full sun. Can be a problem seeding themselves in borders, so keep them in their proper place, on paths and among stones.

RESEDA *(RESEDACEAE)* – **mignonette**

The familiar garden variety is not much to look at, but has remarkable sweet-scented flowers. But that is an annual from Africa, which cannot maintain itself in a natural garden. Much less familiar are the following three species, which seed themselves liberally, particularly on sandy soil:

R. alba Z8–10 ↕ 1m/3½ft ESu–MA ☼

White mignonette. A shrubby branched plant with tall spikes full of small white flowers. Not fully hardy, but seeds itself profusely.

R. lutea Z5–10 ↕ 60cm/2ft ESu–EA ☼

Wild mignonette. Produces lots of tiny, pale yellow flowers on narrow branched spikes.

R. luteola Z6–10 ↕ 1m/3½ft ESu–EA ☼

Weld. Resembles the previous plant, but grows much higher and has even longer spikes, with fewer branches. Familiar under the names weld or dyer's rocket.

SALVIA *(LAMIACEAE)* – **sage**

S. pratensis Z3–9 ↕ 60cm/2ft ✹ LSp–MSu ☼

Meadow sage, although a rather uncommon native plant, is not easy to grow in the garden. This jewel with its large, dark blue, lipped flowers needs a strong soil, rich in minerals and dry, but not manured. Possibly sandy clay? In practice it is a short-lived plant in the garden and seeds itself modestly. The same applies to the following subspecies:

S. pratensis Haematode Group Z6–9 ↕ 90cm/3ft LSp–MSu ☼

This is rather larger, airily branched and has slightly larger flowers.

Above: *Peucedanum verticillare*
Below: *Salvia pratensis* 'Lapis Lazuli'

Salvia sclarea

S.p. 'Lapis Lazuli' does not flower lapis lazuli, but mauve, is early, and stays low (50cm/20in).

S. sclarea Z5–10 ↕ *1m/ 3½ft* ESu–LSu

Biennial clary. Grows into a widely branched plant with ribbed, grey, 'quilted' foliage, smelling of sweat (some people find this pleasant) and a large inflorescence full of pale lilac flowers with striking lilac-pink bracts. Combines in itself all the favourite garden colours. Biennial, but seeds itself well in any good garden soil.

SCABIOSA *(DIPSACACEAE)* – **scabious**
Familiar sun-loving plants with lyre-shaped leaves. Flower stems bear narrow, divided, feather-like leaves. The flowers cluster together in a flat head. They are very attractive to butterflies and other insects. You can sometimes find the rare bee-eating beetle on scabious flowers. Although the plants have been recorded as perennial, in practice they are short-lived, but they seed themselves well. All species like a sunny, dry spot, rich in lime.

S. columbaria Z5–8 ↕ *90cm/ 3ft* MSu–EA ☼

Small scabious. A rather lanky plant, which has to find support from its neighbours or from brushwood, with long-lasting lilac-blue flowers in the summer. Comparable, but much shorter (50cm/20in) and therefore sturdier, are *S. lucida* and the still lower *S. japonica* var. *alpina* (35cm/14in).

S. columbaria var. ochroleuca Z4–7 ↕ *90cm/ 3ft* MSu–EW ☼

As lanky as *S. columbaria,* but goes on flowering endlessly with pale yellow flowers. If it does not freeze in the autumn, the plant will still flower at Christmas. *S.c.* var. *webbiana* is rather sturdier.

SCROPHULARIA *(SCROPHULARIACEAE)* – **figwort**
Genus of coarse water plants with unsightly, small brown flowers that have little value in the garden except for collectors. The following species is an exception:

S. vernalis Z4–9 ↕ *80cm/ 32in* LW–LSp

Yellow figwort. Biennial to short-lived woodland plant with plenty of fine, fresh green 'quilted' hairy leaves and pale yellow flowers in dumpy flower heads in the leaf axils. Interesting for its great mass of luminous leaves and very early spring flowers. Often flowers a second time in autumn.

SENECIO *(ASTERACEAE)* – **ragwort**

S. inaequidens Z7–10 ↕ *1m/ 3½ft* MSu-MA

A shrubby species from South Africa. Perennial, though in practice short-lived in cooler climates, it seeds itself profusely. Decorative, with stems turning red, linear dark green foliage and loose plumes of small, bright-yellow daisy flowers. Not welcome everywhere as it is very invasive and poisonous to livestock.

S. jacobaea Z4–10 ↕ *1.2m/ 4ft* MSu-EA

St James's wort, the common ragwort, is well suited to growing wild in dry grassland. In the garden the seedlings will drive you crazy. The plant is poisonous to livestock, and in the UK it is illegal to allow it to seed on neighbouring land. In any case the plant guarantees plenty of cheerful yellow in late summer. In the first year it forms a rosette of lyre-shaped foliage, succeeded in the second by flower spikes with divided, feather-like leaves and broad umbels of yellow daisy flowers. It may be worth introducing some of the black and yellow striped caterpillars of the cinnabar moth, *Tyria jacobaeae*, so that you can kill two birds with one stone: the caterpillars keep the St James's wort in check, and you will have some wonderful black and red daytime moths in your garden. Very similar, but much taller, is *S. erucifolius,* which likes a heavier soil and so is probably more suitable as a garden plant. Usually short-lived. *S. aquaticus*, marsh ragwort, is also similar, but stays much lower (60cm/2ft) and only grows in damp soil.

SESELI (APIACEAE)

S. libanotis Z4–9   ↕ **50cm/ 20in**   **MSu–LSu**

A lovely plant for dry sunny spots, with parsley-like leaves and lots of broad, domed, cream-coloured flower heads. Falls apart, but flowers so heavily that it forms 'mounds'.

SILENE (CARYOPHYLLACEAE) – *campion*

S. dioica Z5–8   ↕ **90cm/ 3ft**   **LSp–MSu**

Syn. *Melandrium rubrum*. Once you have planted the familiar red campion in your garden, you will spend the next few years trying to get rid of it again, it seeds itself so annoyingly. In the end you will give up, because it is still pretty. The rather untidy plants with their cheerful pinkish red flowers brighten up the gloomiest corners of the garden, where nothing else will grow. With some skill they are manageable. Some of the seedlings produce white flowers.

SISYRINCHIUM (IRIDACEAE)

S. striatum Z7–8   ↕ **60cm/ 2ft**   **MSu–LSu**

A fine plant with iris-like leaves and pale, straw-coloured flowers, half hidden by grassy bracts, on long spikes. Short-lived and in any case often not hardy, but seeds itself well in any good garden soil.

SMYRNIUM (APIACEAE) – **alexanders**

S. perfoliatum Z6–10   ↕ **80cm/ 32in**   **MSp–ESu**

A short-lived plant, which takes a few years to start flowering. Dies after flowering, but seeds itself liberally. In the first years the plant forms a rosette of glossy green foliage, which after the spring disappears again below ground. When it has grown strong enough, the plant forms stiff stems with bowl-like, perfoliate leaves and vivid yellow-green flower heads. The plant displays its talents only on heavy, clay soils. *S. olusatrum*, with trifoliate leaves and less spectacular yellow-green inflorescences, apparently has less stringent requirements on the type of soil.

SYMPHYANDRA (CAMPANULACEAE)

S. hofmannii Z5–9   ↕ **50cm/ 20in**   **MSu–LSu**

A rough-haired plant with, facing to one side, plume-like branched flower heads full of drooping cream-coloured bells of about 3cm/ 1¼in. Seeds itself in dark corners.

TANACETUM (ASTERACEAE) – **tansy**

T. parthenium Z6–10   ↕ **60cm/ 2ft**   **ESu–EA**

Syn. *Chrysanthemum parthenium*. The familiar feverfew that almost everyone has in their garden – whether they want to or not – with divided, feather-like leaves and clusters of small white daisy flowers. There are also several double-flowered cultivars. Troublesome, but may be allowed to grow beneath a hedge.

Smyrnium perfoliatum

TEUCRIUM *(LAMIACEAE)* – germander
Genus whose most notable characteristic is that the flowers sometimes have no upper lip. Mostly small, ground covering, and shrubby, suitable for the rock garden.

T. hircanicum Z7–10 ↕ **60cm/ 2ft** ⚙ *MSu–MA* ☼

A bushy plant with grey-green, ribbed leaves and long, narrow spikes full of small, reddish purple flowers, which keep branching out and flowering on. Does not survive long, but seeds itself liberally.

TRAGOPOGON *(ASTERACEAE)*
Tall, spindly plants with long, perfoliate, grassy leaves and flowers like dandelions, succeeded by strikingly large balls of fluff. The flowers only open in the morning.

T. porrifolius Z5–10 ↕ **1.2m/ 4ft** ⚙ *ESu–MSu* ☼

Salsify. Has large violet dandelion flowers and still larger fluffy 'clocks' of seeds. Used to be cultivated for its edible roots (salsify). Grows anywhere, but only seeds itself reliably on strong, preferably clay soils.

T. pratensis Z3–10 ↕ **1m/ 3½ft** ⚙ *LSp–LSu* ☼

Goatsbeard. The plant flowers throughout the summer with fairly small, yellow dandelion flowers. The large fluffy seed heads provide the plant's decorative value. *T.p.* subsp. *orientalis* has much larger, orange-yellow flowers. Grows in any kind of soil, preferably not too fertile.

VERBASCUM *(SCROPHULARIACEAE)* – mullein
A genus of tall-growing biennials and short-lived perennials, which form a large rosette of leaves and the following year flower with a tall, rather candle-like, branched spike, densely covered with five-petalled flowers with their bottom petal slightly larger than the other four, and woolly-haired stamens, mostly of some other colour. All species will only grow in well-drained, preferably sandy soil. All seed themselves profusely. The various species easily hybridize among themselves, which is why the specimens found in gardens cannot always be ascribed to a particular species with any certainty. In gardens where more than one species is grown, there are likely to be swarms of hybrids. We list only the most common species (there are far more). We are not sure if we have all the names right; some of those used by commercial growers are not to be found in any of the official flora.

V. blattaria Z3–10 ↕ **1.2m/ 4ft** ⚙ *ESu–LSu* ☼

Moth mullein. Forms a rosette of smooth, dark green, serrated leaves, and flowers with tall spikes, with few or no branches. The pale yellow flowers with purple stamens have short stalks and grow separately on the stem. *V.b.* f. *albiflorum*, with white flowers, is found more frequently.

V. bombyciferum Z6–10 ↕ **1.5m/ 5ft** ⚙ *MSu–LSu* ☼

Both the leaf and the tall, unbranched flower spikes are covered in white down. Yellow flowers with yellow stamens.

V. chaixii Z5–9 ↕ **1.2m/ 4ft** ⚙ *MSu–LSu* ☼

Nettle-leaved mullein. Perennial but in practice short-lived plant which seeds itself about profusely with dark green, short-stemmed, almost hairless leaves and candle-like branched inflorescences of densely packed yellow flowers with purple stamens. 'Album' has white flowers.

V. lychnitis Z3–9 ↕ **1.8m/ 6ft** ⚙ *MSu–LSu* ☼

White mullein. Leaves almost bald on top, with white downy undersides and a white central vein, white downy stems with a plume-shaped inflorescence of small white flowers and white downy stamens. The flower buds look as if they have been dusted with

Above: *Tragopogon pratensis*
Left: *Verbascum lychnitis*
Below: *Verbascum olympicum* with *Angelica archangelica* after flowering

flour. There is also a sterile form of this plant with purple stamens, probably a hybrid.

V. nigrum Z5–9   1.2m/ 4ft   ESu–LSu ☀

Dark mullein. Closely resembles *V. chaixii*, but has an unbranched inflorescence and long-stalked leaves. *V.n.* var. *album* has white flowers. The pure form, without branches, is now hardly ever seen, even growing wild. We mostly have to make do with hybrids, probably with *V. chaixii*, which also now hardly ever occurs in its pure form.

V. olympicum Z6–10   2.5m/ 8ft   MSu–LSu ☀

What we know under this name (with some reservations, as it is probably a hybrid) is a large plant with big, pointed, grey-haired (but not downy) leaves, and an enormous candelabra of yellow flowers. The largest species, impressive.

V. thapsus Z3–9   1.5m/ 5ft   MSu–LSu ☀

Great mullein, Aaron's rod. Species with no branches, downy-haired leaves, and a compact, downy-haired 'torch' of small, yellow flowers. Comparable, but with much larger flowers, are V. *densiflorum* and *V. phlomoides*.

VERBENA *(VERBENACEAE)* – **vervain, verbena**

Short-lived or not fully hardy plants with compound inflorescences, consisting of countless very tiny, five-petalled flowers, which are very popular with butterflies.

V. bonariensis Z8–10   1.5m/ 5ft   MSu–MA ☀

Spindly, sparingly branched plant with rough square stems and small flat inflorescences full of small purple flowers. Goes on flowering for ever and fits in anywhere. Gives up at temperatures below -10°C (12°F), but seeds itself abundantly. After mild winters it becomes a shrubby plant.

V. hastata Z4–8   20cm/ 8in   MSu–EA ☀

Fully hardy, but short-lived, shrubby, branched plant with leaves running to a point and slender spikes turning upwards, full of small, purple flowers. Seeds itself abundantly. The cultivars 'Alba' with white flowers and a lovely autumn colour, and 'Rosea' with pink flowers, seed themselves true to colour, provided the common purple species is nowhere near them.

V. macdougallii Z3–8   1m/ 3½ft   MSu–EA ☀

Similar to *V. hastata*, but with rounded, coarsely toothed leaves and thicker, compact flower spikes.

VIOLA *(VIOLACEAE)*

V. corsica Z6–9   25cm/ 10in   LSp–MA ☀

This chapter, too, should have its viola! *V. corsica* is a short-lived viola (but not an annual) with large purple-blue flowers with narrow petals and a yellow centre, which seeds itself generously in sunny, dry spots. One of a group of violas from the mountains of southern Europe, differing from each other in small details, which also includes *V. gracilis* from Greece and the 'zinc' viola (*V. calaminaria*). This last species is probably also a good garden plant, on acid soil. In any case it certainly thrives vigorously in the Jac. P. Thijssepark in the Dutch town of Amstelveen. The whole group is closely related to the annual three-coloured heartsease (*V. tricolor*), and hybridizes readily with it.

Verbena hastata 'Rosea'

Chenopodium botrys 'Green Magic'
with *Atriplex hortensis* 'Red Plume'

Playful
Annuals

More than perennials or biennials, most annuals need bare soil on which to seed themselves. In a natural garden, in which you try to keep the planting as dense as possible, there is in practice little room for annuals. But in the limited space that exists in spite of this (you are always grubbing about somewhere in the garden) there is a good chance of success with the annuals listed in the next three pages. In general these are large, vigorous annuals, which grow fast enough to hold their own among the perennials. Sometimes you lose them for years, but when you cultivate a new piece of garden again, they suddenly reappear. The seeds of many annuals can remain dormant but viable for years, and rapidly take advantage of any bare soil that becomes available. We do not delude ourselves that the list below is anything like complete. There are thousands of annuals, of which probably a respectably large number are prepared to behave in a 'reliable' fashion in a natural garden. That depends on many factors, of which the availability of bare soil for germination is only one. Another is whether the garden is well established or relatively new: in an existing garden, with plenty of different species, it will be more difficult to introduce new annuals than in a virgin garden. But, in any case, don't let yourself be restricted to the list below: try other kinds of annuals as well.

AGROSTEMMA (CARYOPHYLLACEAE) – corncockle

A. githago Z8–10 ↕ 1m/ 3½ft ESu–MSu ☼

A cornfield weed, almost entirely eliminated in the wild because of its allegedly poisonous seeds. Forms a sparsely branched stem with few leaves and large, single, flat, five-petalled, magenta flowers, about 4cm/1½in across. Very beautiful.

AMBROSINIA see CHENOPODIUM

ARTEMISIA (ASTERACEAE)

A. annua ↕ 2m/ 6½ft MSu–EA ☼

Tall plant with grey-green, finely divided foliage, flowering from top to bottom with small knobs of flowers, of a yellow-green colour. The whole plant smells of fresh herbs, like an old-fashioned flower shop.

ATRIPLEX (CHENOPODIACEAE) – orach

A. hortensis Z6–10 ↕ 1.5m/ 5ft MSu–LSu ☼

An inconspicuous vegetable with typical triangular leaves, a plume of small, green flowers, and surprisingly large, round seeds; it used to be popular as a vegetable (too popular: there is a risk that, in quantities, it might cause kidney stones). Much more effective in the garden is 'Red Plume', which is entirely dark red. Seeds itself profusely, but only in ground which has been turned over and manured.

BORAGO (BORAGINACEAE) – borage

B. officinalis Z5–10 ↕ 60cm/ 2ft LSp–LSu ☼

To quote Rob Leopold: 'A familiar culinary herb, a proven source of honey for bees, with a sky-blue inflorescence of fine, star-shaped flowers, about 2cm/1in across, that can be scattered freely in salad to add to the taste. In a sunny location and rich soil your borage will grow 60cm/2ft high.'

BRASSICA (BRASSICACEAE) – cabbage

B. oleracea Z6–11 ↕ 1.2m/ 4ft MSu–EA ☼

If you let the annual species of *Brassica* (broccoli, cauliflower) or the biennial ones (kale) flower and seed themselves about, you will eventually get the original wild annual form back. This flowers in summer. Yellow and rather coarse, but seeds itself very reliably. Looks very bright and cheerful. Colza and rapeseed (*B. napus*) behave in just the same way, but have rather prettier, deeply indented foliage.

BULBINE (ASPHODELACEAE)

B. annua ↕ 2.5cm/ 1in MSu–EA ☼

A small annual from South Africa with cylindrical grassy foliage and – but only in the morning – small, yellow, star-shaped flowers. Seeds itself abundantly.

BUPLEURUM (APIACEAE)

B. rotundifolium Z6–9 ↕ 60cm/ 2ft ESu–LSu ☼

Thorow-wax, with bowl-like leaves that clasp the stems, and yellow-green flower heads above equally bowl-like involucral bracts. Popular in flower shops, it also fits anywhere in the garden.

CALENDULA (ASTERACEAE) – pot marigold

C. arvensis Z9–10 ↕ 30cm/ 1ft ESu–LSu ☼

We limit ourselves to the wild form of *Calendula*, which seeds itself about wonderfully and creeps through everywhere with its tiny, bright yellow flowers, about 1cm/½in across. But if you think that you can do anything with the familiar, large marigolds, go ahead.

Above: *Helenium* 'Kupferzwerg' with (on the right) *Atriplex hortensis* in front of *Artemisia lactiflora* Guizhou Group
Below: *Claytonia sibirica*

CHENOPODIUM (CHENOPODIACEAE)

C. botrys 'Green Magic' ↕ 1.2m/ 4ft MSu–MA ☼

A spindly plant with small, three-pointed leaves, covered all over with small, pale green knots of flowers. The plant is covered in glandular hairs and has an exotic herbal smell, like incense.

CLAYTONIA (PORTULACACEAE) – purslane

C. sibirica ↕ 40cm/ 16in LSp–LSu

Pink purslane. A plant with lozenge-shaped leaves on fragile stems and small, pink flowers, about 1cm/½in across, which can spread aggressively in shady gardens. A good ground-cover plant.

117

Top: *Impatiens glandulifera* 'Candida'
Bottom: *Nicotiana langsdorffii* with *Eupatorium purpureum*
subsp. *maculatum* 'Purple Bush'

COLLOMIA (*POLEMONIACEAE*)

C. grandiflora   60cm/2ft   MSu–LSu

To quote Rob Leopold: 'First it is a soft yellow, later it has a very delicate melon-pink or apricot colour, and the small flowers are in dense flower heads, about 7.5cm/3in across, on slender, firm stems. A noble annual. Do, please, use it somewhere.' But if you do use it, you will never be rid of it! It always seeds itself somewhere in the garden.

CONSOLIDA (*RANUNCULACEAE*) – larkspur

C. regalis   50cm/20in   ESu–LSu

Rare cornfield weed. A slender plant, flowering abundantly with delphinium-like spurs, mostly bright blue, sometimes white or pink. The only larkspur that does not suffer from slug attack. Seeds itself about particularly well on turned-over and manured soil.

IMPATIENS (*BALSAMINACEAE*) – balsam

I. glandulifera Z9–10   2m/6½ft   MSu–MA

Giant balsam is a plant most people don't want in their gardens because it self-seeds so excessively. But it is a nice plant for shady gardens, because it flowers abundantly at a time when little else is happening in the shade, with thick, hollow stems, turning red, and dark pink, spurred, two-lipped flowers, dangling on thin stalks, beloved by bumblebees. Notorious for its exploding seeds and a characteristic sickly smell. *I.g.* 'Candida' is a pale green plant with white flowers. It can be kept well under control, because superfluous seedlings are easy to remove. *I. balfourii* appears to behave like the rest of the species, but stays much more compact (60cm/2ft) and has pale pink flowers with a white throat.

LACTUCA (*ASTERACEAE*) – lettuce

L. sativa Z7–11   1m/3½ft   MSu–LSu

Lettuce? Yes, lettuce. If you let lettuce plants bolt they produce stiff rising flower spikes with a richly branched cluster of tiny dandelion flowers, opening only in the morning. That is fun, but it is breathtakingly lovely in the purple-leaved forms, such as 'Lollo Rosso', which seed themselves true to colour.

LIMNANTHES (*LIMNANTHACEAE*)

L. douglasii Z8–10   15cm/6in   LSp–LSu

Poached egg plant. A low, widely spreading plant covered with large, white flowers with a yellow centre, crawling with bees and butterflies. Grows and seeds itself anywhere, but does best on damp soil.

LOPEZIA (*ONAGRACEAE*) – Mickey Mouse plant

L. racemosa   50cm/20in   ESu–MA

A shrubby plant, which goes on branching out while it is in flower. Has silly little pink flowers, hardly visible, but with two larger petals sticking up above the rest, like Mickey Mouse ears. Seeds itself about well, but beware: the young seedlings with their small, insignificant leaves look like weeds.

NICANDRA (*SOLANACEAE*) – apple of Peru

N. physalodes   2m/6½ft   MSu–MA

An enormous plant, as wide as it is high, and long-flowering with soft blue flowers in lantern-like calyces. 'Black Pod' has black-spotted leaves, black calyces and darker blue flowers. A muck-heap weed that also displays its impressive talents best on well-manured soil. It will only seed itself where there are quantities of manure. Sometimes you lose it for years, but if you spread your own compost anywhere in the garden, there it is again.

NICOTIANA *(SOLANACEAE)* – **tobacco plant**
Large coarse-leaved plants with tubular flowers. They grow best on heavy, well-manured soil. There are many species suitable for the garden; we find those mentioned below the most beautiful. They seed themselves spontaneously, but (again) only on heavy, well-manured soil, on which they sort themselves out very effectively.

N. langsdorffii Z9–11 — 1.5m/5ft MSu–MA ☀
Forms many long arching stalks full of dangling, small, greenish-yellow tubular flowers with blue stamens.

N. sylvestris Z9–11 — 2m/6½ft MSu–MA ☀
Has leaves up to 60cm/2ft long, and large clusters of dangling, pure white tubular flowers up to 8cm/3in long, with a sweet smell in the evening.

NIGELLA *(RANUNCULACEAE)*

N. damascena Z8–10 — 60cm/2ft ESu–LSu ☀
Love-in-a-mist. A very popular plant with sky-blue flowers nestling in delicate, very finely divided calyces, succeeded by vivid green seed pods.

PAPAVER *(PAPAVERACEAE)* – **poppy**

P. rhoeas Z5–9 — 75cm/30in ESu–MSu ☀
The true poppy, which seeds itself abundantly on sandy soil, best, of course, on soil that has been turned over. Some of the large-flowered cultivars are especially delightful: the 'Mother of Pearl' strain, for instance, produces poppies in grey, soft blue, lilac, apricot, old rose, and a marvellous red and white, with the colours running into each other. They are quite sophisticated enough for a mixed border. Then there are the Reverend Wilks's Shirley poppies, which range over the whole spectrum from bright red to pure white. Sow them all mixed up for a brief but stunning display of summer fireworks.

P. somniferum Z8–10 — 1m/3½ft   ESu–MSu ☀
The familiar opium poppy, with large, billowing, grey-blue leaves, and large, white to pale lilac flowers with a centre of thick stamens where bees crowd in the morning, when the flowers have just opened, stoned out of their minds – does the pollen also contain opium? They are succeeded by fat, grey-blue seed pods. There are many cultivars, all of which grow well from seed when they are not too close to any other colours. One selection, 'Danebrog', has fringed scarlet flowers with bold white basal blotches; 'Giganteum' produces extra-large seed pods and delicate pink and lilac flowers; in 'Hen and Chickens' the main seed case is surrounded by a crowd of smaller ones, and 'Paeoniiflorum' are the double forms, which exist in all colours of the rainbow.

PHACELIA *(HYDROPHYLLACEAE)*

P. tanacetifolia Z9–11 — 50cm/20in   ESu–LSu ☀
Fiddleneck. Grown as a food for bees, but not to be scorned as a garden plant, with hairy, double pinnate leaves and small, purple-blue flowers in wide, curling cymes. There are many other – and even more beautiful – species of *Phacelia*, but they do not seed themselves so easily.

RAPHANUS *(BRASSICACEAE)* – **radish**

R. sativus Z6–10 — 1.2m/4ft   LSp–EA ☀
Leave a radish to bolt some time and you will be surprised! It becomes a tall, rather untidy plant that flowers endlessly with white, sometimes pale pink flowers and beautiful, bobbly, inflated fruits (siliquas), like peanuts. Seedlings do not retain the thickened root (the radish) of the parent.

Papaver rhoeas Shirley poppies with *Agrostemma githago*

SILYBUM *(ASTERACEAE)* – **milk thistle**

S. marianum Z8–11 — 20cm/8in   MSu–LSu ☀
Has enormous, prickly, but beautifully glossy, dark green leaves with striking white marbling and purple-red thistle flowers. Seeds itself about moderately, but you can't fail to recognize the seedling.

VIOLA *(VIOLACEAE)*

V. tricolor Z5–10 — 25cm/10in   LSp–MA ☀
The familiar three-coloured heartsease, which seeds itself everywhere and all the time, and is ever welcome. Always multicoloured, but very variable, every seedling has a different signature. *V.* 'Bowles' Black' has dark purple, almost black flowers with a little yellow heart, and grows well from seed.

Agastache rugosa

Verbena hastata with *Molinia caerulea* subsp. *arundinacea* 'Transparent'

After flowering

As summer wears on, the garden gradually loses its colour and its shapes become more abstract. The colours fade until it resembles a rough charcoal drawing, and in winter it finally hardens into an engraving.

You need to take this into account before you begin planning your garden, since plants are out of flower for most of the year. You can, of course, run recklessly around with a pruning knife, cutting down everything that has finished flowering, to make it look as if it is always spring. But before you know it, autumn has arrived, and you end up spending the whole winter looking at a bare expanse of earth. This is not what natural gardening is about. In a natural garden everything should be allowed to finish flowering, not simply to please butterflies and birds, but also because plants in decline can be beautiful: the leaves of the *Inula* turning into coarse doormats, the orange-brown skeletons of the parsnip's top growth, and the black shapes of *Eupatorium* and *Veronicastrum*.

We have sometimes been criticized for putting too much emphasis on plants that have finished flowering, and on winter silhouettes. Some people have attributed this to a fashionable *fin de siècle* feeling, or worse, to a morbid obsession with the impending 'end of time'. Nothing could be further from the truth. The basic link between death and life is quite clear to any nature lover, and there is certainly nothing morbid about it. We find it an intolerable notion that a garden should not reflect this link, and that it should always appear to be spring. There is great beauty in plants that have finished flowering. The evidence is all around you.

Stachys officinalis

Euphorbia griffithii 'Dixter'

This is by far the most exciting section of this book, since it is addressed first and foremost to the fanatics among our readers: those who spend all their 'leisure' time in the garden and like rolling up their sleeves. That will certainly be necessary if you want to incorporate plants from this section. You need nerves of steel for the invasive plants in this chapter, bright green fingers for the capricious ones and an iron discipline for the demanding ones. This section may also be of interest to less fanatical gardeners. It is about very beautiful plants, which can greatly enrich a natural garden. But be warned!

Troublesome Invasive plants

Invasive plants are particularly suitable for a natural garden, because they give it a 'wild' appearance in the shortest possible time. In the wild they are among the most striking plants because they often dominate large areas. Just think of the splendid patches of rosebay willow herb on sandy soils. In gardens, particularly when the garden is a small one, they can be a considerable nuisance, and you should think twice before you include them. You will be kept constantly busy restraining them, to prevent them swamping all the other plants in the garden. On lighter soils, such as sand, that is not such a problem, because you can usually pull the runners out of the ground very easily, but on heavier soils, such as clay, you should think not twice, but ten times before you introduce them. However, there are some lovely species, and the true fanatic never shrinks from them.

ANAPHALIS *(ASTERACEAE)*

A. margaritacea Z3–8 ↕ 60cm/2ft MSu–EA

Pearly everlasting. Resembles *A. triplinervis* (see the 'Tough' section), but is less rigid and more adaptable. Particularly at home in humus-rich woodland soil in half-shade, the plant gently encroaches on other plants, without becoming a nuisance.

ANEMONE *(RANUNCULACEAE)* – **windflower**

A. canadensis Z3–7 ↕ 50cm/20in LSp–ESu

A vigorously invasive species for moisture-retaining soil, with virtually hairless, deeply indented leaves, and cheerful white anemone flowers rising above them.

A. sylvestris Z4–9 ↕ 30cm/1ft LSp–ESu

Looks like a large-flowered, hairy version of the common wood anemone, but flowers later and thrives in dry, sunny places, despite its Latin name (*sylvestris* means 'of the woods'). Often flowers again later in the summer. 'Macrantha' has larger flowers. In stronger types of soil, such as clay, the plant is less invasive than on sandy soil.

ARTEMISIA *(ASTERACEAE)*

A. ludoviciana Z4–9 ↕ 1.2m/4ft MSu–LSu

A tall, upright species with silver grey, willowy leaves. Needs dry, not too rich conditions or it becomes too untidy. Spreads everywhere by thin runners.

A. pontica Z5–9 ↕ 50cm/20in ☼

Roman wormwood. A strongly invasive species with filigree-like,

silver-grey leaves. Good for plugging gaps, but not combined with other plants; if these are larger, the artemisia disappears (it will not tolerate being overshadowed at all), if they are smaller, it drives them out.

ASPERULA *(RUBIACEAE)* – **bedstraw**

A. taurina Z4–9 ↕ 40cm/16in LSp–ESu

Resembles an outsize lady's bedstraw, but with broad leaves and sweet-smelling flowers. Spreads considerably.

ASTER *(ASTERACEAE)*

A. umbellatus Z3–8 ↕ 1.8m/6ft LSu–EA

Forms sturdy stems, rising straight up, with narrow leaves and flattened heads of small, white daisies. A lovely silhouette in winter. Spreads extensively, seeds itself about – in short, quite indestructible. Can even hold its own against stinging nettles.

CAMPANULA *(CAMPANULACEAE)* – **bellflower**

C. punctata Z4–8 ↕ 30cm/1ft ● ESu–MSu ☼

In sunny spots on dry, sandy soil, this plant thrives mightily and flowers with striking, large, cream-coloured bells, dotted with red inside. On other soils or in shade the plant falls prey to slugs. Important as the parent of a number of fine cultivars (see the 'Tough' section).

C. rapunculoides Z3–8 ↕ 80cm/32in MSu–LSu ☼ ▨

An invasive cornfield weed, not a garden plant. Has particularly nasty characteristics: if you leave the plant alone, it does not flower.

Anemone sylvestris 'Macrantha' with
Euphorbia characias

Epilobium angustifolium var. *album* with *Filipendula rubra* 'Venusta'

If you then want to get rid of it, you can't: it has runners like rubber bands. Any runners that remain promptly start to flower: pretty, with a tall spike of lavender-blue bells. If you then leave the plant alone, it does not flower again. It will never be a success. Get rid of it (if you can).

CHAMAENERION see EPILOBIUM

CORONILLA *(PAPILIONACEAE)*

C. varia Z6–10 1m/ 3½ft   ESu–LSu

Crown vetch. The common crown vetch is a brilliant plant for dry, limy soil. With tall, slender stalks carrying delicate pink-and-white spherical flower heads, it forms immense mounds, thronged with bees and butterflies. In fact it is an important food source for threatened species of butterfly such as the pale clouded yellow, the brown hisperia, skippers and blues. Plant it. Only one comment: you have to have room for it, because the plant is very invasive.

DORONICUM *(ASTERACEAE)* – **leopard's bane**

D. pardalianches Z4–8 1m/ 3½ft   MSp–MSu

A beautiful wild woodland plant: with its tuber-like roots it creeps between trees, shrubs and thin grass and produces long-lasting yellow daisies on tall stems. Quite different from the stiff, short-flowering leopard's bane which you see everywhere in front gardens. In the long run it forms flat clumps, covering large areas, but it is not aggressive; it grows comfortably among other ground cover. 'Goldstrauss' has larger flowers, but, for that reason, collapses.

EPILOBIUM *(ONAGRACEAE)* – **willow herb**

E. angustifolium Z3–7 1.5m/ 5ft ESu–LSu

Rosebay willow herb is beautiful, but fiercely invasive, particularly on

acid, dry soil. The wild form, with its tall spikes of pinkish red flowers, is well known. Don't introduce it, it's too much like hard work! If you have seen the white-flowering form, *E.a.* var. *album*, or the soft pink 'Stahl Rose', then you are smitten. But they mean a lot of work too! *E.p.* var. *album* also has much whiter seed clocks than the common form.

EQUISETUM *(EQUISETACEAE)* – **horsetail**

E. hyemale Z5–10 1.2m/ 4ft   MSp–LSp

Horsetails are living fossils; survivors from the carboniferous age; dinosaurs of the plant kingdom. They do not flower, but in the spring form egg-shaped sporangias at the end of their stems. The familiar field horsetail (*E. arvense*) is a troublesome, almost ineradicable weed. Rough horsetail (*E. hyemale*) is also invasive, but is – in moist shady areas – reasonably easy to control. It forms a forest of evergreen, hollow, segmented, blue-grey spikes, about 1cm/½in thick – very prehistoric. The stems are not too closely packed, so other plants can grow up between them.

EUPHORBIA *(EUPHORBIACEAE)* – **spurge, milkweed**

E. cyparissias Z3–9 25cm/ 10in LSp–MSu

Cypress spurge. Rapidly forms dense carpets, like a ground-cover conifer, flowers with cheerful, yellow-green umbels in the spring and dies off with the most splendid autumn colours. Most attractive on barren, dry soil. 'Fens Ruby' emerges purple in spring.

E. griffithii Z4–9 80cm/ 32in LSp–ESu

Quite the opposite of the previous species, this one is most attractive in moist, peaty soil, with narrow, dull green leaves and luminous orange-red flowers and calyces. 'Fireglow' is the most readily available, 'Dixter' also has red leaves underneath that fiery display.

FILIPENDULA *(ROSACEAE)* – *meadowsweet, queen of the prairie*

F. rubra 'Venusta' Z3–9 ↕ **1.8m/ 6ft**   **MSu-LSu**

Martha Washington's plume. Spreads vigorously; a large type of meadowsweet with pink plumes on overhanging branches, at least on moist soil. On drier soil the plant grows less tall and stays stiffly erect. After flowering it provides a sublime winter silhouette.

GALEGA *(PAPILIONACEAE)* – **goat's rue**

A large, untidy plant, like a giant vetch. At least that is true of the familiar *G. officinalis*, which has been condemned by us to the short chapter on 'Demanding plants'. Tidier, but also very invasive, is:

G. orientalis Z5–8 ↕ **1.2m/ 4ft**   **ESu-MSu**

Erect, upright stalks and sky-blue clusters of flowers, about 15cm/6in long. It is very beautiful, particularly on good, moisture-retaining soil and it also flowers far longer there.

GERANIUM *(GERANIACEAE)* – **cranesbill**

G. clarkei Z4–8 ↕ **40cm/ 16in**   **LSp-MSu**

A profusely flowering species with divided, feather-like, indented leaves, which slowly but surely creeps in everywhere. 'Kashmir Purple' has violet-coloured flowers and 'Kashmir White' white ones, both with red veining. Pretty, but can be a bit of a nuisance.

G. nodosum Z5–8 ↕ **35cm/ 14in**   **LSp-EA**

A very vigorous plant, invasive to some extent, and seeding itself around liberally, with shiny green, angular, indented leaves. It goes on flowering endlessly with lilac-blue flowers, and does so everywhere, even in dry shade.

GEUM *(ROSACEAE)* – **avens**

A large genus of woodland and mountain plants, very few of which are suitable for the garden. The spherical seed heads, full of hooked seeds like nails, are a striking feature.

G. rivale Z3–8 ↕ **25–40cm/ 10–16in**   **ESp-ESu**

Water avens. The nodding water avens grows in the wild only in boggy places, but in the garden, even on dry soil, it is an aggressive invader. The following cultivars – all charming spring flowers in pink/brown/apricot – are not invasive, but only grow well on damp, humus-rich soil: 'Beach House Apricot', ' Carlskaer', ' Coppertone' and 'Leonard's Variety'.

HOUTTUYNIA *(SAURURACEAE)*

H. cordata Z5–9 ↕ **45cm/ 18in**

In damp, sheltered places this can really run amok, but in hard winters frost puts an end to it. On dry soil the plant pines away in a short time. Strange plants from a strange genus with strange flowers; inconspicuous, green, in a small cube, supported by four to six creamy white bracts, with stems covered in fine, heart-shaped leaves. 'Flore Pleno' has a large number of bracts (just like real flowers) and 'Chameleon' has leaves with red-yellow-bronze-green markings. Pretty in a pot, but just imagine what might happen if it got out and started invading . . . Everyone is free to ruin his own border, we add diplomatically.

LYSIMACHIA *(PRIMULACEAE)* – **loosestrife**

Plants with regular five-petalled flowers, grouped in bunches in the axils of the leaves, and together forming a spike, sometimes a compact one. All the species mentioned in this book are invasive, and prefer moisture-retaining soil. A fine, less invasive species, like *L. ephemerum*, is on closer acquaintance too ephemeral for us.

Above: *Galega orientalis*
Below: *Geum rivale* 'Leonard's Variety'

L. ciliata Z3–9   ↕ 1m/ ↓ 3½ft   MSu–LSu
Fringed loosestrife. A beautiful plant with dark green leaves in whorls of three round the stems, and nodding, lemon-yellow flowers. 'Firecracker' has chocolate-coloured foliage. It also grows well on drier soil, and then stays a bit lower, but is also easier to keep under control.

L. clethroides Z4–9   ↕ 80cm/ ↓ 32in   ESu–LSu
Gooseneck loosestrife. Has white flowers on a tall, compact spike bending over at the tip. Long-flowering and very popular with butterflies.

L. punctata Z4–8   ↕ 1m/ ↓ 3½ft   MSu–LSu
Dotted loosestrife. A coarse plant with leaves in whorls of four round the stem, and rather dull yellow flowers.

L. vulgaris Z5–9   ↕ 1.5m/ ↓ 5ft   MSu–LSu
Yellow loosestrife. The bright yellow flowers are combined into a terminal plume, and the leaves are in whorls of three round the stem. A European native, but not more invasive than *L. punctata*, and more decorative.

MACLEAYA *(PAPAVERACEAE)* – **plume poppy**

M. microcarpa Z4–9   ↕ 2.5m/ ↓ 8ft   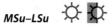 MSu–LSu
An impressive plant, which in spite of its height never falls over, with large, lobed, waxy blue-grey leaves, silver-grey underneath, and beige flowers in plumes that brighten to orange in the evening sun. Prettiest in dry, well-drained soil, and also easier to keep in check there. On heavy ground that is almost impossible. Its colour and shape make it very adaptable; apart from its invasive habit, it is one of the best garden plants there is. 'Kelway's Coral Plume' has a rather stronger colour. The true *M. cordata*, with white flowers, is considered to be a non-invasive plant – or nearly so.

MENTHA *(LAMIACEAE)*

All species of mint are troublesome, invasive plants with little decorative value, cultivated principally for their aromatic leaves. Nice to have, but in a contained section of the herb garden, not in borders. However, the continual battle you would have to wage with mint in the border would perhaps be worthwhile with the following species (and that alone):

M. longifolia 'Buddleia' Z6–9   ↕ 80cm/ ↓ 32in   MSu–LSu
Buddleia mint. This grey-leaved selection with lilac spikes is more decorative, but less aromatic, than other types of mint. Plant in good, moisture-retentive garden soil. Unlike most other herbs, mint does not like dry conditions.

NEPETA *(LAMIACEAE)* – **catmint**

N. sibirica Z4–8   ↕ 1m/ ↓ 3½ft   ESu–LSu
Syn. *Dracocephalum sibiricum*. A troublesome plant, very invasive and also liable to collapse. But yes, so beautiful, it will be worth all the trouble. Long-flowering with sizeable plumes full of large, purple-blue, two-lipped flowers. On heavier, moisture-retentive soils the roots do not penetrate so deeply and its invasive habit is reasonably easy to keep in check, but on dry, well-drained soil the root runners go so deep that you have very little chance of getting them out. 'Souvenir d'André Chaudron' is more compact, so shows less tendency to fall over, and should also be less invasive.

PERSICARIA *(POLYGONACEAE)* – **knotweed**

P. bistorta Z4–8   ↕ 60cm/ ↓ 2ft   LSp–ESu
Bistort, sweet dock. A vigorously spreading plant that thrives in any

moisture-retentive soil, with numerous elongated shiny leaves and delicate pink flower spikes on almost leafless stems. The species is much to be preferred above the cultivar, 'Superba', which has a spike so heavy that the plant falls over.

P. wallichii Z4–9   ↕ 1.8m/ ↓ 6ft   EA–MA
Syn. *P. polystachya*. A powerful invader in moisture-retentive soil, not suitable for a border. Better as a specimen in grass, so that you can mow round it. Forms a mass of luxuriant, pointed leaves and produces many cream-coloured, scented flower plumes in the autumn.

PETASITES *(ASTERACEAE)* – **butterbur** Z5–9

Unstoppable invaders which, thanks to their enormous leaves, up to 1m/3½ft wide, and early spring flowering, still enjoy a certain amount of popularity. But in the course of the summer those leaves will be destroyed by slugs, and the plant cannot be held in check, particularly on fertile soil. So don't use it – there are better large foliage plants (*Darmera*, for a start). This applies notably to the pink-flowering *P. hybridus* and the yellow-green-flowering *P. japonicus*. In all respects smaller and also to some extent more controllable is *P. albus*, with white flowers as early as the end of winter.

PHYSALIS *(SOLANACEAE)* – **Chinese lantern**

P. alkekengi var. *franchetii* Z5–8   ↕ 1m/ ↓ 3½ft   ESu–EA
It is the large, bright orange, inflated calyces, just like Chinese lanterns, that make this plant so decorative. Otherwise it is untidy and unremarkable, and in addition very invasive. Not suitable for a border, but fine for some forgotten corner. Needs well-drained soil.

PHYSOSTEGIA *(LAMIACEAE)* – **obedient plant**

P. virginiana Z4–8   ↕ 1.2m/ ↓ 4ft   MSu–MA
An attractive, erect plant with narrow leaves and thin spikes of pink, two-lipped flowers, which are quite willing to be twined in another direction. Forms a compact bush, which in time spreads to such an extent that the plant merits a place in this chapter. 'Summer Snow' flowers white, 'Summer Spire' a vivid carmine-pink. Both cultivars flower earlier in the summer than the common species.

SAMBUCUS *(CAPRIFOLIACEAE)* – **elder**

S. ebulus Z3–9   ↕ 1.5m/ ↓ 5ft   MSu–LSu
Dwarf elder. Grows only on a heavy, clay soil. And how! It pushes out all other plants in the vicinity, so don't plant it in a border. Very pretty, with characteristic compound elder leaves and wide clusters of creamy white flowers, followed by black (poisonous) berries on dark red stalks. Does not turn woody, so disappears completely below ground in winter.

SAPONARIA *(CARYOPHYLLACEAE)* – **soapwort**

S. officinalis Z4–8   ↕ 70cm/ ↓ 28in   MSu–EA
Bouncing Bet. An amusing plant, but one really for a wild garden, as it spreads untidily. On well-drained soil it forms enormous mats with large, pale pink clusters of phlox-like flowers. 'Rosea Plena', with double flowers, blooms even more handsomely.

SENECIO *(ASTERACEAE)* – **ragwort, groundsel**

S. fluviatilis Z6–9   ↕ 1.5m/ ↓ 5ft   MSu–EA
Broad-leaved ragwort. Vigorously spreading plant for any moisture-retentive garden soil, with straight, erect stems with narrow leaves and wide umbels of bright yellow daisy flowers. Very attractive grown in large clumps.

Above: *Lysimachia clethroides*
Below: *Macleaya microcarpa*

Above: *Persicaria wallichii*
Below: *Nepeta sibirica*

Above: *Symphytum azureum*
Below: *Thermopsis montana*

SINACALIA *(ASTERACEAE)*

S. tangutica *Z6–9* 1.5m/5ft LSu–MA

Syn. *Senecio tanguticus*. Chinese ragwort. Beautiful, but a troublesome and invasive plant for damp, peaty soil, with irregular, deeply cut leaves and pointed plumes of small yellow flowers, succeeded by splendid fluffy seed heads.

SOLIDAGO *(ASTERACEAE)* – **goldenrod**

S. gigantea *Z3–10* 1.5m/5ft LSu–EA

This is the species that flowers so attractively on railway embankments. In gardens you see yet more examples, mainly hybrids. But, however hard we try, we can't admire them. Let's leave it at that.

STACHYS *(LAMIACEAE)* – **woundwort**

S. sylvatica *Z3–9* 1m/3½ft ESu–MSu

Hedge woundwort. There is something to be said for having this plant in the garden, with its deep dark red spike-like inflorescence which fits in everywhere. There is also something against it: its invasiveness is not too bad, since the runners have shallow roots and so are easy to remove, but the plant grows so fast that it is almost impossible to control it. Moreover, it seeds itself everywhere. If you still want the plant in your black-and-red colour scheme, we wish you luck!
S. palustris is similar and behaves identically, but with its unremarkable lilac-pink flowers lacks the special appeal of *S. sylvatica*.

SUCCISELLA *(DIPSACACEAE)*

S. inflexa *Z3–9* 80cm/32in LSu–MA

A long-flowering plant with small, pale blue spherical flowers, about 2cm/1in long, on tall stems above rosettes of narrow, pale green leaves. Attracts lots of butterflies and other insects. Because the plant forms runners above ground, it is easy to keep in check. Seeds itself on a grand scale, but the seedlings, too, are easy to remove.

SYMPHYTUM *(BORAGINACEAE)* – **comfrey**

S. azureum *Z4–9* 50cm/20in MSp–LSp

Unstoppably invasive species with grey-blue leaves, flowering vigorously with azure blue flowers in cymes. Only suitable for growing wild in grass or between shrubs.

S. ibericum *Z4–9* 40cm/16in MSp–LSp

Syn. *S. grandiflorum*. Evergreen ground cover for the shady garden, with whitish yellow, or sometimes pale blue or pale pink flowers. Easy to keep under control, as is *S. tuberosum* with its pale yellow flowers. Both species have problems in a hard winter.

TANACETUM *(ASTERACEAE)* – **tansy**

T. vulgare *Z3–9* 1.2m/4ft MSu–LSu

Garden soil is usually too fertile for this fiercely invasive species: it grows too high and falls over. Only suitable for growing wild in lean grassland.

TEUCRIUM *(LAMIACEAE)* – **germander**

T. scorodonia *Z5–9* 50cm/20in MSu–EA

Wood sage. The strongest point of this plant is that it thrives in dry shade on acid, lime-free soil. There are very few plants of which the same can be said. In a short time, by means of runners and seedlings, it covers a large area with dark green, wrinkled leaves, and it flowers in late summer with spikes of small, pale green flowers, forming a striking background for countless bumblebees.

THERMOPSIS (*PAPILIONACEAE*)

T. montana Z3–8 ↕ **90cm/ 3ft**   **LSp–ESu** ☼

A pretty but invasive species with a cheerful, yellow lupin-like inflorescence in early summer, and afterwards stiff, ascending seed pods, close against the stem. For sunny dry places. Goes well with other invasive plants, such as *Nepeta sibirica*.

TOLMIEA (*SAXIFRAGACEAE*) **– pick-a-back plant**

T. menziesii Z6–9 ↕ **60cm/ 2ft**   **MSp–ESu** ☼☼

Known mainly as a plant for the house, where it never flowers. In the garden it has pretty chocolate-coloured flowers with yellow stamens on tall stems. Hardy in sheltered places among trees and shrubs.

TRACHYSTEMON (*BORAGINACEAE*)

T. orientalis Z5–9 ↕ **50cm/ 20in**   **ESp–MSp** ☼☼

Abraham, Isaac and Jacob. A fast-spreading plant with enormous rough-haired, heart-shaped leaves which does not grow well in wet places. Suitable as ground cover in shade. Produces small, borage-like lavender-blue flowers in clusters before the leaves appear, but the flowers often suffer from late night frosts.

Trachystemon orientalis

Campanula lactiflora seedlings

Troublesome
Capricious plants

It may seem strange to devote a chapter to unreliable plants in a book dealing with reliable ones, but we have several good reasons for doing so. First of all, the chapter is about plants with a strong appeal, which plainly add something to a natural planting: all kinds of species which you might well want to use, bearing in mind doubts about their reliability.

   This brings us to the second reason: it is not as if we know for certain that they are unreliable. In saying that they are unreliable we are not prepared to stake our lives on it. Plants which we know for certain are unreliable are not included in this book. This chapter is about plants that are quite unpredictable: for some people they will grow without problems in the same place for years, for others they just will not 'take', for no clear reason. If a bog plant does not grow in dry sand, that is logical. This chapter is about an unreliability for which there is no rhyme or reason. Several of the plants listed below have grown for years without a murmur in our own gardens, but we know that other people have had great problems in keeping them, while others again complain that they are too invasive.

   In short: these are capricious plants. Plants that we keep on trying, because we think them so beautiful. Plants we think you should try too. Who knows, they may well be reliable in your garden. You never know your luck.

ACHILLEA *(ASTERACEAE)* – milfoil

With the exception of the two species listed elsewhere in this book, we must class all species of *Achillea* as unreliable. This is a great pity, because their characteristic, flat, pancake-like flower heads are, from an architectural point of view, very desirable in a composition, and cannot be replaced by any other species of plant. There are many umbellifers that also have a flat flower head, but they are less dense and architecturally less satisfying.

We do not know if the tall *A. filipendulina* and its cultivars (except for 'Parker's Variety') have ever lasted long anywhere. Fine hybrid cultivars, such as 'Taygetea' and 'Moonshine', sometimes keep shining for years in dry lime-rich locations, and then give up for no particular reason, to say nothing of the many finely coloured *A. millefolium* cultivars. They are quite unpredictable. *A.m.* 'Red Beauty', which is very close to the wild species, does not disappear, but is invasive, and after a few years suddenly acquires white and pale pink flowers among the dark red ones. That is at least something, if rather strange. We know that 'Wesersandstein', which because of its unreliability has not been cultivated anywhere for ages, has in fact survived for fifteen years in the Priona gardens, accompanied by the weed sheep's sorrel, in an extremely acid, dry spot where other garden plants don't want to grow. So perhaps it is possible to grow it after all? Every nursery has a number of attractively coloured cultivars to offer. Don't be discouraged from trying them by our experience. We wish you luck – plenty of it!

Above: *Achillea* 'Feuerland'
Below: *Aster* x *frikartii* 'Mönch'

ASTER *(ASTERACEAE)*

A. amellus Z5–9 60cm/ 2ft MSu–EA

If you like 'real' flowers, you should try this *Aster*, because it has large, strikingly coloured aster flowers with yellow centres. On rich garden soil in full sun it should last for several years. How many, we don't know. The best are 'Rosa Erfüllung', mauve-pink, and 'Sonora', lilac-blue; the latter has so far lasted a full ten years in Hummelo.

A. x frikartii Z5–9 70cm/ 28in MSu–MA

A cross between *A. amellus* and *A. thomsonii*. 'Without doubt this is the finest aster for long display,' says Graham Stuart Thomas of it, and 'It is one of the six best plants, and should be in every garden. (Please do not ask for the names of the other five!)' Of course we would love to know what these other five best garden plants are. We entirely agree that this aster should be in every garden. Unfortunately it will sometimes fail after a hard winter, which is why we put it in this chapter. Then you just have to acquire a new specimen, because it is really fantastic, blooming uninterruptedly from late summer with large violet-blue asters, which are welcome in any combination. All this enthusiasm is exclusively for the cultivar 'Mönch'; the other cultivars usually offered, 'Jungfrau' and 'Wunder von Stäfa', are feebler, both in colour and stem.

Hybrids 1.4–1.6m/ 4½–5¼ft EA–LA

A number of lavishly blooming, small-flowered hybrids have been developed for the cut-flower trade, because they produce a mass of colour. Some of these do well in the garden quite late in the season. In the long run they do not seem to be very persistent, and probably have to be taken up after a few years and divided. 'Herfstweelde' flowers pale lavender-blue with overhanging clusters, 'Ochtendgloren' is a sturdy pale mauve-pink form and 'Oktoberlicht' has wide-spreading stems and white flowers.

CAMPANULA *(CAMPANULACEAE)* – bellflower

C. lactiflora Z4–8 1.6m/ 5¼ft ESu–LSu

Without question this is the most beautiful *Campanula*, flowering long and lavishly with small, but very many bellflowers in sprays. But it is still a bit of a problem. On dry soil the species appears to be fully hardy, but does not flower as beautifully every year: some years the plant does not grow more than 1m/3½ft high before collapsing, and

in other years it forms strong stems of a good 1.5m/5ft that stay firm, and flower throughout the summer. It is not self-seeding on dry soil. On wetter soil, on the other hand, the plant easily dies in winter, but seeds itself profusely. It can justifiably be called capricious. But none other than Graham Stuart Thomas says: 'One of the finest of hardy perennials.' Could it be one of the five species he didn't want to name with *Aster* x *frikartii*? The species flowers lavender-blue, 'Loddon Anna' pale mauve-pink. 'Pouffe' forms a pale blue mound about 45cm/18in high; 'White Pouffe' stays even lower (30cm/1ft) and flowers white.

C. latiloba Z4–8   ↕ **1m/ 3½ft**   **ESu–MSu**

Syn. *C. persicifolia* subsp. *sessiliflora*. Wide open lavender-blue bells are held stiffly against the spikes, over almost its whole length, above pretty rosettes of leaves. *C.l.* 'Alba' flowers white and is taller (1.4m/4½ft); 'Hidcote Amethyst' flowers a soft mauve-pink. Most reliable on good, well-drained soil.

C. persicifolia Z4–8   ↕ **1m/ 3½ft**   **ESu–MSu**

Short-stalked and slightly drooping, and also has less widely open blue bells and narrower leaves. There is a white form of this species, *C.p. alba*. It needs to be divided regularly if it is to go on flowering.

DICENTRA (PAPAVERACEAE)

Pretty and familiar they may be, but we dare not stake our lives on *Dicentra*. They are perennial and grow well in almost any soil, but for some reason sooner or later they will disappear. Their competitive strength leaves something to be desired: they need to be pampered. (Lift them, put new soil under them, and maybe they will recover.)

D. formosa Z4–8   ↕ **40cm/ 16in**   **LSp–ESu**

Beautiful plants with fern-like indented leaves and clusters of pink flowers like small medallions. There are some fine cultivars with grey or metallic leaves, but we do not mention them, because they all have the same problem: within a few years they grow into enormous clumps and then suddenly they are gone. Why?

D. spectabilis Z3–8   ↕ **60cm/ 2ft**   **MSp–ESu**

Bleeding heart. There is good reason for the Latin species name *spectabilis*, for spectacular they are, with their fine indented leaves and dangling pinkish red hearts, split in two – at least, when you are successful, for they are very sensitive to late night frosts. A cool, but sheltered spot, good soil and regular manuring should guarantee a long life (they say). *D.s.* 'Alba' flowers a dazzling white and is, if possible, even more beautiful.

ECHINACEA (ASTERACEAE)

E. purpurea Z4–9   ↕ **1m/ 3½ft**   **MSu–EA**

Purple coneflower. It is extremely frustrating to have to admit that *Echinacea* is not reliable, with its spectacular, bright pinkish red, large daisy flowers with orange-brown raised centres, swarming with butterflies. They will not tolerate any competition from neighbouring plants: within two years they will have disappeared. If you keep the soil around the plant bare and make sure that it consists of rich, well-drained leaf mould, they will last longer. But that hardly fits the idea of a natural garden. Why then do we list them? Because we, too, keep buying new plants and putting them in gaps in the border: at least we get one summer's pleasure from them, which is something. And we keep hoping, against our better judgement, that in the end we will be able to find the right spot for them, where they will be blessed with a long and happy life. Do we have to resign ourselves to the fact that our winters are too wet and our summers not warm enough for them? Or should we hope that the advent of global warming will – as far as *Echinacea* is concerned – also have some benefits in store? While there is life, there is hope.

To add to the agony, we also give the names of a few cultivars, which are even more beautiful than the common species: 'Green

Above: *Campanula latiloba* 'Hidcote Amethyst'
Below: *Echinacea purpurea* with a comma butterfly

Edge' flowers white with a trace of green and fine petals projecting outwards, 'Rubinglow' with larger flowers, and 'Rubinstern' with redder and flatter projecting petals. More are steadily being selected. Perhaps one day there will be a form, possibly crossed with one of its sisters (*E. angustifolia, E. pallida* or the yellow-flowering *E. paradoxa*) which we will be able confidently to call dependable.

ERIGERON (ASTERACEAE) – fleabane

Hybrids *Z5–8*   ↕ 50cm/20in   ESu–MA   ☼

Amusing plants with large daisy-like flowers with countless very fine ray-florets and a yellow heart. 'Dunkelste Aller' flowers purple, 'Sommerneuschnee' white. Intolerant of competition. 'Among the most popular, prolific and easy of hardy perennials,' says Graham Stuart Thomas. But you will need to lift them every few years, divide them and plant again.

EUPHORBIA (EUPHORBIACEAE) – spurge

Without much difficulty we could give a summary here of a large number of Asiatic species, each one more delicate than the next, all of which will either just survive in cooler climates or maybe not. However, we will limit ourselves to a trio of closely related species, which on good, well-drained soil will grow reasonably well, but – because occasionally a plant dies without reason – cannot be given the adjective 'reliable'. They owe their greatest garden value to the fact that, unlike most other species of *Euphorbia*, they flower in summer. All three species have a wide, richly branched, yellow-green inflorescence and a quantity of narrow leaves with a striking white midrib. *E. cognata* grows thinly up to about 50cm/20in, *E. schillingii*, probably the most reliable, becomes tall (1.2m/4ft), with the young shoots a transparent red, and *E. cornigera* is a compact plant, 45cm/18in, which flowers profusely.

GYPSOPHILA (CARYOPHYLLACEAE) – baby's breath

Familiar plants which produce clouds of small white flowers. They are popular in bouquets. You might also want to scatter them through your borders, but that will only be successful on a heavy type of soil (clay), which is well-drained with plenty of gravel in it. Stagnant water and high humidity are absolutely taboo. When all the conditions are right they can live to a ripe old age.

G. altissima *Z3–9*   ↕ 1.6m/5¼ft   MSu–EA   ☼

A tall species with a limited show of small, whitish-pink flowers.

G. paniculata *Z4–9*   ↕ 80cm/32in   MSu–EA   ☼

The most familiar species: one enormous cloud of tiny white flowers. Rather more effective – the form usually used for bouquets – is the double-flowered cultivar 'Bristol Fairy', but this is fairly short-lived.

G. 'Rosenschleier' *Z4–9*   ↕ 35cm/14in   ESu–EA   ☼

A low-growing pink cloud with double flowers, for filling in gaps.

SALVIA (LAMIACEAE) – sage

S. azurea *Z5–9*   ↕ 1.8m/6ft   MA–LA   ☼

A tall, rather leggy plant which in a warm spot and after a hot summer flowers an incredible azure blue, with racemes of small flowers, at a time when the rest of the garden has withered. Is fully hardy, but does not flower well everywhere.

S. hians *Z6–9*   ↕ 80cm/32in   ESu   ☼

A beautiful species from the Himalayas and therefore sensitive to too much damp in winter. Very sturdy, with large purple-blue flowers with a white lower lip.

Salvia hians

Above: *Selinum wallichianum*
Below: *Sidalcea* 'My Love'

SELINUM (*APIACEAE*)

S. wallichianum Z6–9 1m/ 3½ft MSu–MA

Formerly described as *S. tenuifolium*, but that has proved to be a different species. Perhaps the most beautiful umbellifer there is, with lacy, finely divided leaves and a mass of greenish-white flower heads in late summer, or, in other words, a large, wide and long-lasting cloud of refinement, which fits in anywhere. What a pity that we can't issue a certificate of guarantee for it.

SIDALCEA (*MALVACEAE*) – **prairie mallow Z5–8**

A summer-flowering border plant with silky shining flowers, like a small, single hollyhock. Grows best on a heavy type of soil, but even then we can give no guarantee of good behaviour. The strongest species is the slightly invasive (for as long as it lasts) white-flowering *S. candida*; the strongest cultivars seem to be the pink 'My Love' and the reddish pink 'Oberon', which is even better than the familiar pale pink 'Elsie Heugh'. All species grow to about 1m/3½ft, the greatest chance of success being – again – on very good soil. On sandy soil it is not even worth starting.

VERONICA (*SCROPHULARIACEAE*) – **speedwell**

V. spicata Z4–8 50cm/ 20in ESu–EA

A lovely plant, with a spike-like inflorescence densely packed with truly blue flowers. 'Spitzentraum' has grey foliage as well. The hybrid cultivar 'Pink Damask' grows taller (80cm/32in) and is long-flowering with pink spikes. Both are sensitive to too much wet (mildew!) and, for that reason, in the long run will not do well in damp climates.

VIOLA (*VIOLACEAE*)

V. cornuta hybrids Z5–8 25cm/ 10in LSp–MA

With the exception of 'Boughton Blue' (syn. 'Belmont Blue') and 'Milkmaid', all the *V. cornuta* hybrids are short-lived. They seed themselves about all right, but the seedlings will flower a different colour. The only chance of a longer life is to lift them each year and divide them. So we won't describe this species in detail, but for something so attractive it is always possible to find a gap. Here is a selection: 'Ardross Gem', blue and yellow; 'Nellie Britton' (syn. 'Haselmere'), mauve; 'Irish Molly', yellow, brown and gold; 'Molly Sanderson', almost black; and 'Moonlight', soft yellow.

Lavatera cachemiriana and *Artemisia* 'Lambrook Silver' with *Salvia verticillata* 'Purple Rain'

Staking

Falling over is a problem affecting many tall wild plants. In the wild it does not matter; the surrounding grass falls with it and the plant still succeeds in raising its flowers above the grass, at least high enough to be pollinated by insects, and in the final analysis that is the plant's only ambition. Our ambitions go further. We put tall plants at the back of a border to flower high above the others, and not to fall down behind the other plants so that we can't see them.

So, one fine day in early summer (preferably not too late) we go out, full of good intentions, armed with bamboo canes and twine, and proceed to the back of the border. As we describe it now, it sounds as if we actually enjoy doing it, but of course, we don't. It's awful! The twine always gets into knots or is caught up behind the wrong stalk, you keep dropping your scissors where you can't find them in the foliage, there is a big stone just where you want to push a bamboo cane into the ground, and to top it all, when you have at last squeezed yourself into an unsteady position, on one leg, between some tall plants, the telephone rings in the distance. It takes enormous self-control to keep your temper.

You can save yourself a great deal of such misery by cutting back the plants before mid-summer. Of course that is quite tricky; it works particularly well with clump-forming plants, like phlox, and of course, it keeps them lower. If you really want plants 2.4m/8ft high at the back of your borders, then you must as far as possible choose ones that never fall over, such as *Eupatorium*, *Verbesina* and *Vernonia*. Obviously we could provide a list here of plants that never need staking, but it would be of relatively limited value. In a garden with large trees almost all plants collapse, because they angle themselves away from the trees; and near the coast, or in an area without trees, they all blow down.

Even under ideal conditions, in a garden protected from the wind and with no tall trees, a savage thunderstorm with gusting winds can wreak havoc. There will always be some that have to be staked: these vary from garden to garden, and you learn by experience. Sometimes you are just too late, either because you did not feel like doing it at the right time, or because a plant flops that never fell over anywhere else before. Then the only answer is to cut down the whole plant – but sometimes it is worth waiting a few days. The plant may pick itself up again and suddenly seems much prettier in its fallen state than it was earlier. Fantastic – at least you don't have to tie that plant up.

Examples of plants that droop prettily after falling over are *Stipa calamagrostis*, *Gillenia trifoliata* and *Veronicastrum virginicum* 'Temptation'. They can be planted a little further forward, so that they can fall over the edge of the grass or the paving. But here, too, the rule is: every garden is different, and everyone must find out for themselves which plants droop gracefully, and which ones need staking. Good luck!

Delphinium elatum

Troublesome
Demanding plants

In theory we pay no attention to demanding plants in this book. Not because we begrudge you the pleasure of spending hours busying yourself with much-loved specimens, but because it is in conflict with our aim: a book about plants that can be used to create a natural garden without having to pull out all the stops. Because for those listed below you do need to pull out all the stops. However, we have included them because they are very familiar and well-loved garden plants, which can still make an important contribution to the natural beauty of a garden. We have even devoted a special chapter to them – albeit a very short one.

ACONITUM *(RANUNCULACEAE)* – monkshood

A. lycoctonum Z4–8   ↕ 1.2m/ 4ft   MSu–LSu

Wolfbane. The yellow monkshood is a very attractive plant with deeply indented dark green leaves and high-capped, soft yellow monkshood flowers in long, thin plumes. Grows reasonably well on good moisture-retaining garden soil, though it is clearly less strong than the purple monkshood. The great problem with this plant is its tendency to fall over: we know no way of supporting the weak stems without its being very obvious. One option is to let the plant lean against a shrub, but then most of the very fine inflorescence is lost. Difficult! A number of local species, which in the wild have a compact and sturdy habit, such as *A. lamarckii* and *A. kirinense*, about which we used to be enthusiastic, have proved just as weak as the others in the garden.

BOLTONIA *(ASTERACEAE)*

B. asteroides var. latisquama Z4–9   ↕ 2m/ 6½ft   EA–MA

Forms an enormous cloud of white aster flowers on stems 2m/6½ft tall in September: wonderful! Exactly what you need in your borders. It is also extremely strong and grows everywhere. But it needs to be put in scaffolding from top to toe, tied up stem by stem, if it is to reach that height. And when it flowers, keep your fingers crossed that it does not rain, because then the flowers become just a dirty, tangled mess. Once in a while it does well!

DELPHINIUM *(RANUNCULACEAE)*

There is still room for delphiniums in this book: right at the back! It is a familiar story. Delphiniums need very fertile, lime-rich and well-manured soil if they are to thrive. They have to be lifted every two or three years and manured again. They must continually be supported right up to their flower heads, or the stems break. They cannot be planted near other tall plants, because then the slugs make short work of them, so it is difficult to combine them with anything. If you leave space round the individual plants, you can scatter shell-sand on the soil round them; slugs will not usually cross it. (As you know, we don't use synthetic pesticides.) If you are prepared to do all this, you can take up the challenge, for they will always be a challenge, with their stunning masses of blue flowers. We list only the strongest species:

D. elatum Z2–9   ↕ 1.8m/ 6ft   ESu–MSu

Grows wild in the mountainous regions of southern Europe, but still rare everywhere. Parent plant of most garden hybrids. With its slender inflorescence it is not so liable to collapse. The colour of the flowers varies: you come across all shades of blue.

GALEGA *(PAPILIONACEAE)*

G. officinalis Z4–8   ↕ 1.5m/ 5ft   MSu–LSu

Resembles a giant vetch; usually lavender-blue, but there are also white and pink cultivars. Whether they will grow in all types of soil, we beg to doubt: in any case not in poor soil. On fertile soil it becomes unmanageable; very pretty indeed, but how pretty is the forest of stakes you need to keep the plant standing?

Top: *Aconitum lycoctonum*
Bottom: *Galega officinalis*

From left to right: *Angelica gigas*, *Lobelia* 'Eulalia Berridge' and *Gaura lindheimeri* 'Whirling Butterflies'

Failing the test

Many plants have failed the test we set them. We do not consider them sufficiently reliable to include them in this book. Apart from the plants which did not even pass the qualifying examination, such as alpines and marsh plants, several plants may be eligible for a resit. Not in this book, because it is complete, but, who knows, perhaps some other time. They are all plants we are very fond of, but of which we dare not say: just put them in the garden, they will manage all right. The most we could say would be: only if you look after them with great care will they perhaps get by.

Angelica gigas does not seed well every year. Why, we don't know, but it means that you may suddenly find you have lost it.

Aconitum heterophyllum, of which we put such a fine photograph in our last book that it caused a run on them. We forecast that it would have a great future. We don't know what that future will hold, because unfortunately it abandoned us.

Centaurea glastifolia. It is sad, but it is just as unreliable as its sisters. What is the matter with *Centaurea*?

Diascia cultivars. Never used in the past because they could not stand up to a hard winter. Recently widely cultivated because they unexpectedly appeared to be winter-hardy after all, and yet more recently dismissed because they did not survive the exceptional lows of recent years.

Gaura lindheimeri 'Whirling Butterflies' is a wonderful gap filler, but you have to buy a new batch every year.

Heuchera x *brizoides* is quite nice with its little red flowers, and also quite reliable. However, it falls into the category of 'examiners' prejudice'. We just don't go for it. The same goes for the *Heucherella* crosses.

Kniphofia varieties have been omitted because on closer acquaintance we think they need too much attention to survive severe winters unscathed.

Lavatera 'Barnsley' has to be brought through the winter by means of cuttings, otherwise you may lose it.

Lobelia hybrids are divine, but only for people with green fingers.

Lysimachia ephemerum is just not hardy enough to withstand the winter without protection.

Primula florindae, the only reliable one among the Asiatic species, is still, however, a bog plant.

Scabiosa caucasica needs to be renewed regularly if you want it to flower successfully.

Tiarella wherryi is quite reliable when you look after it properly, but is still rather too tender for us.

Index

Publisher's acknowledgments English language editions
Translators Guy Shipton, Alastair Weir
Copy editor Andrew Mikolajski
(First Edition Translations Ltd)
Editors Michael Brunström, Sarah Mitchell

Gardens open to the public in the UK

Scampston Walled Garden, Scampston Hall, Malton,
North Yorkshire YO17 8NG
Tel: 01944 759111 Email: info@scampston.co.uk
Web: www.scampston.co.uk

Trentham Gardens, The Trentham Estate, Stone Road,
Trentham, Stoke-on-Trent Staffordshire ST4 8AX
Tel: 01782 646646 Email: enquiry@trentham.co.uk
Web: www.trentham.co.uk

Pensthorpe Waterfowl Trust, Pensthorpe Road, Fakenham,
Norfolk NR21 0LN
Tel: 01328 851465 Email: info@pensthorpe.com
Web: www.pensthorpe.com/norfolk-gardens/millennium/

RHS Garden Wisley, Woking, Surrey GU23 6QB
Tel: 0845 260 9000 Web: www.rhs.org.uk/wisley

Gardens designed by Piet Oudolf that open to the public in North America

The High Line, 529 West 20th Street, Suite 8W · New York, NY 10011.
Tel: (212) 206-9922 Web: www.thehighline.org

The Lurie Garden, Millennium Park, Chicago, Illinois
Web: www.luriegarden.org

The Battery Conservancy, The Battery, New York

Gardens open to the public in The Netherlands

The Priona Gardens
Schuineslootweg 13-7777 RE Schuinesloot
Email: prionagardens@gmail.com
Web: http://prionagardens.blogspot
Opening times will be given on the garden's Facebook page.

Oudolf family garden
Broekstraat 17-6999 DE Hummelo
See web: www.oudolf.com for opening times.

Nurseries in the UK

Cotswold Garden Flowers
Sands Lane, Badsey, Evesham, Worcestershire, WR11 5EZ
Tel: 01386 833849 Fax: 01386 47337
For mail order: Tel: 01386 422 829 Fax: 01386 49844
Web: www.cgf.net Email: info@cgf.net

Marchants Hardy Plants
2 Marchants Cottages Mill Lane, Laughton, East Sussex BN8 6AJ
Tel/Fax: 01323 811737
Web: www.marchantshardyplants.co.uk

Orchard Dene Nurseries (wholesale only)
Lower Assendon, Henley-on-Thames, Oxon RG9 1GA
Tel: 01491 575075 Fax: 01471 413850
Web: www.orcharddene.co.uk Email: enquiries@orcharddene.co.uk

Phoenix Perennial Plants
Paice Lane, Medstead, Alton, Hampshire, England, GU34 5PR
Tel: 01420 560695 Web: www.phoenixperennialplants.co.uk

Quercus Garden Plants
Rankeilour Gardens, Rankeilour Estate, Springfield, Fife,
Scotland, KY15 5RE Tel: 01337 810444 Email: colin@quercus.uk.ne
Web: www.quercus.uk.net

Binny Plants
Binny Estate, Ecclesmachan, West Lothian, EH52 6NL
Tel: 01506 858931 Email: contact@binnyplants.com
Web: *www.binnyplants.com*

Nurseries in The Netherlands

Coen Jansen Vaste Planten
Ankummer Es 13a 7722RD Dalfsen
Tel: 0529 434086
Web: www.coenjansenvasteplanten.nl

Kwekerij Kabbes
Jelke Sjoerdslaan 4-9262 SL Suameer
Tel/Fax: 0512 372521
Web: www.kabbes.nl

De Kleine Plantage
Handerweg 1-9967 TC Eenrum
Tel: 0595 491604 Fax: 0595-491433
Web: www.dekleineplantage.nl Email: info@dekleineplantage.nl

De Hessenhof Nurseries
Miranda and Hans Kramer
Hessenweg 41-6718 TC Ede
Tel: 0318 617334 Fax: 0318 612 773
Email: hessenhof@planet.nl Web: www.hessenhof.nl

Nurseries in North America

Not all of these provide the plants which Piet Oudolf uses,
but some provide native species or others which create 'the look'
in the relevant climate zone.

Midwest Groundcovers www.*midwestgroundcovers*.com
  (wholesale only)
Missouri Wildflowers Nursery. www.*mowildflowers*.net
Northwind Perennial Farm. www.*northwindperennialfarm*.com
North Creek Nurseries, PA. www.*northcreek*nurseries.com
  (wholesale only)
Plant Delights Nursery, NC. www.*plantdelights*.com
Plant Creations Nursery in Homestead, Florida.
  www.*plantcreations*.com
Rancho Santa Ana Botanic garden is all natives and perennials.

Niche Gardens
1111 Dawson Road, Chapel Hill NC 27516
Tel: (919) 967 0078 Fax: (919) 967 4026
Email: mail@nichegardens.com Web: www.nichegardens.com

Forestfarm
146-43 Watergap Road, Williams, OR 97544
Tel: +1(541) 846 7269 Fax: +1 (541) 846 6963
Email: plants@forestfarm.com Web: www.forestfarm.com

FURTHER READING

The New Perennial Garden, Noel Kingsbury, Frances Lincoln, 1996
Designing with Plants, Noel Kingsbury and Piet Oudolf, Conran
  Octopus, 1999
Planting Design: Gardens in Time and Space, Noel Kingsbury and Piet
  Oudolf, Terra/Timber, 2005
Planting, the New Perspective, Noel Kingsbury and Piet Oudolf,
  Terra/Timber, 2013